ON LEAVING
A PRAGUE
WINDOW

David Brierley

WARNER BOOKS

A *Warner* Book

First published in Great Britain in 1995 by Little, Brown and
Company
This edition published in 1996 by Warner Books

A CIP catalogue record for this book is available from the
British Library.

ISBN 0 7515 1684 8

Typeset in Berkeley by M Rules
Printed and bound in Great Britain by Clays Ltd, St Ives plc

Warner Books
A Division of
Little, Brown and Company (UK)
Brettenham House
Lancaster Place
London WC2E 7EN

David Brierley was born in Durban in 1936 and spent his early years in South Africa, Canada and England. After graduating from Oxford he taught in a French *lycée*. He spent fifteen years working in London advertising agencies before becoming a full-time writer in 1975. His novels have been set all over the world, from behind the former Iron Curtain to the rainforests of Latin America. In 1992 he moved with his wife to France where they now live in a lovingly restored farm cottage.

Praise for David Brierley

'Super-skilled graft of fiction on to history . . . An authentic winner' *Sunday Times*

'If you want espionage in the le Carré class, this is it' *Observer*

'Tough . . . witty . . . in the best tradition of suspense fiction' *New Yorker*

'[The] brilliant description of a damp and cold life after Dubcek makes one want to read it by the fireside; and the paranoia will keep you looking over your shoulder' *Sunday Telegraph*

Also by David Brierley:

Big Bear, Little Bear
Shooting Star
Czechmate
One Lives, One Dies
Cold War
Blood Group O
Skorpion's Death
Snowline

This is for Jackie
who has met Monsieur Bien Cuit
shaken hands with the Mad Baker
survived the repas de la chasse
and heard the nightingales

CHAPTER ONE

The Russians are going.

The Russians are going.

Are they going naked? On Charles Bridge over the Vltava River they have left booty. It is like an army pillaging in reverse. Newly emerged entrepreneurs have set up stalls. There are the stalls selling watercolours of Hradcany Castle and Old Town Square. There are stalls selling cassettes of Dvořák and Frank Zappa and other honorary Czechs. There is the man with the wind-up gramophone and dancing puppets – see Gorbachev and Thatcher hop to a polka. There are stalls selling rings and necklaces – see, there is Olga, the pretty one with her eyes that ask a question and her lips half open with a promise until you've bought a trinket and are sent on your way.

Yes, the communist winter has thawed and the first magazines are on sale with women who've taken their clothes off in the warmer climate. Men, eyes caught by this display of freedom, stop to stare. Fulnek's eyes are caught too and his step falters. He looks an ordinary man who lives a blameless life but such breasts and such poses would have tempted Ghandi. Then he turns his head away and walks on. After all, Fulnek is a man of the cloth.

There are other stalls with crowds two and three deep. Here are small heaps of Soviet army caps – see the red star. Run a hand over the rough cloth of the trousers. Feel the weight of the boots. Is the belt the right size for your waist? Here is a Soviet officer's uniform jacket. Maybe he was an Afghanistan veteran for you can see the darker patch where the decoration has been removed. The medal is for sale separately. They say that six times as many medals are sold as uniforms and that in a garage in the district of Karlin an entrepreneur is turning out more each day.

There are no Soviet army pistols on the stalls. For those you have to consult another kind of entrepreneur, a new breed. These seemed to step fully formed out of the shadows. In truth they are not new. They were always there. They just wore a different guise.

What happened nearly one and a half years ago was dubbed the Velvet Revolution. Was that boastful or hopeful or relieved? In time some people turned peevish, as people do. It's not the Velvet Revolution, these sour-sayers muttered, it's the Pick-pocket Revolution. Those who dipped their hands in and stole people's dreams were men like Broucek.

See, there is his Mercedes parked in that corner at the end of the bridge while he lunches in U tri Pstrosu. You can't drive over Charles Bridge, though he would like to. Convenient, a short-cut to his office. If you drove a tank across, who would try to stop you? Broucek knows a man who could get you a tank, a second-hand T64 maybe, old but well maintained, only one owner. The Russians are going home but it is said they are willing to part with a tank. Cash down. No korunas, no roubles. For this is the spring of 1991. Dollars are the future.

The bridge is lined on both sides with statues grey with city grime, apart from the white hairstyles donated by birds. The statues are all of saints, though not even Fulnek can name them all. In medieval times justice was administered here. Wrongdoers were caged in wicker baskets and dipped in the river. Fulnek pauses to look down and ponder. Doubtless in those days you could catch some fatal disease from a dip in the water. It's just a thought.

CHAPTER TWO

You must absent yourself for a while.
    How long? Fulnek had asked.
    A week, two weeks. For as long as it takes us.
    Why?
    We consider it wiser.
    But tell me why. Another degree of frost had entered the atmosphere. It was not for Fulnek to consider the collective wisdom of this synod. *Where should I go? What should I do?*
    Reflect.
    Learn.
    Find the path again.
    Which was precisely what Fulnek was trying to avoid. Was he meant to cry, beat himself with whips, repent of his life?
    Confess everything because everything is known. Confess because confession is good for the soul. Recant like a heretic at the stake as the flames lick the soles of the feet. Betray like a partisan whose fingernails are ripped out. Admit guilt like the Stalinist faithful and beg for death to further the Stalinist cause. Fill your heart with shame and remorse. Return to days of honest toil, nights of monkish calm. Retrace your steps to the crossroads where you took the wrong turning.

And if all this had not actually been said, there had been pauses which Fulnek had been expected to fill. He had left the room with silence at his back. There had been no handshakes, no goodbye.

Later, reliving the scene a dozen times, other details came into Fulnek's mind. It hadn't been completely silent as he left. There had been the sound of rough breathing and papers shuffling. Also, there'd been the smell of beer in the air though it wasn't yet ten in the morning. For courage, to propose a toast, for an early celebration.

He thought of their eyes, so bright and fixed on him. But as he switched from one face to another, the eyes had dropped.

There were some you couldn't trust. Everybody knew that.

Ah yes, the wall. As high as Fulnek remembered.

The wall as chastity belt. That's what the sly had said. Jump and you still couldn't get a hand on the top. The young women of the village were safe, though they didn't want to be. The young men were kept in by the wall in case their urges proved more powerful than their vows.

Of course it was possible by standing on someone's shoulders to reach the top of the wall and clamber over. But the authorities in those days were merciful, or at least realistic: if a passion was so strong, it would defeat any obstacle. The sin should be, if not forgiven, glossed over. Only when the sin became too obvious, too noisy . . .

So, Fulnek decided, the wall as a chastity belt that could be breached.

But then in more recent times the wall had served other masters, other purposes. The wall as guarantee of secrecy.

When They took the place over They had liked it for its high wall, no doubt of it. Walls keep people out: burglars, murderers, rapists. Walls keep people in: prisoners, suspects, the damned. Also walls help keep sounds in.

Fulnek filled his lungs and let the breath out slowly. He turned round, hands clasped behind him, back to the wall. Had They liked the wall for that reason too? Had They stood prisoners up against the wall, a strip of cloth for a blindfold? There was a ritual to such events. A last cigarette, bourgeois traitor, They would say. A match, enemy of the people. A final puff, imperialist scum.

They used to talk like that. In Their hearts They thought like that still.

So, our Czech cigarettes are not fancy enough for you, American spy. What do you expect – Lucky Strike? That was how They taunted Petr Letov, though he wasn't an American spy but a Trotskyite revisionist, or was it a Maoist deviationist, anyway some tongue-twisting ist. Letov had replied: Smoking might kill me but only slowly, and I think you are in a hurry to get back to Prague. They had hated Letov for that. They couldn't shoot him slowly so They shot him in places where his death would be slow and They could appreciate its finer points.

Such had been the times.

Seen from a distance, arms clasped behind him,

Fulnek looked a quiet man. No drama to him, you said. Step closer and you noticed the set of his jaw and tightness at the corners of his mouth. Closer still – but no, you wouldn't crowd him today. In his eyes you saw bruises, fury, steel. Things that shouldn't be there. You stepped back to give him space. He wore a dark overcoat on this early spring day. It was unbuttoned because he didn't notice the nip in the air. He was fuelled by something within.

With the wall protecting his back he gazed out. After the storm had cleared, the sky was blue but the road ahead muddy. More, he thought, go on. On your cheek you feel the sun, weak but promising. Watch your feet on the treacherous path because at any moment you can slip, trip . . .

Abandoning this line of thought, Fulnek forced himself to take in what lay in front. Down the slope he had climbed was a line of willow trees, as if there was a river. In fact a ditch. Beyond that was Benevice, a compact village huddled round a church. That's where the girls had been. But the high wall might as well have been the Iron Curtain, and the ditch the Atlantic, and the girls in America for all the possibility there had been of meeting them.

Beyond the village were ploughed fields. A railway line slashed the fields. North, the railway ran to Kolin where you kicked your heels while you waited for the connection to Prague. Beyond the tracks, right on the horizon, were the chimneys of the engineering works and the cigarette factory, and suburbs of apartment blocks. Peeping between them and no more important were the three spires of the cathedral of Kutna Hora.

He let his eyes rest there a moment, though he couldn't love the place. Gothic is cold. Gothic oppresses. Gothic is God made granite, disapproving of colour and laughter. It showed the same stern spirit as you saw in the apartment blocks which had been named after Gottwald and Husak and other worthies. Imagine having an ugly cement block called after you. It took a vain and stupid politician not to see that as an insult. What were the buildings called now? The country had enjoyed an orgy of name-changing though it was said true believers had squirrelled away the old nameplates, biding their time.

Enough. Fulnek turned aside. Enough of spires and chimneys and hopeless cement slabs. He walked the length of the stone wall that for a couple of centuries had kept young lives uncorrupt. He could see nothing of the buildings inside except the steeple of the chapel. He arrived at the entrance where a discoloured patch of stone showed where the brass plate had been fixed: Seminary of the Holy Name. They had taken that down, of course. What had They called it then? Nothing, apparently. The Place of No Name for people with no names.

There was a solid wood gate tall enough to let in a haycart. Inset in the gate was a door. Fulnek rattled the handle and to his surprise the door swung open. In the days before They took over, the door had been kept locked and you pulled on a metal lever to make a bell tinkle inside. The caller was inspected through a crack in the door to ensure it was not a girl from the village. A female was allowed in only if she was – as the statutes had it in dubious Latin – *senex et harrida*.

When They took over They ripped out the old bell and replaced it with a buzzer. You pressed a button and a man came out of the guardhouse and put his eye to the spyhole. You knew he was there because the spyhole changed colour. It turned brown and gazed at you as unblinking as a lizard. Then the bolts were slid back, the key turned a lock, you answered respectfully and were admitted, and the door slammed shut.

What is your name?

Fulnek, Alois.

What is your age?

Forty-seven.

Where were you born?

Pardubice, not far away.

I don't need geography lessons from you. State your business here.

And what was it? Fulnek pushed the door open and stepped inside and wondered. Why come? A middle-aged man seeking out the place of his youthful hope? Morbid curiosity to find out what They had done to the place? Running, hiding? Washing away guilt? Looking for strength?

Motives. The twentieth century has had a bellyful. Motives as reasons, motives as driving force, motives as justification. They are always for the best and always result in the worst. Who trusts motives any more?

To cheer himself up Fulnek shouted out loud, 'I've come to steal the sacristy silver.'

But of course They'd done that Themselves long ago.

He was expecting the chapel to be like this. The door opened when he pushed it. The wood round the lock was splintered. Someone with more experience of firearms than Fulnek would have judged it had taken a two-second burst from a machine-gun.

'Someone in a hurry to say his prayers.'

In this strange time Fulnek found comfort in the sound of his own voice. Speaking to yourself was meant to be a sign of madness but in the old days he'd watched the communist hulks who had led the country into ruin and never seen their lips move.

As he took a couple of steps inside, the smell struck him first. Some of the buildings that had been thrown up in the last quarter of a century – the V.I. Lenin Memorial Apartments, the Peace and Friendship Workers' Hostel, whatever they were now called – were already turning into modern ruins. Their smell of crumbling concrete was different, sharper, catching at the throat. The chapel was two hundred years old and its smell was of damp stone, leafmould and something else. It came unbidden into Fulnek's mind: women's genitals.

He sighed.

'Look,' he cried out, swinging an arm round. The wooden pews had gone, chopped for firewood.

'Look.' He pointed up the nave. The pulpit, the crucifixion, the icons, the candlesticks, the Madonna and child attributed to Manes had all gone. The Madonna's disappearance was a particular blow. Her hair, her cheeks, the breast she offered the baby were possibly a little lush for Manes but not for the young seminarians. Her lips had been parted in a way that would have been provocative in one of the village girls. Her eyes had followed wherever you went in the chapel. She had been the object of fervent prayers. Gone.

'And there.' The font and the organ had vanished. The stained-glass windows gaped. Gilded putti lay on the floor, smashed, as brutish soldiers clubbed the skulls of children with their rifles. On a wall someone with a spraycan had written RAMBO! Never mind the politics, relish the violence.

He filled his lungs, closed his eyes and let out a bellow.

'Forgive them, Father, for they—'

The air was filled with clapping. It was the broken cherubs brought to life by his roar. He opened his eyes and it was pigeons flapping in the rafters.

All that remained was a confessional at the west end. It was a double confessional with a cubicle for a priest in the middle. Why hadn't that been taken away for firewood? When he got close he understood why. It had been used as a urinal. He perched on the priest's seat, his head resting against the grille through which sins were whispered into a receptive ear.

Are dreams a sin, Father?

They can be.

Even though we have no control over them?

They are yours, nobody else's. They are manifestations of your soul, of hidden desires. In what way have you sinned? Tell me your dream.

In my dream the Madonna came to my bedside and I put my lips to her breast as if I was the holy babe.

Yes, go on. Go on.

When my teeth bit her nipple it was not milk but vinum sanctum that poured into my mouth in a stream. Tears splashed on to my skin from her eyes and I asked why she was weeping. She answered they were a virgin's tears.

Is that all? Is there more?

There is more.

You must tell me, Alois, tell me. Even if it is very bad, Lojza, you must tell me.

He meant: *Particularly if it is very bad.*

Tears because she was still a virgin. And so . . .

Well now. But Fulnek's memory faltered as he heard something. He had to strain his ears to catch it. The faraway roar of the surf when you lift a seashell to your ear. No, more the scrape of waves on pebbles, wave dragging after wave. He tried out explanations. It was the echo of ten thousand confessions. It was some electronic device They had left hidden behind the panelling. It was the Madonna sobbing over her virgin state. It was the blood pushing through the arteries close to his ears. There was so much blood in a man. The heart pumped and pumped without a day of rest.

There was a new sound from outside. He recognized the squeak of the door set in the entrance gate. Had the wind blown it open? There was no wind. He heard the hinge protest as the door was closed. Someone had gone out. Very faintly came a sound that might be a key turning in the heavy lock.

'Hello! Who's there? Can you hear me?'

Fulnek was outside, striding to the entrance.

'Is this some kind of a joke?'

He twisted the handle. The door wouldn't open. A dread started in him that this wasn't a joke at all. Or if it was a joke, it was the kind that only They would play. He kicked the planks.

'Hey, you out there, whoever you are.'

Finally he beat on the old oak gate, pummelling with both fists, shouting in a voice rising with panic.

'Don't go away. Don't lock me in. I haven't got a key. In the name of God, come back.'

His voice died in his head. He could hear heartbeats and rough breathing, his own. Then once again the sound like waves drawing back on a beach. He recognized it as footsteps on the grit of the path.

The spyhole! Why hadn't he thought of that? But when he put his eye to it he found the view blocked. Whoever was out there had put an eye to it, thinking the spyhole worked both ways. There was the sound of metal on metal, a struggle with the old lock, and Fulnek stepped back as the door in the gate opened. At first just a crack. Then enough for a head to poke round though no head appeared. Whoever was out there had that caution acquired over the years, of not opening a door willingly to people who kicked and hammered at it.

'Thank you,' Fulnek said, more to give courage to the unseen person. 'I didn't want to get locked in. I'd have been a skeleton the next time you came.'

It just slipped out. He'd made something of a joke of it but wasn't smiling. Of all the ways to die this would be the most poignant: in a seminary that had been taken over by the security police but now lay derelict.

The door pushed open further and a head appeared, a pair of dark eyes made a swift circuit behind Fulnek before settling on his face. Why was I expecting a man? he wondered. Because when it had been a seminary no women had been allowed in except the wizened harridans who collected the laundry, prepared soup, swept the floors. This woman would have been inspected through a crack in the door and turned away. Even in her late forties she had too much life in her eyes. In her youth she must have been striking, but her face frowned as if it had been a beauty that had brought her constant trouble. Her skin was pale, accentuated by her black coat with the collar turned up.

'Don't be absurd,' she said in her practical woman's way. 'You'd have found a ladder and climbed over the wall.'

It was spoken as if she knew all about men, ladders and escaping over walls. Studying her face more intently he decided the frown was from determination, a match for his own.

'Who are you?' she asked.

'Alois Fulnek.'

'I mean, what are you?' They both hesitated, taking stock of each other, but she was the one who went boldly on. 'You don't behave like one of Them or you wouldn't have been shouting for help.'

'This is where I trained in the days before They took the place over.'

'A priest?'

She kept her eyes on him. In her voice he could hear unspoken thoughts: You don't have the look of a priest. You don't smell like a priest. You don't have any of the conflicting faces priests wear: self-contained/ outward-going, fastidious/jovial, virtuous/venial, open/ elusive, serene/troubled. Perhaps elusive a bit. Perhaps troubled a bit more.

'You?' she said with renewed doubt.

There was more staring. These days, when you didn't

know a person's past, trust was so much a leap in the dark. Then she relaxed a fraction because she seemed to recognize something in Fulnek's face – the way his eyebrows tightened as if he was experiencing a spasm of pain.

He said, 'You mean I don't wear fancy dress.'

It was his day for making jokes. It's nerves, he told himself, it's not facing reality. Or is it something simpler – wanting to see the woman's face soften. What makes her smile? When did she last laugh? When did I?

'For taking mass, of course I do. But otherwise . . . it seemed to set me apart so much.' Which was in part what was intended. He realized that only when it was too late.

'Well then,' she said at last and came fully into the courtyard. She closed the door and held up the key. 'There's an old priest in the village, Pavlicek—'

'Good heavens, is he still alive?'

She studied Fulnek a moment. The man was an idiot. 'Obviously.'

'I never thought he'd still be alive. I went and asked at the café.'

'He gave me a key to get in but he wouldn't come with me. I told him I wanted a prayer said, a blessing, but nowadays he is . . .'

She spread her fingers against her forehead and tapped.

'Gaga,' Fulnek said. Father Pavlicek had seemed old when he was training at the seminary. Now he must be in his eighties, maybe nineties. A priest's calling was no defence against a softening of the brain.

'Gaga if you like,' she said. 'I suppose the prayer of a

gaga priest counts for as much as a prayer from a priest with a fully functioning mind, does it?'

'God understands,' Fulnek said. 'God makes allowances for our imperfections.'

'Still, I wouldn't have felt easy about it. I'm not a churchgoer myself but I wanted a prayer from a believer.' She shrugged. 'Perhaps Father Pavlicek wouldn't properly have grasped what he was praying for. But you, however . . .'

She turned back to lock the door, to keep other intruders out or Fulnek in.

'Who is the prayer for?'

My husband, was the answer he expected, or my son or my mother. But she gave him a name.

'Vaclav Bodnar.' She inspected his face. 'Doesn't the name Bodnar mean anything to you? Think a long way back.'

Bodnar, Bodnar? Ah. The name rang a bell, a distant one from the darkening past. But he said, 'Bodnar, no, I don't think I recall a Bodnar,' because he wanted to hear it in her own words.

'Nineteen sixty-eight,' she began. She was walking away and he had to hurry and bend his head to catch what she said. 'Were you here then?'

'I left the year before.'

'Just as well. They would have kicked you out into the snow because They had a better use for this place.'

'Prerova,' she said.

'Mrs Prerova, do—'

'Prerova. Just call me that. As if I was a prima baller-ina. First name Milena but don't use that. Sometimes

They would call me that, whispering in my ear as if we were lovers. Tell us, Mila, don't hide anything. Oh Miluska. They'd croon as if I was a baby. A finger tickling under my chin and then the hand dropping down, you see, here. A smile mocking me, booze on their breath. Oh Miluska . . . As if we shared some intimacy. That's the way They were, thinking They owned our lives.'

She was walking on ahead of him, firm steps, head up, eyes on the future. Just the way her elbows jutted out said: Don't come too close, I don't know you yet, use my formal name.

Beside the chapel ran a gravel path being recolonized by grass. Beyond the chancel end of the building the path gave out altogether in a muddle of unpruned shrubs, brambles and tussocks of grass. The stalks of last year's flowers were on the lilac. When those bushes were last flowering and those nettles stinging, Fulnek thought, were They in this place? He could still feel Their presence. It was in the silence, as if They were holding Their breath and watching. And then They were going to hiss, Oh Miluska . . .

Prerova stopped and swung round as if he'd spoken out loud. 'People call it *lustrace*, you know?'

'I know.' It was the search through files, sniffing out villains, skeletons, ghosts. The idea was that the past could be cleaned. *Lustrace* quickly became a ritual, with its own rules, dogma and sins.

'Mr Havel becomes President, the secret police are no more and the communists have disappeared from power. Like going to the theatre, there is a bang and a puff of smoke, and by some trick the scene has changed. Truth will make us free. Truth will guarantee democracy. But if the secret police have gone and the communists have gone and the informers have gone – where have they gone to?'

She didn't expect an answer. Fulnek had no answer, in any case. Or if he did it was the answer that everyone had: that after the puff of smoke has cleared, some of the old players have changed their costumes, others are learning new lines, others are waiting in the wings for the moment to make their next entrance, others have slipped up the aisle and are mingling with the audience.

'Sometimes They went overnight,' she said and snapped her fingers. 'Sometimes They seem to have been gone for months, for years, never to have existed at all except in a nightmare. They didn't go empty-handed. They took Their files with Them. Not just by the armful, by the truckload. Where did They take Their files to? Where are They hiding Their evidence?'

'They didn't get away with all the files.'

'They dropped a few. They forgot a few cupboards.'

'They burned them.'

'The sky would have been black with smoke, blacker than Kuwait,' she said. 'They kept the files because They know their value. Think of the possibilities for blackmail.'

'Yes.' Fulnek considered the many ways people could be bullied and threatened. You could be telephoned in the middle of the night when you were muddled by sleep. You could find someone had fallen into step beside you as you walked down the street. You could be summoned to appear before a committee.

In two minutes your life could be reduced to ruins. 'Yes,' he said again.

It was the seminary's graveyard they picked their way through. The village had its own cemetery so this was for the priests who had died here, in number thirty-four, and the single probationer who died while Fulnek was there. He had a fall and broke his neck. Fulnek paused to read the headstone: Tadeas Slabina. 1944–1966. He rests with God. Thin man, gaunt face, troubled eyes, hair slicked straight back. It was the eyes that Fulnek saw, fixed on some inner turmoil. He'd been on his way to rest with someone else, was the rumour, and it wasn't his rosary he tripped over.

'Not him,' Prerova said.

Fulnek ran his eye across other headstones, speckled with lichen and moss. Many of the older inscriptions were in German. Reasonable enough: the Habsburgs had been the paymasters of the church. The communist state simply inherited an old tradition, one hand clutching the purse, the other clutching the church warmly by the throat.

'Over there against the wall.'

A low mound had been recently cleared of weeds. There was no headstone but a plain wooden cross had been stabbed into the ground. This too looked recently done. On a wall a large X was splashed in faded white paint. The kiss of death. A tiny posy of snowdrops lay on the grave. These weren't hothouse blooms bought from a florist but more like flowers filched from gardens in the village.

'That's his grave.'

'Vaclav Bodnar's?'

'Yes.'

'You're certain?'

'Yes.'

Suddenly she was shy with words. She could spew out invective against Them because she was a pressure cooker of emotions and experiences. But here was something close to the heart that was difficult to share. Everybody had a wound they licked in private. Fulnek nodded. She had her pain, he had his pain. It was a bond between them.

'There's no name, no date, nothing,' he objected, prompting her.

She swung round on him. 'I tell you that's Vaclav.' She rubbed her eyes with the back of her hand. 'There's someone at one of the ministries – not a bad man, because we all had to live somehow. I'd known him a long time ago when we'd been students. We were never that close because I liked to watch Ibsen and he liked to watch Spartak. That's got nothing to do with what I'm telling you. It's just that we went out together when we were young but nothing came of it. Nothing much. So a month ago I was in Kotva in Prague – you know?'

'I know,' Fulnek said. Built by Swedes, staffed by sadists, used by the unfortunate, the largest department store in the country.

'I needed certain garments.' She frowned at the priest a moment before gesturing at her bosom. 'Underwear. I was in the department when I saw him – my friend from long, long ago. I recognized him and called his name and cried out, "What! Does your wife send you shopping for her bras?" One or two people looked at him and he went radish-red in his cheeks so I realized he wasn't shopping for his wife.'

She paused and her eyes stood guard in case the priest should pounce on this hint of sin. She shook her head: why was she bringing out all these personal details?

'We had a beer and talked about old times and he said he wasn't interested in football any more and anyway Spartak were rubbish now . . .' Again she broke off and when she restarted she had her story under control. 'He had never risen higher than being chief clerk in the transport pool because he wouldn't join the Party. He'd been responsible for cars and drivers for the big bosses, and occasionally with special requests. One request was on the day that Vaclav Bodnar disappeared. More than twenty-two years ago but it stayed in his mind. Things do when they trouble you. He had a telephoned order – nothing put on paper – for a van without windows to take a prisoner. Is it going far? My friend needed to know whether the driver would be away overnight. He was told to keep his nose out of business that wasn't his, and the next moment he was told where it was anyway, or close enough. "Near Kutna Hora," he was told, "a place where they used to train priests how to take confession though there's nothing they could teach us." That was what had stuck in my friend's mind. A former seminary that had become the country home of certain torturers. It was on that day that Vaclav Bodnar vanished and was never seen again so my friend put two and two together.'

'He provided transport for Them,' Fulnek said, 'though he knew They were torturers?'

'We all knew They were torturers. We all knew They beat, kidnapped, lied, locked away, murdered. But They gave us cheap beer and plenty of sausage and we kept quiet. Most of us kept quiet. Isn't that so?'

She fixed him with a stare. You for instance, her frown said, you Mr Priest in sheep's clothing, what did you do? Did you sign Charter '77, see the inside of interrogation cells, inspect at close range a secret policeman's fingernails?

'Pah,' she said, and with a wave of her hand wiped these doubts from the air between them. 'When I saw him next—'

'The friend you met when you were out shopping? You kept contact?'

'And why not? Are we all to be chaste like priests? We'd have nothing to confess and you'd be out of a job.'

For a moment she was ferocious before her face lit up with a lovely smile.

'Don't be cross with me.'

'I'm not,' Fulnek assured her.

'It's just my way. In the meantime my friend had done some research and he gave me a name: Benevice.' She gestured beyond the wall where the village was. A man might stab out a finger like aiming a gun but she raised her arm and let the hand droop in the general direction. It was a gesture from the theatre, a grande dame offering her hand for a kiss. 'A week ago I took a day off work and came here. The gate was locked so I went to the village. I started with the church because someone there would know about a place that had been a seminary. The church was locked and I was told there were no longer any services because the priest was too old and somewhat . . .' Her fingers tapped her forehead. 'I asked where he lived. A little cottage with snowdrops by the front door and a rusty bicycle planted between the rose bushes. The bicycle hasn't been used for years. He's keeping it to ride to heaven on, ringing the bell.'

A sunny glimpse of smile came again. Just her way. Fulnek was joining her in a smile and wondering how she must have looked all those years ago when she languished over Hedda Gabler and her friend cheered on Spartak and how alluring she still was despite the unkind Czech diet with its beer and dumplings and chocolate cake – such thoughts were dancing in his head when they both heard the car.

Their smiles were silently packed away. Fulnek felt a wave of sadness. This was Their legacy. Something as simple as an unexpected car could still cause your heart to skip a beat. The engine seemed to race and he listened to it. Was it straining to climb the hill or was it in a hurry to get at them? Common sense said it was sightseers or pilgrims.

The high wall hid the car, hid them too. The car stopped by the gate and the engine cut out. There were voices, male, but it was impossible to tell how many. Like flies in a room. One fly, two flies, more than that it is a relentless buzzing. A door slammed, a second door slammed. Now a voice rose clear over the wall because They'd never needed to lower Their voices.

'Nobody goes in, nobody gets out.'

Prerova looked at Fulnek, then at the chapel as if it might provide sanctuary. It was Them, there was no serious doubt in either of their minds. Rage welled up in Fulnek. This is our country, it doesn't belong to Them. It is our fledgling democracy, it's not Their old tyranny. But Their old tyranny was half hidden in the shadows, impatient to step out if you took liberties.

Fulnek touched her forearm and jerked his head for her to follow. Not the chapel because there were only the confessionals to hide in and they'd look there. He led her to the long building that was at right angles. The door was unlocked and once they were inside and the door closed Fulnek considered securing it. There was no key but there were bolts top and bottom. No, even the dullest thug would know that bolting was an inside job.

The building was of stone, colder and darker than he remembered. Ignoring the corridor to the right Fulnek led the way upstairs. The staircase was impressive to the half-landing but nearer heaven the way was narrower. Nine windows threw light on the corridor and at the first Fulnek stopped and, standing back, he looked out. Prerova pressed against his shoulder.

The wall was what caught your eye. Fulnek no longer saw it as a chastity belt but as a leftover bit of the Berlin Wall. To the left was the gate, shut. The car outside was hidden. Part of the track leading to the village was visible. To the right was the chapel. Beyond was the patch of graveyard and that was where the two men had gone. They stood either side of Bodnar's last resting place, breathing clouds of cigarette smoke. Were they expecting grave robbers? One man stooped to pick up the posy of snowdrops. Letting it drop again he kicked it at the wall. It tumbled back to earth like a shot dove.

They were such ordinary-looking men. One wore brown workman's overalls and had thinning hair. The other was plump and wore a narrow-brimmed hat so his hair was hidden. They turned and the one wearing the hat pointed at the chapel, then at their building. This was where the novices had been housed. Another block further away held the old refectory, the offices, the priests' quarters. At least that was how the arrangements were when it had been a seminary. Fulnek pulled away from the window.

'Follow me.'

They were the first words spoken since the two men arrived. They had brought back the bad old days when words could be traitors and silences could mean a host of things. Prerova wanted to dart through the first door but he tugged at her arm.

'Let go.' Pale sun from the window showed the anger in her face.

'This way.'

The fourth door he pushed open and found himself stepping back a quarter of a century. There was the same curtainless window giving on to the stables. There'd been no horses but he remembered a tribe of cats that nobody seemed to feed. They survived by eating mice and other of God's creatures. Under the window stood the same plain table and wooden chair so hard you couldn't concentrate for long. The same locker, the same metal sheet nailed over a cracked floorboard, the same iron bed, cold, narrow, empty. The blankets and sheets were gone but the stained mattress had been left. He hadn't been prepared for the shock of the past and it brought him up short, Prerova knocking into him. He could almost touch and taste and smell his old life. The long nights came vividly back. He couldn't sleep, he was wrestling with the devil. God knew his thoughts, God was watching his every move, God was testing him. He'd believed all that. God had created him but hadn't got the mix quite right. He'd lain awake with his eyes on the cross on the wall that caught the light from the stars up in heaven. He looked for the cross now. Gone, of course, but amazingly the dusty outline of it still showed.

The sound of heavy footsteps below brought him back. The partition still held a hanging closet, the wood of its door matching the panelling. There was space inside for Prerova and himself, and with the door closed flush with the panelling they could have vanished down a secret passage.

A pause, a break, the breather between rounds while the boxer fills his lungs, wills his pulse to slow, and tries to piece together a strategy for dealing with the relentless machine that keeps raining blows on him.

The closet was stifling, with air so dead it lay heavy against his skin. He sent his ears out on patrol: are They downstairs still, are They on Their way up, at the half-landing, at the end of the corridor? The rest of his body was growing aware of Prerova's physical presence. He felt her fingers now, a light touch on his thigh, searching, moving away. It was his hand she found and locked on to with an iron grip. For security? For strength? Fulnek had none to spare. She laid her head on his shoulder so that he had a faceful of hair. It was in his nose, tickling, building to a sneeze. He opened his mouth to breathe and hair spilled inside.

There was a crash. Somewhere in the building. The closet door baffled Fulnek's sense of direction. Was someone lashing out with a foot? Banging a closet door? Suppose They find us. Suppose They don't find us and set fire to the building. Stone walls don't burn. Wooden floors and partitions burn. Smoke us out. Shoot us down like animals fleeing a forest fire. Don't panic. But there were times when panic was the reaction of a rational man.

The closet was pressing in on him. Like a coffin. Dead already. I should pray. O Lord, he thought, Lord who loves us all, who protects the weak and defence-less . . .

Who hadn't saved Vaclav Bodnar.

A shout from outside. Bellowed louder. 'Honza!' Answering shout from just down the corridor. Next words a jumble of sounds.

They've found the criminals! That's it! It was two other people and they've been discovered cowering inside a mouldy cassock and we're saved. Hallelujah!

And the stupid thing, Fulnek thought, the stupen-dously grotesque thing is I don't know who the woman is or what her connection was with Bodnar. She hasn't told me about Bodnar. She hasn't told me why she's here. But here she is, body pressed against me in the dark as close as a man and a woman can be, our hands clammy together, the smell of the perfume she wears in my nostrils.

The door to the room opened. It swung back and hit the wall just as it always used to until Fulnek had put Saint Augustine's Confessions there as a doorstop. He felt the slam of the door all the way through Prerova's body. He felt the tightening of her grip. He felt rather than heard the catch in her breath.

I can't have brought Them here, he reassured himself, she must have. My quarrel is not with the thugs of the overthrown society. They have come because she has shown interest in a man murdered twenty-three years ago. She has been asking questions of an old lover in Prague, asking questions in the village, asking questions of a priest so senile he is probably still mumbling answers to anyone who bends close to him.

There was a protest from bedsprings. The man would have sat on the bed before lowering his head to look under. Grunt as he got upright. Overweight, too much beer, not enough exercise persuading suspects to sign confessions. Footsteps crossed bare boards. There was a pause. And in the stillness there was a fart, rattling out, ending in a squeak. The footsteps retreated to the corridor.

Thank you, Fulnek said to himself. A symbol. The old régime vanishes, leaving a smell lingering in the air.

'O Lord, we ask Your blessing on Your servant Vaclav who died before making a final act of contrition. You, who know all things, understand the reason for this. Whatever his sins, whether of the body or the spirit, they are as nothing compared to the evil that was done to him. In his life he showed great love and compassion. Keep Vaclav safe in Your hands, we beg you. Let him enjoy everlasting peace.'

But there were others in more need of prayers to be saved: the torturers and murderers. Did he have it in him to pray for their souls which were undoubtedly damned? Those who were still alive still had time for true repentance. Could he find the right words? Would he bring bitter grief down on Prerova? He was stalled by confusion. Prerova stood across the grave from him. Her gaze had been fixed on the ground as if her eyes could penetrate through to the wounds on Bodnar's body. She had picked up the posy of snowdrops and held it against her left breast. She lifted her eyes to Fulnek and gave a slight nod. Enough.

'Amen.'

She dropped the snowdrops on the grave.

CHAPTER THREE

This was the school train. It was the end of their day and they had pent-up energy to work off. Shouts, whistles, shoves. Girls had not been invented. These were all boys. From their treble voices and smooth chins they still had the fence of puberty to jump. Girls had not been invented, not yet.

There was Prerova, of course. She sat opposite Fulnek, legs and face angled towards the window. She was enthralled by ploughed fields, a pond ringed with alders, dabs of forgotten snow tucked under bushes. Or she was inspecting Fulnek's face reflected in the glass. Or her gaze was inward, on the long-ago past or scenes from the seminary.

She broke a long silence, speaking as if those men hadn't come in the car, they hadn't hidden themselves in the closet or prayed over the grave. She could pick up a conversation as if nothing had happened. But she stored happenings. In private she could turn over each event: this is a treasure to be hoarded, this is trash to be thrown away, this is a wound to be avenged.

'The Prague Spring, yes?'

The question wasn't clear to Fulnek but he answered, 'Yes.'

'To me it was the Prague Summer because on the twenty-first of June I met Venca.'

It was as if Vaclav Bodnar had slipped into a seat beside them. They were on more intimate terms. Venca, meet Lojza. Strange, Venca, but you don't smell as if you've been dead nearly twenty-three years. You are coming more alive by the moment.

'We joked about how badly we arranged it – the shortest night of the year. But he said it was for the best or we would have died of love.'

She swung her eyes on him and they were puzzled. She set out to give him a piece of information but her own personal life had a habit of intruding.

'I shouldn't be telling you this.'

'Why not?'

'You a priest. That is, if you are a priest.'

'People tell me things. Not always. But people do confide in a priest.'

'It's not a question of confiding. It's to do with experience. You don't know how reckless love can be.'

Fulnek said nothing. He could hear her voice even when she'd stopped speaking. Almost a quarter of a century had passed and it was not just love for Bodnar he could hear, not exactly. It was obsession. A double obsession. With him and with Them. Already in his mind he was jumping forward because the scandal or crime was part of his memory. Not such big news as the humiliation of Dubček, packing him off to be a forestry official; nor as shocking as the immolation of Jan Palach. Bodnar was a mystery. She would tell him in her own time.

'He used to say we could live on black coffee and

love, and we were lucky because even if the coffee ran out we would never starve. He used to say that love-making was true socialism with a human face: from each according to his ability, to each according to his need, and to Them nothing at all. He used to say that if They published a five-year plan for love, we'd fulfil our norm in one.'

The train slowed, continued uncertainly before coming to an unscheduled halt. And with it Prerova's talk. There was no signal, no station or platform or even name-board. Three boys got off and ran down a path that disappeared into a band of bushes. The land rose gently up a field hazed green by winter wheat. At the far side were three houses showing smoke from their chimneys. A boy to each house? That was too neat, Fulnek decided. Life didn't arrange itself like that. Life distributed its favours and disasters in random fashion. He didn't discover where the boys went because the train started with a jolt. And Prerova with it.

'We used to get dressed and go to the Viola. You wouldn't know what it was like.'

'Tell me.'

She sat forward.

'It was a sardine can, a beehive, a Turkish bath. You understood what those clichés really meant. Students make more noise, smoke more cigarettes, drink more coffee. You bang the table, you don't want the waitress, you have just squashed those moral bugs Brezhnev and Kosygin. You won an argument by shouting loudest. This was a revolution in the making. In there we were free and soon we would be free throughout the country. On the wall – if you can penetrate the battlefield smoke haze as far as the wall – are cartoons. Let's see. There's one of a screaming woman giving birth to a Russian bear with Brezhnev's eyebrows. I can see a guillotine basket of skulls with Lenin's balding head lying on top. I can see Karl Marx raping a woman on the Czech flag, and lining up for their turn are Lenin, Trotsky and Stalin, all with bulges in their pants. You know Déjeuner sur l'Herbe? Well, there was a cartoon of naked women in the background while Brezhnev and Kosygin sprawled on the ground with a picnic of tanks and rocket launchers. Note how women are violated, women are helpless, women are victims. Venca said to me: You've got to be strong; if we're going to beat Them, we can't do it if half the nation is dithering in the background and waiting to service the men.'

She moved back in the seat and gave him her brilliant smile. 'So, Mr Priest, you want to hear all about it?'

'They were brave times,' Fulnek said, 'brave people and brave ideals.'

Prerova didn't trust his preacher's trick with repetitions. The smile faded.

'What do you know about bravery? What experience do you have? After bravery comes death.'

Her mouth was so firmly shut the lips were a thin line. She turned towards the window again. She saw whatever she saw: heroic gestures, a lover's intensity, maybe just the drab houses that stood a little back from the track.

Fulnek's attention slipped back to his own past and he heard again the baying dogs eager to be let loose from the van and saw the police with guns in their hands. They were roaming his church, peering under the pews. While they searched the young man who had come in wide-eyed and panting was wedged behind the organ pipes. Had Fulnek been brave then? He'd certainly been frightened. No, no one, certainly no escaped prisoner. God would applaud the lie.

They rocked together in rhythm as the train swung over the points into Kolin Station.

Something in their design makes rail junctions cheerless. At Kolin a breeze always sneaked inside your clothing. Prerova gave a convulsive shiver and Fulnek had the idea she'd welcome a man's arm around her shoulders.

'You never married him?'

She'd gone deaf.

Fulnek wanted more of her story and persisted. 'Man like him, the two of you so much in love, heady times, I'm surprised you didn't rush to marry. Or did you?'

Her face was half turned aside and she regarded him with one eye. She pondered a bit as if selecting from a range of possible truths. At length the answer came. 'Because he was married already. That's why. That's reason enough. You disapprove? You're shocked? God is sad?'

'God has witnessed it all a million times. Nothing surprises God. To tell the truth I cannot even say if He absolutely disapproves. If two people are honest in their feelings, well, God gave them the capacity for love. There is little enough love in the world without people wilfully denying it. I have to stress that is not the orthodox view of the church. The theologians and the bishops teach that—'

'Spare me the sermons. We had Them preaching Their dogma at us for forty years so it's nice to have a rest. No hard feelings but I can't stomach moralizing. All right?'

There was silence for a time. Fulnek was indeed shocked. Preaching? He was doing the opposite. He was showing friendship, interest, sincerity. He wasn't judging. Maybe – the possibility entered his mind – he'd been a touch pompous.

Prerova had taken refuge from the weather and him in the waiting-room. She had moved a chair close to the window on to the platform so that when Fulnek followed inside and sat down she was in front of him. They were the only people in the waiting-room, and it was as cold as the middle of winter. Prerova had hunched down into her coat. The pose reminded Fulnek of a photograph he once saw of a soldier waiting in the snow for the order to go into battle. The same frozen stiffness, numbness at the approaching H-Hour. It was a photo from the last war, Hitler's war. He couldn't remember if the soldier had been German or Russian. It didn't matter. The boy was most likely dead.

They didn't speak. We're a married couple having a row, Fulnek decided. No, it's a variation on the confessional. Now it is the priest's turn to confess. Mr Priest, as she called him, why did you never marry? Can you explain? Don't try to hide behind your priest's cassock because you don't wear one.

Was she scowling? Eyes closed? From his position he couldn't see her face.

Now she was rummaging in her bag. Cigarette pack and lighter, a little throw-away model with a green transparent tank for fuel. Smoke hovered over her like a depression. Why did he think of the Viola café? She and her lover would have been smoking, arguing, passionate, their eyes catching fire.

Was it his imagination? Was her neck growing stiffer under his gaze? Her head was held higher like a banner going into battle. With a screech of chair legs on the floor she swung round.

'You're judging me. Just stop it. You know nothing.'

'I was thinking,' Fulnek said, surprising even himself, 'that if I'd been in Bodnar's place and met you, I would have acted exactly the same way.'

Her eyes grew immense as if to swallow him. A barely understandable loudspeaker announced the arrival of the train to Prague.

This was a real train, all the way from Bohumin on the Polish border. The windows framed grannies, commercial travellers, off-duty soldiers, functionaries from various ministries. There should have been more romance to it. In the old days you could count on an adventuress, a couple of runaway lovers, a spy with a plan of the docks at Gdansk. Or, in even earlier days, the docks at Danzig.

She led the way down the corridor and slid back the door to an empty compartment. They sat opposite each other, which made the silence awkward. She turned her face to the window as the train left the station but caught the reflection of Fulnek's eyes. His last remark hung between them. What had possessed him?

She construed the remark this way and that. Should she treat it as a joke? As something to ease the tension? A priest showing his human side? Best ignore it. It was a mistake. It never happened. It was the hand that brushes against a breast in the metro. That wasn't a fondle, that was the lurch of the carriage.

'Nineteen sixty-eight,' she said. It was spoken in a tone of wonder, so long ago. She still favoured the window. 'Spring and summer. Winter was just round the corner but we didn't believe that. The hot weather came and it seemed everything was a heaving ferment. The country, politics, the future, our own lives. You know how it is, do you?' She was facing him again. 'Perhaps just once it happens: that your own personal life and events in the wide world march in step. You're one with all humanity. You're part of history. You, your lovers, your friends, everybody around you are making it. You feel absorbed by . . . by . . .'

'By love?' Fulnek suggested. 'By God?'

'By the first, certainly. Venca would open the door – my parents were spending the summer with my mother's sister – he would burst in, love, life, laughter, delight, amazement fizzing out of him. "Do you know what I learnt from Franta? Do you know what the Brno police chief has proposed? I bought these roses this morning, sorry if they wilted. Did I tell you I love you? Guess who's resigning tonight. Kiss me, kiss me hard."' She was suddenly alive, her hands gesturing, her body moving, her face alight. 'He'd been one of the radical reporters on the radio. Digging out stories, interviews, conferences, demonstrations, investigations. What stupid long words. News, news. He was always breathless, always running. In my mind I can't remember ever sleeping. Common sense says we must have. It made no impression on me. In bed, yes, but not asleep. Sometimes when he wasn't working, I was, and we'd miss each other. When we met we tore each other apart.'

She stared at her hands and went quiet.

'What is your work?'

'In those days I was in the theatre. In a way I still am. Then I was an actress. Now . . .' A hand jerked and fell back on her lap like a dying fish. 'Let me tell you how Venca and I met. At that time there was a small theatre club in a cellar not far from Central Station. It was called The Other Place. No, don't ask me – I don't know what place it was other to. It specialized in fraught modern drama. Experimental. Daring. Searing indictments of everything. Often naked. That was when Venca noticed me. The third and fourth tits from the right. That's what he said.'

She inspected the priest's face closely to see if he was shocked. Fulnek was thrilled. He wanted nothing better than for her to go on speaking. He said, 'Was he always outspoken?'

'He said exactly what he thought. That's all very well if you happen to be having charming thoughts or seductive thoughts. If you have subversive thoughts . . .' She lifted a hand, all the fingers out-stretched, dismayed by such innocence. 'He would say to me, I love you with all my heart. So to all these communist hardliners he would say, I loathe you with all my soul. You have to choose your time to make criticisms like that. He was an entire generation too early. He was a fool. He was my lovely foolish Venca. He was too impetuous, too generous with himself and what he found out.'

She broke off again to stare through the window. The train was passing a factory surrounded by a vast carpark set among fields. There was no village in sight. The workers must have been bussed in from somewhere for the carpark was mostly empty tarmac. A chimney spat pollution at the countryside.

'Do you read poetry?' she asked, as if poetry might be a forbidden pleasure for a priest. 'Hrubik?'

'I've read some of Hrubik.'

'Anger, love and hope . . . Do you know it?'

He continued:

'That three-ply rope
Binding us together
One to another
Like lover to lover.'

She concentrated on Fulnek as if he was reading for a part before a beautiful smile lit up her eyes. 'Good. Excellent. I used to think Hrubik was crazy. We were outraged. What had our grand passion to do with the anger and hate They filled us with? Now I think Hrubik saw more deeply. Venca loved me but he would come in fuming at President Novotny. He would be throwing away his clothes shouting, "When is that bastard Novotny going to pack his bags?" In my mind I would translate that into: When is my darling Venca going to pack his bags? He still hadn't left his wife completely. She had her claws well dug in. Most of his clothes were at their apartment rather than mine. Private lives, public times, bound together, yes? There were manifestos to argue over, demands to be drawn up. An old printing press had been unearthed and Venca liberated some rolls of newsprint, which was in short supply.' Her face had turned serious. 'One night he came to me very angry and I thought his wife had been taunting him or sobbing or scratching or threatening suicide. She had many tricks except the most important: how to make Venca feel passionate. No, it wasn't her. It was a great scandal, a great corruption, and he was going to investigate it, dig out the dirt, the names, the dates, how much money . . .'

The doorway darkened. Two men stood there, but not ticket inspectors. They wore hats and raincoats and could have been anything. They could have been teachers or clerks or typesetters or librarians. They murmured something to each other. Then, looking each way down the corridor, they slid open the door.

'These seats are free?'

Prerova looked at them with a deadpan face.

'Yes,' Fulnek said.

The two men sat and lit cigarettes and did not speak. No one spoke. It was a silence of the kind there used to be.

The real trouble, Fulnek decided, was the checking each way down the corridor before coming in. It was what They used to do. The habits of years weren't discarded as easily as clothes. They could be normal travellers. Of course. Just been in the refreshment car enjoying a pilsner. That was it. They are travelling without luggage just as we are. They've come all the way from the Polish border in the refreshment car and didn't have seats anywhere else in the train. Yes.

And there was no reason They should be interested in us, know we would be on the train, even know what we look like. None at all. No.

Still, Prerova had lost the thread of her story and Fulnek didn't prompt her.

The train rattled through suburbs, industrial zones, small-holdings to Liben. Then, with all the caution of someone making a clandestine rendezvous, the train slipped into Central Station. The two men, who had kept their hats and coats on throughout the silent journey, nodded before stepping out. Once again they glanced right and left before moving off. It was what muggers did. Or guilty lovers. Who else?

'Maybe,' Prerova murmured. 'Maybe not.'

Even out of power They still had the power to silence people. It was Their legacy. It was fading fast but something trivial – a word, a gesture, looking each way – could still bring it back.

A great scandal, a great corruption. Her words. For that a man had been kidnapped, taken to a secret police hideaway, suffered unknown terrors, was murdered and buried, with a white X to mark the grave.

For a small scandal, a small corruption, what was the punishment? To be kept in suspense, to have the future an abyss in front of you. Will the next step take you over the edge, falling? Will you be pushed?

Waiting to learn the future was part of his punishment. All the judges and jailers and inquisitors in history had known that. The future yawned ahead. It was the yawn of nerves, fear. To fill the void was a sudden urgency.

'Wait.' They were crossing the concourse of the station and it seemed she was to disappear into the evening rush hour. 'Prerova.' It was the first time he had used her name since the introductions.

She swung round on him, her coat swirling about her calves. It was how certain ladies swung round when they laid eyes on a Western businessman coming out of one of the expensive hotels. Fulnek had observed this though the ladies, noting his lacklustre shoes and creaseless trousers and lumpy jacket, had never swirled for him. He would have disapproved if they had put on a display for him, naturally he would. He would have liked the opportunity to disapprove.

It was Prerova who was disapproving. She scowled at him, or at something just by his elbow. Fulnek let his eyes slip sideways and found he was standing next to a dispenser that announced itself boldly in English as Men's Shop. It sold condoms. He did a priestly shuffle to mask the machine.

'You were coming to the climax,' he said. 'The corruption Venca had uncovered. You can't leave me like that.'

She sighed. It was a sigh Fulnek recognized, a woman's sigh evolved through hundreds of generations at the demands of men.

'Come.' She offered an arm to link with his.

Fulnek thought he was being led to the Esplanade Hotel but she swept past the entrance. 'You could not afford a drink there on a priest's wages. And besides, those big hotels . . .'

End the sentence how you like, she seemed to be

saying. She had had a disappointing experience in a big hotel. She was contemptuous of the German guests who sneered at the cheapness of everything but counted every last koruna of their change. She was wary of a place where, in the old days, a careless word in front of an attentive waiter could go in one ear and out through a telephone call to Them.

She pulled him down a side street for two blocks and into a narrow doorway with a sign above proclaiming The Jazz Hole. 'It used to be The Other Place until after the Soviet tanks rolled in and Dubček was banished. They didn't like the searing social criticism but it was the nudity They really hated. We carried on for a while until it became clear that naked bodies were ideologically unsound. As well as everything else. They are prudes. Mind your head going down.'

It was perpetual dusk in the cellar. They passed an empty rack for coats and went into a room with a bar at one end and eight tables with accompanying chairs set in two ranks in front of a diminutive stage. A man with a tenor saxophone and a man with a xylophone were fooling about. They were middle-aged, paunchy and altogether looked like a pair of janitors. Which, Fulnek conceded, may very well have been their fate in the old days.

Prerova had commandeered the telephone that sat on a corner of the bar and was reordering her life. 'Didn't I cover for you when you went to Karlovy Vary with whatsisname, Elephant Trunk? . . . Well, that's what you called him, darling, I didn't like to enquire . . . It's come up at short notice . . . Of course it's a he, at least . . .' Here she cast a glance over at

Fulnek. 'Bozka, in theory it's a he, the practice . . . No, darling, not one of those. It's too complicated to go into now . . . You will? Blessings, my sweet, and may all your nights be long ones. Ciao.'

She brought two glasses of apple juice over to the table where Fulnek had been watching the musicians and listening to half a telephone conversation. A third man had wandered in, pudgy like the others, an over-coat like a woollen blanket draped around his shoulders, carrying a leather instrument case. Trumpet, from the size of it.

'That Bozena, really, all she'll have to do is sell the programmes at the beginning and the orange juice at the interval.'

Fulnek waited for the explanation.

'I'm at the Palace of Culture. I told you I was still in the theatre. That's what I do. Stand round with a tray of programmes.'

'Can't you get back on stage now?'

'There's a pit twenty years deep where my career should have been.'

That's what They did – stole people's lives. Do this, do that, They had ordered. Stop acting, stop reporting. Dig this grave, now step into it. A man wandered out from behind a curtain and sat at the piano. He laced his fingers together over the keyboard to flex them and the knuckles cracked. As he began to play, Prerova took up her story. She could have been waiting for the music to cover her voice. Even now.

'Sometimes we went to the zoo. Sometimes we talked in bed. Whispered, I mean, not loud. Sometimes we went to Kampa Island and stood with his hands on my shoulders and my hands on his hips. Facing each other like lovers but he could see past my head and I could see past his. Whenever anyone drew close he would stop talking and kiss me instead. So it was terror and delight in one. Terror, I mean it. Beyond fear. I was terrified for him because he said he could be killed for what he had found out. Terrified for myself too because he'd shared his secret with me. It was money, of course.'

She broke off to watch another couple who'd arrived. They took beers from the bar and sat a little way off. Nowhere could be very far off. Thirty people would be a crowd in this room. Is this where she appeared naked – on that stage? Perhaps just there where a man was screwing a mouthpiece into his clarinet. His moustache stood out in perfect detail. You'd have been able to count every hair on her body.

Satisfied, she started again. Cautious, she leaned so close her shoulder brushed his.

'When I said money, I don't mean money like we understand it, or even Their ordinary corruption. We all know the pigs had Their snouts in the trough. They had Their Mercedes, so what? We didn't have to walk, we had our trams. They had Their hunting lodges, we had our *chata* even if it was knocked together from wooden packing cases. They dined in *salons particuliers* at the Alkron, we could queue for a sausage from a stall outside. We had no cause to be jealous. Besides, jealousy is a bourgeois sin, jealousy is out. No, this was embezzling from the state on a grand scale. Having stolen our country from us, and our lives, They had scaled a new peak and were stealing Their own loot.'

She drew a breath. 'We were walking up Petrin Hill, stopping as people do to catch our breath and look back over the city. Venca put an arm round my shoulders and bent his head so that his lips were close to my ear.'

And that is what she did, leaned so that her mouth was near Fulnek's ear. The jazz group had grown to a sextet and provided background music to her soft voice.

'He whispered in my ear: "I love you, my darling, you are my enchantress, my Cleopatra. I met a man today – Vilem, to give him a name – who comes from near Presov. He has been here since Monday doing the rounds of the ministries. Agriculture, Land, Natural Resources, you name it. And your ear is perfect. If I blow in your ear is it like an express train roaring through your soul? Vilem said he'd been turned off his land which was wanted to build a paper mill. I don't know all the details yet – perhaps his land was to be flooded when a dam was put up. I can see beads of moisture at each side of your nose. Is it the sun warming you? Is it me? Vilem said that surveyors had come over a year ago and a new road was half constructed. Then everything came to a halt. The workmen have removed the machinery. So please, why was the land taken from me, why have you stopped building, and can I have my land back? I can feel your eyelashes when you blink, a butterfly caressing my cheek. And this honest but simple man was thrown out on his ear, told not to be a nuisance, not to concern himself with matters of economic policy that were beyond his understanding. But all I want is my farmland back, he would protest. Finally he was picked up on the street and taken in for questioning. He didn't know who by. Nobody wore a uniform or showed identification. Was he a trouble-maker? Was he anti-state? Was he a Zionist? Was he in the pay of the Americans? And this fellow couldn't make head nor tail of it. No more than I can understand how one touch of your hand sends twenty thousand volts through my body."'

Prerova leaned away. Fulnek's ear was burning. She was an actress. She had never left the stage. All her life she had used voice, face, body. She needed to win her audience, even if it was only one man. She lacked patience, was never wholly still, always occupying herself with theatrical business. Now she lifted her glass, using both hands, and dipped her face towards it. It could be some exotic bloom grown in a hothouse. Her lips touched the glass in a kiss, and all the time her eyes looked over the rim at him.

'How did Bodnar—' Fulnek swallowed and began again. 'How did Venca find the man Vilem?'

'Met him in a pub, picked him out of the gutter, I don't know. Most probably someone in one of the ministries whispered something down the telephone. They had Their informers, we had ours.'

She released him from her intense gaze, looking to the pocket stage. Her eyelids drooped a moment as she saw the past, herself in the spotlight where now the drummer laid a cigarette in an ashtray and set the tempo, calling in English, 'One-two, one-two-three-four.' She peered around the audience which had swelled to eleven and back to Fulnek.

'I may have got it wrong,' she said. 'The first time he

whispered it in my ear we may have been in bed. I know the second time we were climbing the hill, he stopped and swept his arm out over the city.' She gestured round the stage, the audience, the murals showing reclining nudes, male and female, with their backs turned. 'This was during the unreal time. It was before the Soviet tanks rolled in, but we didn't know they were coming. It was after Dubček had been summoned for fraternal consultations at the Soviet border, but we didn't know much about that either. The Railwaymen's Club, Platform Three, Cierna nad Tisou was where our fate was being sealed but we thought it was here. Venca said: "Prague is a city of betrayals. People lean too far out of windows and never say goodbye. People plead to be executed for crimes they didn't commit in order to advance the cause of the system that is murdering them. If foreign politicians betray us, our own politicians are spurred to even greater efforts. Friends betray friends. Wives betray husbands. Colleagues betray colleagues. Everybody betrays the system which betrays them. Perhaps one day you will betray me." I bit him. I grabbed hold of his wrist and twisted his palm up so I could sink my teeth into the ball of flesh under his thumb until I tasted his blood. I would rather have killed him than betray him. I would have shot him and as he lay dying I would have held him in my arms. He understood that. He nodded his head. The pain of my bite meant nothing. He said: "They are betraying Their own creation. The rot is very deep in Their soul. A lot of money, a lot of corruption. I'm almost there, not quite but almost. And when I know the truth, I'll publish."'

She fell quiet. The trumpeter was announcing *Down the Road a Way*, a tribute to Miles Davis in his lyrical and tender style. 'Man walking on eggshells' was how the trumpeter summed up his feelings. He flexed his lips before kissing the mouthpiece.

'Why was that man Vilem being threatened? What became of him? Did Venca find the truth?' Fulnek asked. He held on and held on until he was forced to prod again. 'Did he publish anything at all?'

She shrugged.

What kind of answer was that?

'Did he get to the bottom of the corruption?'

'You don't get to the bottom of corruption,' she said, 'you get to the top. I don't know if he got to the very top or not. I know he got too close.'

'But he didn't print anything?'

'Questions! Always questions! You'd make some interrogator yourself.' She scowled and relented. 'He was with me one night, then I didn't see him for twenty-four hours, then the Russians were suddenly driving up and down Wenceslas Square. Tourists with tanks. That day it was like the clock stopped for everybody. I waited in the flat and he never came back. I thought: he's out getting a story, he'll come bursting in with it. I thought: he's out shouting at the Ivans to go home. I thought: he's in detention somewhere. There were rumours of truckloads of demonstrators being taken to Spartak Stadium. I thought: he's in a bar getting blind drunk. Then I thought: that wife of his has got her claws in him. He had no telephone so I went to his apartment. I wasn't frightened of her. It was Venca I was frightened for.

'Red Army, tanks, police all along the way. I don't remember what my plan was. Didn't have one, I expect. It was just Venca I was going for. Scream at the wife, fight her for her man, tear her hair out. I would have. Believe me, I would have. I climbed up the stairs of his block and when I stepped into the corridor I understood at once. A man stood smoking a cigarette at the far end and a second man came off the wall behind me. Men with square faces and hats, like on the train this afternoon. Talk about first-night nerves. The trick is to go straight into your performance and carry your nerves with you. I simply went to the first door and rang the bell. Some grandfather answered and I asked for Maria. There was no Maria. There has to be – and I'm peering round his shoulder. There is no Maria living here. So I switch to pantomime, overacting for the sake of the audience of two. Big look at the number on the door. Demanding Maria, the number is right, what's his game hiding her? Then, discovering my mistake: I'm in the wrong building. I should be in Block D, confusion, silly me, thousand apologies, bless your sweet grey whiskers. I walked back ignoring the man at the head of the stairs and got out. I kept my hands deep in my pockets, they were shaking so much. They had taken Venca and were waiting to pick up his contacts. I never saw him again. Never.'

She made a gesture and let her hand drop.

Curtain. That was it. End of show. There was no more. Except there was. Fulnek was sure of it. But she'd relived enough pain for one day. He'd watched her performance and seen the actress die. Now she was a widow and needed privacy to mourn Bodnar. She pushed herself up from the chair and he watched her walk towards the door. She swerved as if to sidestep an obstacle and came back.

'*Los desaparecidos*, you know, like they had in Argentina and El Salvador? Well, we had them first. Venca was a *desaparecido*. They disappeared him.'

This time she didn't loop back on the way out. Her widow's coat swung behind her. Her heels clicked as she climbed the stairs.

Woman walking on eggshells.

CHAPTER FOUR

I t was the clink of metal that woke him. Or the man's voice. Lying in bed Fulnek strained his ears. He could feel the patter of his heartbeat. He'd been dreaming something about a wrecked chapel and the sounds had merged into the dream. He strained to recapture flickering images. He was in the confessional and a penitent entered the other box. Grunting, straining, deep breaths from beyond the grille. Woman giving birth? Then an unmistakable noise and smell. A man's voice: Pal, got any paper your side?

The dream evaporated like steam. From outside came a drawn-out screech of metal. Fulnek thought of Them. How would They know he was here? How had They known Prerova would be at the seminary?

Out of bed, by the window, he edged back the curtain. He had a view of the communal courtyard and a man hauling away a dustbin. It was whatever-it-was past one in the morning. He found something menacing about removing garbage in the dead of the night. Prague 1991 could be a fourteenth-century village getting rid of the corpses of plague victims under cover of darkness.

This was his temporary bolthole in Prague while the committee deliberated. Absent yourself, they had said.

This room was where his body retreated. His mind, that was a problem. Images didn't absent themselves but suddenly swarmed in. Mouth screaming abuse, cheeks shining with rage. Her eyes pale, dry, too mad for tears. Then the eyes darken, the face dissolves into another face, Prerova's.

He flung himself into a corner with his face shut in by two walls. Eyebrows, cheekbones, nose hid in the blackness. I'm a five-pointed star pressing against the cold plaster and the plaster is pressing right back. This was where he liked to pray best. The outer world was excluded.

'Lord, keep her safe this night. Give her the peace to sleep. Forgive her her sins for we are all sinners. We are all human. We are.'

He hadn't included her name but God knew. Fulnek thought of Prerova's frown, he thought of her smiles, he thought of the click of her heels going upstairs and the switch of her calves one in front of the other as she paraded in front of him across the station concourse. He thought of her whisper in his ear, he thought of the gestures acquired from the theatre of life and love. He thought of her hand finding his in the secrecy of the closet.

'Keep her safe from Them. Keep her in the palm of Your hand. Their evil isn't dead, only hiding.'

What had drawn Them to the old seminary? What was it in Their past?

'Bodnar. Her Venca. Another sinner but his sins pale in the brightness of his love and the joy he brought. Bless him, Lord, bless the adulterer, the fornicator. His love redeems him. Amen.'

Footsteps in the passage made him turn his head. The door handle moved. Finding it locked, there was a knock.

'Mr Fulnek, are you all right?'

'All right? Why shouldn't I be?'

'You're talking out loud. Groaning.'

It was the voice of his landlady. He'd spied the sign in the window Zimmer frei. She would have preferred a German tourist with a pocketful of Deutschmarks but it was too early in the season.

'Was I?'

'I could hear you in my room, Mr Fulnek. I told you I don't allow visitors at night.'

'So you did.'

Fulnek unlocked the door and her eyes flicked from his face to the bed.

'Who were you talking to?'

'God.'

She took a step back. Behind her in the shadows was a movement. The two Persian cats she kept for breeding were swatting at each other with their paws. It was some courtship ritual.

Fulnek said, 'I'll pray for you too.'

They were so different from God. Weren't they?

Fulnek was drifting, not yet asleep but with his thoughts slipping.

We gave a capital letter to God's name for His infinity. So why did we do the same for Them? Did we see divinity in Them? All knowing, all seeing, all powerful?

Both were givers and takers of life. Forgivers and condemners. To whom people had dedicated their lives, confessed sins, suffered punishments. We had also hidden our faces from both in awe.

Now They had fallen from Their throne and God was alone.

They said God was dead and God had answered Them.

Sighing, turning over, the comparison dissolved in the shadows.

Socks, pants, shirts, toothbrush, razor. Fulnek had made a pilgrimage to Kotva. Mounting up the escalator he cast an eye over the ladies' underwear department where Prerova met her most recent lover. Prerova would have bought things here too. There were lacy bras and frilly knickers in satanic black but would they stretch round sturdy Czech bodies? Prerova, he thought, yes. Purchases made, he wandered along Na prikope and stopped for coffee and cake.

One week, that committee, the synod, had said. Stretching to two weeks.

Appalled, he stared into the cup as he stirred. It was a black whirlpool.

It was important to keep going. It was important to keep the brain busy, not to brood or be bitter or build fantasies or even try to plan a future. The past belonged to our mistakes, the future belonged to God.

For a few moments Prerova stared, as if she had never met him. Her eyes wandered to the left where the stairs came up, to the right where the next apartment's door was shut, down to his shoes to see if they showed traces of mud or whether he had been delivered to the entrance of the building in comfort, up to Fulnek's face again.

'How did you find out where I live?'

'They told me—'

'They?'

'I went to the Palace of Culture,' Fulnek explained. 'I asked for Bozena. I didn't know her surname. But—'

'But you wouldn't be the first man never to find out her surname.' Finally a smile crept up to Prerova's eyes. 'And you got out alive. She eats men for breakfast. That's afterwards, if you see what I mean. Like that spider. Come in, won't you?' She stepped out of the way. She looked tired, edgy, a little lonely.

'I brought you these.' Fulnek handed her the bunch of flowers he had been holding behind him. They were roses, their buds drooping, the way Bodnar used to give them.

'Oh.' She held the roses away from her, frowning into them. 'Thank you.'

I shouldn't have, Fulnek told himself. It makes me out to be a suitor. Or an errant husband. He stood in the doorway to the kitchenette while she stuck the flowers into a vase. He stood aside to let her carry the vase to the sitting-room, then out of the way again as she returned to the stove. She set to making Turkish coffee. The silence was growing awkward. She's regretting yesterday, Fulnek decided, talking about the past, laying it out like the naked dead.

Her flat was in Zizkov, a district the unkind said was given over to thieves and gypsies. She noticed Fulnek peering about him and said, 'I inherited the apartment from my parents. They died in a coach crash years ago and I've never moved.' If she'd had a career and become a great dame of Prague theatre she would be living off Wenceslas Square in one of those overheated apartments that could be on a grand boulevard in Paris.

She carried the coffee through to the sitting-room, making small talk. 'Some people say you should drop an aspirin in the water with roses. Have you heard that?'

'What good does that do?'

'Cure their hangover?' Her smile was pale, wintery. 'Pardon me for being blunt – you've come for something, Father Fulnek?'

'Call me Alois. Or . . .' He stopped. 'Alois will do.' With Lojza the image that terrified him last night flashed through his mind: the crazed eyes, the glistening cheeks, the mouth open in a scream. What it was screaming was I hate you, Lojza, hate you.

She leaned back, stretching one arm along the back of her chair. 'So what brings you?'

Fulnek looked away across the room at a solid desk in dark wood with carved legs that ended in bear's paws. He swung back to her. He said, surprising himself once more, 'To see you again.'

She sighed. Men. A nod of her head. If she nodded for each man with a silver tongue she'd known she'd be dizzy.

'Voilà, you see me.'

Fulnek looked at her, down at his tiny cup of coffee, up at her.

'You're strange for a priest. Are you absolutely sure—'

'It is one thing I am sure of.'

'Venca had no time for the church. He said the church was on the margin of life. You couldn't take priests seriously. You couldn't take them seriously as leaders in the struggle and you couldn't take them seriously as, well, as men.'

Yes. Well, Bodnar had been busy in the struggle and someone had taken him very seriously indeed. Concentrate on that, Fulnek told himself, keep your mind on Bodnar.

'After Venca disappeared,' he began.

Prerova nodded.

'When he didn't return, what happened?'

'Don't you remember?'

'I don't remember anything in the paper. Of course there were rumours.'

'Rumours?' She didn't like the word. 'Rumours? Where were you?'

'Brno.'

'Rumours in Brno?'

'The cathedral. Restoration work. Pushing a barrow, lifting stones. Someone has to do it.' He opened his hands in front of her. 'A cathedral is a perfect place to pick up whispers.'

'Bodnar Must Live.' She halted, memories of the times crowding in. Soldiers in uniform, police in uniform, police out of uniform. Thugs with a hunger to use their fists. Sirens, shouts, screams. The way a crowd shudders, ripples spreading out like a stone tossed in a pool. March, demonstrate, throw leaflets in the air, run down side-streets, dodge in doorways. Learn to disguise yourself with *Rude Pravo* like a good little apparatchik.

'It was a campaign, a crusade. It was dangerous because They had kidnapped him. What we were doing was anti-Party, anti-state. You risked a beating, risked your career. Some novelist would write a piece: *Why Bodnar's fate is the fate of us all*. We'd get it printed clandestinely, drop the leaflets around. The novelist would be sent to stoke the boilers in some factory. We had our very own Gulag, the boiler rooms of Prague.'

Meanwhile I was restoring an entrance porch, Fulnek thought. Be honest: I was a labourer helping the mason who was doing the restoring. It was practical work, made a difference, improved the quality of life. Something like that.

'You can't have a campaign without a committee. Planning the next event, what banners to carry, what leaflets to print, which embassy to march on. Some committee! We are world leaders in committees here in Czechoslovakia. Everybody gets together in a small room, smokes cigarettes and talks. Actors, professors, writers, radio reporters, musicians, painters, photographers. For a time we had a member of the proletariat. She was someone who had worked at the Viola so she was allowed to make the coffee.'

Prerova was on her feet now, the adrenaline flowing.

'It's a funny thing. You can never really pinpoint the moment things begin to go wrong. Like a marriage, you know? No, I suppose you wouldn't.'

'You think we spend our lives on our knees, our eyes on the angels? Do you think we don't get tearful husbands, desperate wives? Do you think we close our ears in the confessional? Do you think I know nothing about marriage? Or committees?'

'Not this committee. After about three weeks – only three weeks – it grew on us that things had gone wrong. The authorities knew what we planned as soon as we did. Maybe before. They'd raid the studio where the posters were being designed. They'd be in the front row of a crowd. They'd be the thugs in boots who kicked people's insteps and spat in their faces. They had a spy on the committee, must have had, so that was the end of that.'

Fulnek nodded. He understood. There was always a Judas.

She was standing over him, looking down.

'Except me. One woman, one mad woman. But one woman can make a noise. Bodnar Must Live! Free Bodnar! Let Bodnar Out Of His Cell! Let Bodnar Go! I'd scream it and run to scream another day. Or chain myself to the railings under Wenceslas's statue and not run. And one night They came to get me.'

Sometimes bad things got censored out of the memory but Prerova had perfect recall. She'd been with a girlfriend to the cinema. A night out to forget her troubles. She was returning to the apartment towards midnight. In those days there were fewer cars so she noticed the car parked outside the Dobruskych and the men sitting in the car. Three men. Perhaps they'd come out after dinner and were having a last cigarette before going home, except the Dobruskych closed at ten. Also, it was not the kind of restaurant you got in a car and drove out to. It served liver, dumplings, cabbage and beer but the wise avoided the first three. She thought of crossing the road but then she'd have to cross right back to enter the front door of her building.

And besides, she was fearless, she was a campaigner for Venca, she was a committee of one. These considerations flitted through her mind in the time it took to walk a dozen steps. She was parallel with the car, she was walking past it, she truly thought she was past it and was getting tetchy with herself for having a flutter of nerves when the rear door opened, a man grabbed her round the waist and she was bundled into the back seat.

'Yes?' Fulnek said.

She focused on him, his face tilted up to her. He seemed to be waiting. Had she been speaking only inside her head?

'Down there.' She jerked her head at the window. 'Three men in a car.'

In the back seat she had a man squashed each side of her. The engine started and she screamed. A man clapped a hand over her mouth and she bit and tasted blood. He swore and the man on the other side knocked his elbow hard into her and when she turned her attention on him she found herself peering into the nostril of a pistol.

'They drove me across the river somewhere beyond Smichov. I remember passing the station. They didn't speak much. No point in asking them anything. They were just the delivery men. The place they took me to was one of those nineteenth-century villas that are falling apart. No style, not one of the big shots, I thought. I was pushed into a room, an office or study or den. He was waiting for me. Still youngish. Got his way to make in the world. That's how I'd judge him now. Then . . .'

Then she saw a man of thirty-something, dark hair and moustache. His body filled his suit but it looked brawn rather than fat. The eyes that held hers had intelligence in them, or certainly shrewdness. She heard the door close. She saw the windows had shutters and bars. What could she do? Hit him with the desk lamp? She knew she would only get out when he said so.

'And?' Fulnek prompted.

'And? And what, for God's sake? What do you want from me? You expect me to show you what it's like being raped? How do I do that?'

'No. No, don't go on. Please. I understand.'

'You do not understand because you don't feel what I felt. That would be an impossibility. It was more than what he did. It wasn't just what he said. It was what he thought. I was raped by what was in his mind. He didn't get his men to rip my clothes off and hold me down, one to each limb. He didn't put a pistol in my ear and threaten to blow my brains out. He said: "Get undressed, take everything off, I'm going to fuck you." That's what he said.'

The priest's brow went into a brief spasm. It was not the language, it was the picture in his head that hurt.

'He said, "You don't do what I tell you and I'll have your mother picked up. Ondrej will fuck her. I've seen that Slovak slob fuck a goat. You or your mother. That's your choice."'

'Don't tell me. I don't want the details.'

'My choice, he said. What choice? Would a mother choose for her daughter to be raped? What choice did I have? The bastard knew I would agonize about it for years before I went to sleep, that I'd blame my mother. Democracy is about choice, so we're told. A People's Democracy is about the kind of choice I was given. "Take your clothes off."'

Fulnek's face had disappeared into the darkness of his hands. Prerova's sitting-room was blotted out but not the scene she was describing.

'He stood waiting. I was wearing a sweater and skirt and slip underneath. I took them off and then I looked at him. He was watching. You know how a man watches a woman undress? Do you, Father Alois? Desire makes the man's eyes bigger. His eyes are eating her up. He doesn't smile because mating is a serious business, the survival of the species. But he was watching and smiling. I remember that face. A smile touching the ends of his mouth. He was enjoying his power. "Everything." I took off my underclothes and looked at him again. The smile was gone. He was staring. The look on his face . . . I haven't forgotten it. His expression had changed. Now it was like someone at the butcher's saying, "Two pork chops," and paying close attention while the butcher gets out his knife and slices through the meat . . . Can you hear me? Are you praying in there? Because if you are I want you to ask your God to turn up the burners when that man gets where he is heading.'

'I don't want to hear any more.' Fulnek could have moved his hands to cover his ears but he kept them over his eyes. He could have got up and left. He could, he could . . .

'Don't you want to hear the best part?'

'No.' He could, but he didn't.

'The act itself? You think I'm talking about that? The climax? He unbuttoned his fly. He didn't even take his trousers off. He wasn't the meat on the butcher's slab. He told me to lie on the floor. When I didn't he screamed in my face, "Get down, whore!" Any self-respecting whore would have kicked him in the crotch. He gave me the choice again. "You or your mother." He was playing with me. I remember getting down on the floor and he was on all fours. He grabbed a fistful of hair and held me tight in case I tried to bite him. I remember thinking: if Venca was alive, he'd kill him. Thinking: if Venca was alive . . . It was the first time I'd admitted his death to myself. That was when he did it. I was raped and widowed all in the same moment.'

She was quiet. Her relentless march through the badlands was over. So Fulnek thought as he took his hands away from his face. Prerova had fetched a bottle from somewhere and poured a glass. She knocked it back, refilled the glass and handed it to Fulnek.

'Drink it.'

It was plum brandy. The bottle was without a label, the brandy distilled in someone's barn, and it burned Fulnek's throat. It reached his stomach and he had the sensation of a hundred ants biting.

'So, the best part.' Prerova hadn't come to an end, merely been renewing her courage for the final act. 'He'd finished and buttoned his fly and was standing over me. "Get up."' She had a voice for the rapist, a clipped bark like a Nazi on parade '"I didn't say to get dressed yet."'

While Fulnek watched, Prerova unbuttoned her

blouse down the front. Slipping one hand inside her bra, she wriggled a shoulder to make the strap slip off and eased the right breast out of its cup.

'See?'

How could he not? She was so close Fulnek could reach out . . . reach out and button up her blouse.

'God,' he whispered.

'Is that swearing or praying?'

Running from high on the breast in a long curve that ended under the nipple was a white scar.

'He did that with a razor, an old-fashioned cut-throat one. He didn't cut deep but there was still blood everywhere. He emptied the ashtray in the palm of his hand and rubbed the ash in. The idea was to make the scar more prominent. He said: "You've done your last strip on stage. There isn't a director who'll give you a nude scene now." Oh, that hurt. I was crying and there was nothing I could do to stop myself. He said: "Forget about Bodnar. You won't see him again. Concentrate your thoughts on yourself. Nobody rapes the same woman twice. If your loud and stupid behaviour puts you in my way again . . ."'

She ran a finger across her own throat.

Prerova had tidied away the slivovice bottle and made another pot of coffee.

'You know what the doctor said when he was fixing this up?' She gestured at her breast. 'I told him I'd been holding a glass against my chest when I slipped and fell. He said, "Tell me what brand of cigarette the glass was smoking and I'll give it up." I thought about that doctor afterwards. Man with a sense of humour like that is a man you can trust. I thought about going to see him later . . .'

Fulnek had the sense of her pulling back. She had things to tell him and things to keep to herself.

'You've no idea who raped you? His name, position?'

'No.'

'You didn't try to find out?'

'First I was in shock, then I was frightened, then I had other things on my mind. My chest was all strapped up and I lost my job. Anyway, have you already forgotten what the times were like? He was one of Them. Suppose I found out his name; who would I go to to lay a complaint? Do you know anyone who went to police headquarters with a charge like that? Anyway, I had no name. So, comrade, who are you laying this complaint against? Unknown, but a man of some small power. What is the complaint? Rape. What violence did he give you before intercourse? Not before but— Did you struggle? Shout for help? No but— Your name and address, comrade. Oh yes, friend of the late Vaclav Bodnar. We'll be keeping a close eye on you to make sure you aren't the cause of any further trouble. That scar? Is it rape or assault you are complaining of? Do you have any witnesses to the assault? What was it you told the doctor who attended you? Your assailant said it was to prevent you appearing nude on stage – but that is already barred. Do you admit to taking part in illegal activities? So on. By degrees I become the accused.'

Such were the times.

'You never found out who he was?'

'Weren't you listening? He had frightened me and I

had other things to worry about. I told you – there was no authority I could go to.'

Her hand was rubbing at her breast, the right one. The scar might itch. Or she was too preoccupied to know she was doing it. Or it didn't matter because Fulnek was a man of the cloth even if he favoured a jacket and trousers.

'Then, all these years later, you learn where Venca is buried. On your second visit someone tells Them and They come after you.'

'Or after you. We don't know which of us . . .' She shook her head. 'No, it was because I knew Venca.'

'We don't know who. We didn't even catch a glimpse of the car.'

'In nineteen sixty-eight I saw the car.'

'It won't be the same one.'

'Isn't a priest meant to be good at listening? Then listen. In nineteen sixty-eight I saw the car parked outside here. At that time there was only one lamp in the street but it showed up the number plate.'

That was over twenty-three years ago. Fulnek asked, 'Are you saying you remember the number plate? After all this time?'

'Yes.'

There was a pause. The actress in her played her scene. A little cold coffee remained in the pot. She poured that and drank. She smiled at Fulnek, seeing that she had his full attention.

'Do you believe in symbols?'

She seemed to expect a serious answer. Life in Prague was full of symbols. What was the flag above the President's palace but a symbol? What was the

Presidential guard in their Amadeus uniforms but a symbol? What was President Havel but a symbol? A priest believed in more symbols than anybody. The wafer was the body of Christ and the wine was his blood and transubstantiation made that true. Except, except, Fulnek looked at them, tasted them, and they remained wafer and wine. For him the symbols stayed symbols.

'Of course.'

'The number was CS.02.48. That was the month and the year They had Their coup. I'll remember that until my dying day. Was it chance Their car had that licence number? Some inflated ego? Didn't he make—'

The doorbell silenced her. It rang twice, brief bursts, and was followed by the click of a key in the lock and the rattle of the handle. The front door opened and closed, leaving a moment of silence.

'*Ahoj.*'

Prerova's face softened.

'Shit, it's started snowing,' a voice said from the hall. 'Either that or God has dandruff.'

'Olina, in here,' Prerova called out. And to Fulnek, 'Olga, my daughter.'

CHAPTER FIVE

'Just a minute. You know me, don't you?'

'Mr Broucek.'

'Know my name. Know who I am. I've been here before.'

'Yes indeed.'

'Tell me where the hell telephoning gets you. I'll tell you where it gets me: in the backside. I'm sitting here waiting while you find out something you already know.'

'It's the system, Mr Broucek. Can't beat the system.'

Broucek leaned his head against the back of the seat. He lit a cigarette and stared into a cumulus cloud of smoke. That's some system. Do what isn't necessary, antagonize people, waste everybody's time. That was the old system. No wonder it broke down and was thrown out.

The gatekeeper was at his window but Broucek didn't look at him.

'That's all right, Mr Broucek. Go right ahead. You'll be met at the front door. Mr Radl is expecting you.'

Broucek might not have heard. The gate opened, the car swept forward, but he remained staring up at the smoke.

Triumph of the system. The system went into spasm and heaved and strained until it produced. Produced what?

He turned his head to look through the window. The drive from the gatehouse to the front door wasn't much above a hundred metres. He counted two gardeners. It was not a time of the year when there was much for a gardener to do, which accounted for the fact that neither was doing anything, just standing and smoking and watching the car roll by. Gardeners who were not gardeners were part of the same system. The only system he had put any store by was the personal system: someone you shake hands with, someone you telephone, someone you call in a couple of girls and take your pants down with, someone who is bound to you as you are to him. That was the system that he and Josef and others had always worked. It was their system within the system. The personal touch.

The car stopped at the bottom of the steps. Broucek said, 'I don't know what time I'll want you. Some time after lunch. They'll look after you in the kitchen.'

'Right, chief.' The driver's eyes flicked up to meet his in the mirror.

'Just call me Sir. We'll get on much better with that.'

Chief. This was Czechoslovakia, this wasn't Africa or some banana republic. Everything was taking time to settle down in these brave new democratic days.

So. He smoothed the lapel of his jacket as he climbed the steps to the front door. The style of the building was rococo. On this scale he found its charm cloying. Like a third éclair.

*

What was it like to live here? What was it like to be Josef Radl, Pepa to his cronies, sixty-seven years old, widowed, rich, full of influence still, an aristocrat of the Husak years? He kept his head below the parapet now. He had the sort of power that came from knowing exactly the right person to telephone, the right tone of voice to use, what crime, what sin, what weakness to put his finger on and press. Pepa, they said, knew where all the bodies were buried. Pepa could exhume your past and, provided you saw sense, could bury it again. What was it like to go into exile ninety miles from the capital, in a corner of South Bohemia, and spend your days in this third éclair? How did you cope?

Pepa drinks a little more, people said.

What kind of people would say a thing like that? Only those who had known him in the past, had gone away to do his bidding and come back to celebrate. He used to pour the champagne (and none of that German Democratic fizz-piss) and raise his glass in the only toast that mattered: To us.

He drinks a little more but can you blame him?

So Broucek lifted the bottle from his briefcase and handed it to him.

'Antonin, this is good of you. The Famous Grouse.' Radl smiled his appreciation. 'They make good whisky in England.'

'"Distilled, blended and bottled in Scotland",' Broucek read from the label. 'It means it's made in Scotland.'

'Our great English speaker,' Radl said.

'You know I never took to Russian. I always believed the future was in English.'

'That was foresighted of you. So tell me, is it written on the label in Scottish or English?'

'English.'

'And isn't there a Queen of England? And wasn't Thatcher Prime Minister of England? Scotland is in England. Here.'

They touched glasses.

'To us.'

They drank the whisky off in a gulp. Radl ran a finger across the label on the bottle like it might be the perfectly rounded contour of a breast.

'Did you see that photograph last weekend? Our President balanced on top of a horse? Fellow imagines he's the new Masaryk. I can't say the horse looked too happy, sagging under that weight. You know what the horse is thinking?'

'Tell me, Pepa.'

'The horse is sighing and saying to itself: One at a time, one at a time.'

Radl refilled their glasses. Broucek, holding up his glass, said, 'To hell with the President, here's to the health of the horse.'

There was a log fire burning. They stood in front of it, warming their backsides, supping whisky, dipping into a dish of salted almonds. Tell me your news, Radl demanded, tell me your gossip. Radl pretended he heard nothing in his Bohemian backwater but that was just his way. Tell me if Kadlecek and Kysil have stopped quarrelling. Is Sramkova still screwing the Italian Military Attaché? Explain, if you can, what a country like Italy is doing with a Military Attaché in the first place. You might as well propose – have a drop more of

your English Scotch whisky – it makes as much cock-
eyed sense as Gaddafi appointing a Minister for
Zionism.

The level in the Scotch bottle had dipped towards
the half-way mark when a manservant announced
lunch. Seated at table in the dining-room, Broucek was
even more aware of his surroundings. There was no
place for the eye to rest. On the floor was an
Azerbaijani rug with an intricate pattern in muted
brick red, violet, buff and pink. On the walls were gilt-
framed portraits of somebody's ancestors. Between the
paintings hung weapons from forgotten battles:
broadswords, pikes, épées, halberds. Pistols were in
pairs. They had curved stocks that would fit comfort-
ably in a highway robber's fists. There were stags'
antlers and a boar's head roaring defiance. Look up
and you were dazzled by a chandelier. Look down and
it was the reflection of the lights that sprang out of the
french-polished wood. Beech from the estate?
Chestnut? Broucek didn't know about wood. It was
very dark – maybe ebony. There were lace doyleys,
gleaming cutlery, a cruet like a bandstand, Moser crystal decanter and glasses, candlesticks, ashtrays,
cigarette box, a heavy silver lighter of vaguely Doric
inspiration.

How could a man live alone with all that?

They were served pork loin smothered with a cream,
mushroom and paprika sauce. There were potato
dumplings and bread dumplings and sauerkraut.
Broucek had heard reports of cuisine minceur which
left your stomach and your wallet feeling light. This
was cuisine lourdeur, made to soak up bottles. Rosé

wine was poured in their glasses and the bottle left in an ice bucket on a stand at Radl's right elbow. It was Gracie, flowery, sweetish. A girl's wine, was Broucek's opinion. Still, Radl was growing older. When your powers began to wane, you preferred your wine sweeter and your girls younger.

'Now tell me about the new democratic Minister,' Radl said. 'I hear bad things of him. I hear he ran an audit on foreign travel expenses. I hear Jarda was bawled out for an eight thousand franc bill for lunch at the Tour d'Argent. Why, I remember a certain esteemed Special Assistant,' and his eye lingered a moment on Broucek, 'who would put in a claim for eight thousand francs just for sandwiches. Are we to starve under democracy?'

No, Broucek concluded, rumours of his declining powers were premature.

There was a ritual about these occasions which Broucek knew well. There was the booze, a river of it, which was why he took the precaution of coming with a driver. There was a meal, with a manservant passing the dishes before withdrawing. During the meal Broucek – like all the ones who had known each other before – brought him up to date with the dirt and the deals. This was important to Radl in his rural St Helena. He drank, he put away food, he listened. Later he himself would talk.

'I'm told the Minister doesn't know a damn thing about the world.'

'Not much.'

'Does he know he doesn't know?'

'He's starting to find out.'

'He's an idealist?'

'He's an innocent.'

'Could be it's time he lost his virginity,' Radl said. He divided what wine was left between their glasses and plunged the bottle neck down in the ice bucket.

'Educating him . . .' Broucek's face showed pain. 'Is it worth it? Is it even possible? He lives in an unreal world, which is an unusual qualification in a Finance Minister. Take this privatization business. There is a strong case for simply giving away small businesses to the people who are running them. They already know which suppliers to bribe and how to fiddle the books to keep the tax inspectors happy. But the Minister is in love with the English – it is a contagion I think he caught off Havel – and he says: Look at all the money the government in London made by selling off state-owned things. Our treasury needs money so we'll do that. They auction off a few shops and restaurants and little businesses. Then he throws up his hands and cries out: Who are these people who have so much money they can afford to buy a restaurant? How did they amass it?'

'They are our people,' Radl said with a certain relish. 'Let him keep his innocence a while longer.'

Under the Azerbaijani rug was a footstud that Radl pressed. The bell rang in the kitchen and the servant appeared to clear the dishes.

'And another bottle.'

They were served strawberries sprinkled with sugar and Cointreau. Whipped cream stood in peaks.

'Are these your own so early, Pepa?'

'No. I tried last year. The boys stoked the boiler that

feeds the greenhouse all through the winter but it made no difference. Bloody plants sulked until their own good time. My theory is they need a period of freezing.'

'So where do these come from?'

'Spain. One of those costas.'

'I don't think they have a period of freezing there.'

'Tonda, listen. These come from Spanish strawberry plants and they understand the way of the world. They know damn well that if they don't work they'll be dug up and thrown on the heap. Our strawberry plants are different. They need the lash of winter to perform.'

'There are a lot of strawberry plants wandering around Prague right now that don't act as if they've had any lashing lately.'

'And the Minister – he hasn't grasped that yet?'

From somewhere a pair of red setters had appeared.

'Sometimes I go out after hares with them. They lack the discipline for pheasants.' Radl stooped to fondle the ear of one. 'They're company for me.'

Radl's wife died four years before but he hadn't remarried or brought a female companion to live in. There were no women in evidence at all. Radl's name had been linked with other women in the past, actresses naturally, singers, designers and once, more exotically, with the Assistant Director of the Greater Prague Sewage Authority, a striking statuesque blonde. She'll make full director, Radl had said, because she's a woman and in essence a woman is a functioning sewage system. It was during this time that his wife committed suicide. Now, well, certain of his powers must be waning. The evenings would be lonely. He drinks a little more.

'We'll fertilize the rose bushes,' Radl announced.

The dogs bounded ahead as they walked down a gravel path. Gardeners kept pace with them, one to each flank, a respectful distance away, out of earshot.

'What are these roses called?'

'Peace.' Radl aimed a steaming flow like a horse's over naked branches. No old man's troubles there. The bushes were still earthed up as a protection against killer frosts.

'Ceaucescu, the great *conducator*,' Broucek began.

'The great arsehole.'

'Old Nic, he had microphones planted among his rosebushes.'

Radl was shaking the last dewdrops on to the earth. 'Listen in on the greenfly. Find out if any are planning a coup.'

'Caterpillars in my version. But I think you've heard it?'

'I'm just smiling with relief.' Radl zipped up his fly. Picking up a stick he hurled it away for the dogs to fetch. They raced after it, barking, then quarrelled over who should have the honour of bringing it back. 'So, caterpillars in Ceaucescu's roses.'

Broucek took back the story. 'One caterpillar says: "It's the *conducator*'s birthday next month. To honour the great event, I'm going to turn into the biggest Red Admiral ever. And you, comrade?" "To build communism in the Golden Era of our glorious leader, I've vowed to eat every leaf on these bushes." The first caterpillar is aghast. "That's terrible. The branches will be totally bare." "That's communism."'

Side by side they strolled. The dogs were tussling

over the stick until Radl wrenched it out of their jaws and hurled it away overarm. He stopped again and Broucek with him. There was a view of the house through a clump of Colorado spruce.

'So,' Radl said. A more serious tone had entered his voice.

Finally, Broucek decided, we reach the meat at the bottom of the goulash.

'What's your opinion?' Radl asked.

Of what? Broucek looked at Radl, who nodded towards the house. He'd never asked Broucek before.

'For my taste . . .' Broucek hesitated. 'It's a bit rich.'

'It was her choice.' His wife's, Broucek understood. 'Two thousand castles in Bohemia and Moravia and she chose this. The local army command had been using it and there was a lot of hard work to be done. Back in the early 'seventies, this was. At that time we used it just for weekends away from Prague and during August.' He began walking again. 'Last December I had a visit. The long-ago owners. They made no appointment, they just turned up as if they could walk right in. Two of them came: a very old woman who walked with a stick and had to sit down on every chair she saw and her grandson, some little prick who wasn't thirty. They'd heard the law was going to be changed to restore confiscated property and they wanted the place back.'

Radl called to the dogs and fondled their ears. His dogs, his home.

'Their name is von Walderberg. That translates as Of-the-Forest-Mountain. Stupid name. Show me a mountain here. They couldn't speak Czech. Not even the old woman, though she said the family – The Family, making it sound important – had been here for a couple of centuries. Aristos.'

'What did you say?'

'You see, Tonda, I knew about the von Walderbergs. I'd found out all about them from the Interior Ministry. I told her, "I speak German because for my generation it was necessary, but I'm not German, I'm Czech, I was born Czech and I shall die Czech. But you . . . Your husband had been a member of the Sudeten German Party and when Hitler marched in, you all took German nationality, and when the communists came to power you left and since nineteen forty-nine you've been living in Germany. So far as I am concerned you and all your family were collaborators. Your husband was an officer in the Wehrmacht and fought right through Russia until he was killed on the retreat from Stalingrad. I have many friends who don't have my good manners. They would kick someone like you out and throw your stick after you. As for your grandson, if he tried to live here, he would be in the woods one day and have a fatal hunting accident." The old lady was still looking down her aristocratic nose. So I said, "If you're thinking of hiring some lawyer in Prague to pursue your claim, well, I have certain friends who could pay him visit and point out how in the new democratic Czechoslovakia he could lose an awful lot of business through representing old Nazi sympathizers. Especially if his office burned down and all his files were incinerated."'

'Have they been back?'

'Would you?'

Radl looked at Broucek. For all the drink they'd had, for all the years of drink, his face looked very hard. It wasn't the hardness of muscle, it was the hardness of his will.

'You see, they made a mistake half a century ago. Mistakes, even long after, can be fatal.' There was something of a pause. Broucek could feel himself breathing. Each breath seemed so heavy. 'Before I telephoned you yesterday,' Radl went on, 'I had a visit from Sizling. From Jiri.'

'Shit.'

'Someone is sniffing around.'

'Is that what that shit says?'

Radl turned on him so sharply he alarmed the dogs, who came racing up barking. Radl lifted a hand and prodded one thick finger into Broucek's chest.

'Just keep your mouth shut.' He waited to make sure Broucek understood. 'All right, I don't know what it is between you and Jiri. You always have something bad to say about him. Did he do something you can't forgive him for? Something I should know about?' Broucek held Radl's eyes but didn't answer. 'Or was it you who did something wrong and can't forgive your bad conscience? Maybe that's it.'

Radl's eyes were not angry, just cold and noticing. What they noticed was Broucek's colour. The whisky, the wine, the Hungarian apricot brandy that had come with the coffee, were all in his cheeks. Yes, a guilty conscience, some bad act towards Jiri Sizling that now made Broucek feel bad. He'd find out, some other time.

'So,' Radl picked up what he had set out to say, 'someone is sniffing about, with an interest in things that happened a long time ago. Certain events. We do our best to reinvent the past but we're not God, there are always details we overlook. I still do some fishing and I'll tell you what it's like. You are standing on the bank of a backwater at the bend of a river and you see, almost see, you sense a fish there. A big bastard of a pike. It's a murky pool and perhaps all that registers is a change in the shadows in the water. This big pike is nosing through weed. Hungry pike. Killer teeth. Looking for something to sink those teeth into.'

The dogs had lost interest and frisked away. The two men resumed walking. The gardeners, like frigates protecting a battle group, kept pace.

'What, er,' Broucek wasn't too happy with Radl's image but he stayed with it, 'what murky pool, precisely?'

'The chaos of nineteen sixty-eight. You remember the time? I was number two in the Foreign Settlements Department. And I still was after Dubček, after all the reformers were unmasked as fascist agents of American imperialism and the fraternal tanks of the Soviet Union rolled in to defend socialism.'

'So long ago.'

'But you remember. You were a young man in a hurry and like hotheads from Cain onwards you displayed an excess of zeal. It's when you first came to my attention. You were a threat to us.'

'What I did was bring to your—'

'Listen! All these years and I've never told you this. So listen. You threatened us with the knowledge you'd acquired of certain events. The information had come from a man who then decided it was too much of a struggle to go on living. But you weren't dead. You were very much alive. Have Broucek disposed of – that was the advice people kept giving me. But I asked: Who is this man? Don't be too hasty. We could always make use of a man with such a streak of ruthlessness. I brought you into the ministry, got you a title. Special Assistant. Nobody wanted to enquire what was so special about what you did. I saved your life, Tonda, just as I'm saving your life now. Or I'm telling you to save your own life.'

Looking again into Broucek's face, Radl saw the whisky, the wine and the Hungarian *barackpalinka* had all drained away. They had reached the boundary wall. Radl turned and led the way back.

'Tell me what the danger is,' Broucek said. His voice was lower, quieter.

'Jiri heard from someone at Benevice.'

'Benevice?'

'Have you forgotten? I would have thought it was like your first woman.'

'I haven't forgotten. I just can't credit it's something from all that time ago.'

'Dead and buried but not forgotten. Apparently two people visited the old seminary, though they didn't arrive together. There was a woman, who talked first to the old priest in the village. Afterwards a man. Jiri's friend went and picked up a couple of pals and together they drove to the seminary to ask a few questions. You know, names and nature of business. But they never got a peep of the man or the woman.'

'They'd run away?'

'They'd certainly disappeared.' Radl shrugged. 'I wasn't there. However there is a certain grave in the seminary – no name but marked, I'm told. Some flowers were left on the grave. So it is someone who knows about Vaclav Bodnar, someone who is sniffing around his life and how he died.'

Broucek's head was throbbing. It's that Gracie. Damn woman's drink. Kicks you in the head like a woman, too.

And still Radl went on. 'It's a bad time for this to come up. For you there would never be a good time but for me – and so for all of us – it's terrible timing. There is a banker, an English banker, flying in tomorrow. Since I used to be Deputy Minister what could be more natural than he should want to consult me about investment opportunities? But you see, Tonda, he's from the same bank.' Radl let that sink in. 'All right, I shall suddenly catch 'flu and be unable to see this English banker. So I'm sending my trusted assistant. You. You can see what a terrible time it would be to have the dead man coming to life. You cannot afford it.'

In the reception area of a motel on the outskirts of Prague, Broucek was jammed into a cubicle. He juggled with a cigarette, a glass of gin, the telephone, coins and his little black book. His driver waited outside in the car. Twiddly music dripped from hidden loudspeakers.

Ivana, Ivana, Ivana. His brows were contracted in thought. Hairy legs.

Eva. Talks too much.

He drank, he smoked, he turned a couple of pages. Teserova. Teserova? What was her first name? Sod what her first name was, it wasn't a baptism.

There was no answer.

How about Dasenka, kid with the go-on-amaze-me look. Take her some bubble gum. It gave her a kick. She did weird things with it.

It was a man who answered when he dialled.

'Ah, is Dasenka there? I want to speak to Dasenka. Yes.'

'Who's that?'

Broucek frowned. 'Who the hell are you?'

'Her father.'

'Fuck.' He banged down the receiver.

He noticed a lanky youth with a problem complexion standing by his shoulder. He gripped a tray with a saucer holding two tablets.

'What do you want?'

'You asked for these.'

'If they're aspirin. Another gin to wash them down.'

He chewed the aspirins, swallowing most of the bits dry. Shit, what a day. His head throbbed in time with his heartbeats. It wasn't just what Radl had said, it was the tone he'd used, that hard tone as if he was no better than those Forest-Mountain people. Pepa drinks a little more. It was true what people said. Bloody Gracie, final monster finish-the-bottle apricot brandy for the road. He turned his attention to the telephone again. He needed someone very badly. Someone who could hold his head together and make him human again.

'Anca, my dove.'

'This isn't Anca.'

'Who is it if it isn't Anca? You answered the phone.'

'It's my phone so I answered it.'

'Who are you?'

After a pause the woman said, 'Marie.'

'Lovely name, that. Knew a Marie once. A cracker, she was. Listen, Marie, I think we should get together. I can be there in, oh, half an hour at a guess. Depends on how fast the little runt drives. Also on just where you live. What's the address? Let me write it down.'

'Who are you?'

'What do you want? No, not you, Marie. Don't you go away.'

The youth had brought his drink. Broucek gave him money then rinsed his mouth clean of aspirin.

'Better. You're still there?' Broucek spoke again into the telephone.

'I've never heard your voice in my life. I don't know who you are.'

'My name is Antonin. Tonda to you. Let's start friendly.'

'Well, Tonda, you got a wrong number. I don't know you from a bowl of soup. Don't be offended – actually I don't give a shit if you're offended or not, but I'm keeping things polite. You sound as if you're as drunk as a Finn. I have never met you and I am absolutely positive I don't want to meet you drunk or sober.'

'Just a minute, woman. Don't you talk to me like that. Don't you dare. Who do you think you are?'

There was a click and the telephone started to hiccup in his ear. Taking the receiver away he glared at it.

'Me pissed? Just listen to you.'

The telephone went on hiccupping at him. He slammed it down.

'Drunken bitch.'

He knocked back the rest of the gin and returned to his black book.

A little after nine, his driver dismissed, Broucek was in an apartment in the unlovely district of Dejvice. He knew the woman quite well, at least as well as any other man who shared her bed. He had arrived with a bunch of flowers and a bottle of sparkling wine to add life to the cocktail in his stomach. Temporarily he had mislaid the woman's name but she responded to Blondie.

'Do something new, Blondie, do something different.'

Sometimes she danced naked while he watched from the bed. She turned on the radio and found a German station playing dance music and began moving in front of him. He waved an arm in the air, conducting, but it seemed to be different music that he heard in his head. Tomorrow, tomorrow is another day. Another day, another problem. Tomorrow belonged to Bodnar.

'Who?'

'I didn't say anything. Where's your inventiveness?'

Jesus, he asked in his head, should I go out and find someone else? Make it a threesome? Man of my years appreciates new tricks. He rolled off the bed and began to crawl. His shoes, jacket and trousers were heaped against the wall. He wore his shirt and tie, underpants and socks. He took an indirect path over the rug to the dressing-table, where he plucked a rose out of the vase of flowers he had brought.

He said, 'You need a partner.'

'You? You couldn't stand up for two minutes. I don't think any part of you can stand up.' She nodded her head at his underpants.

'This. Blondie, come here. Open your legs.'

He thrust the stem between her thighs. The bud peeped out of her pubic ruff.

'Ow, that hurts.'

'Rosebud,' Broucek muttered.

'Bloody thorns more like.'

'You're a cultured sort of bitch, aren't you? Been to university, got a degree, screwed all the right professors. Think of *Citizen Kane*. Film Orson Welles made. Welles being all sly about Randolph Hearst and Hearst not being able to do a damn thing.'

'You're drunk.'

'Hearst's mistress. That's the term he used. Her rosebud. Get it?'

'You're stinking drunk. You're raving. What is it?'

Broucek was staring. Like a playing card flipped over, his mood had changed in a second. 'You're not rosebud.'

'I'm not rosebud. Well done. Of course I'm not rosebud. What's the matter with you?'

'You're Blondie. Well, Blondie, I had some news today.'

'What news? Something to boast about? Out celebrating? Done yourself a little too well?'

'Shut up. Dead man telling tales.'

'Dead man.'

'Live woman.'

'What woman?'

'I'll find her.'

'You're absolutely out of your mind. Woman from your past? Caught up with you, has she?'

Broucek had slumped back on the bed. His face was white and greasy with sweat. His eyes were focused on something only he could see.

'Blondie . . .'

'What is it? Want me to dance some more?'

'Sick.'

'What?'

'I'm going to be sick.'

CHAPTER SIX

The noise came from a long way off and went on for a long time before Broucek grew aware of it. His eyes closed, he struggled to identify the noise and isolate its source. All of him was at war. His body was in open rebellion. His brain was divided into two opposing camps. Ignore the noise and it will go away. No, said the other side, the noise persists, gets louder, has an urgency about it. The more alert side of his brain embarked on a journey through space, blackness illuminated by starbursts. The starbursts were as regular as the thump of a funeral drum. The drum was his pulse, each beat a stab of pain. The noise was suddenly and dangerously close. He opened his eyes. In half-light he made out the telephone on the table beside the bed. His bed, his telephone. He picked up the receiver and peace was restored so he dropped the receiver back. Twenty seconds later the telephone rang again. This time he answered it with a grunt.

'Are you receiving me well?'

Receiving him well? In all honesty, no. Broucek felt as awful as on any morning in his life. But his brain made the supreme effort and commanded: *Do not deny it.* This was the introduction They had always used among themselves. No name given or asked, just a voice you recognized speaking these simple everyday words. The wrong answer, an equivocation, a joke, a plain *No* would end the conversation. *No* meant it was unsafe to talk, the phone was not secure, a third party was present.

Was there?

He heaved his shoulder round, his stomach heaved with it. He was alone.

'Well, thank you.'

'You sound . . . Never mind. Listen. This is an early warning about a tremor. Tremor from a long time ago.'

Tremor, a tremor. Broucek knew it was important to concentrate. Radl had used a different phrase: 'sniffing about'. Different but the same.

'I've been warned.'

'What?'

'Yesterday. I was out in the country having lunch. Lengthy affair. He drinks a little more, you know?'

Was it secure to say the lunch was with Pepa? It didn't matter because his caller broke in.

'This is new, my friend. It only came to my notice late yesterday afternoon. I tried to telephone all evening but you were still out to lunch.'

'I see,' Broucek said.

He said nothing more because he didn't see. Something new, something else, some further indication of trouble from the past.

'We have to meet.'

'All right,' Broucek agreed.

With great caution he swung his legs out of bed. The room also swung before righting itself. He was naked. His clothes were all in a heap. He had no recollections of undressing. How did he get home? Taxi? Where from?

'When? This morning?'

Blondie. Broucek remembered being with her. He remembered her pirouetting, arms raised over her head, the brown eyes of her nipples watching him. Something else hovered in his memory.

'I have somewhere else I must go this morning.'

'This is important.'

'So is what I have to do,' Broucek said. Benevice. Bodnar's burial plot. Flowers on the grave. Flowers! They grew clearer in his memory.

'Tonight then?'

'When I get back I'll be in touch,' Broucek said.

On the carpet by his feet was one rosebud, somewhat crushed. He remembered. Suffering Jesus.

In Prague the local offices of the Party had dropped out of sight. There was a greater need for hairdressers and stationery shops and stand-up cafés. A few lingered, locked up, silent except for echoes of old May Day parades on curling posters.

There was no metropolitan haste to abandon the past in Benevice. The Party office in the main street had a light on. A poster in the window called for Peace and Socialism. Sizling's informant had his desk close enough to the window to watch passers-by. Being in the Party office rendered him invisible because no one looked his way.

Of course Broucek used to be a Party member though he drew the line at attending Party meetings. It was necessary for his special position at the ministry, useful for contacts, vital for perks. And of course he no longer was a member. Indeed the most thorough search of records would find no trace he ever was. Apparently Sizling's informant had no such shyness.

'You can call me Mirek,' he confided, as if in other circumstances it might be Bedrick or Karel. 'Take the weight off your feet, make yourself comfortable.'

Comfortable is what Broucek did not feel. The window on to the street seemed to frame him. There could be someone on the opposite pavement out to catch him, some spy with a camera and a satirist's eye: Peace and Socialism and Broucek. Apart from Mirek's desk there was a low table such as you find in a dentist's waiting-room covered with magazines, a cupboard, four straight-backed chairs. It was like any other office apart from certain marks on the walls. The cream paint showed lighter patches where photos of fallen leaders once beamed or looked inspirational.

'That's your car down the road? The Germans really know how to build them. Cars, tanks, you can't beat them.'

Broucek's gaze was still doing a circuit of the room: the telephone on the desk, the central light fitting, the heavy ashtray on the low table, the lamp with a solid base.

'Got you.' Understanding came to Mirek's face. 'Music lover, you must be. What's your taste? Tchaikovsky's 1812 Overture, stuff like that?' He brought a transistor radio out of a desk drawer and tuned the dial to a station playing rock music.

They sat side by side on the hard chairs. Competing with the music, Broucek leaned towards Mirek to speak.

'Jiri sends greetings and warm wishes. He speaks highly of your help. I find this,' he waved a hand to indicate the Party office, 'interesting.'

'Interesting, yes, that's just what it is.' Mirek beamed at this choice of word. 'You see, we're not like Prague here, never were. None of your backroom deals, walks in the park, no-name telephone calls. We're peasants, that's what we are, plain speakers. No good saying to someone, "Need you to do me a favour," and giving him a wink. He'll just think you've got something in your eye and need him to take it out.'

Mirek gave a nudge with his elbow in case Broucek hadn't got it. His smile showed stained teeth for a moment.

'Party secretary's position used to be good in a dump like this. To be honest, now it's worth shit. In the old days you knew what everybody had going. Also I run the repair shop down towards the crossroads. You passed that, can't have missed it. Bloody gold mine, that was. It still can be . . . interesting, your word. Only now you've got to be more cautious. Sometimes a truck running down to Brno will develop a little trouble. They overload them, see, that's what they do. He'll pull off the highway into the repair shop, we'll close the doors and I'll see what I can do to help sort out the overloading problem. Usually he'll be out and back on the road in five minutes. That way his time sheet doesn't show anything funny. Fancy a beer this time of the morning?' He moved to the cupboard and returned with bottles and glasses. 'Cigarette? Local produce, good and fresh, factory over the way. We all help each other, see.'

Mirek kept an elaborately straight face when he stopped speaking. You get my meaning or you don't. He raised his glass.

'To opportunities, to the future.'

They drank.

'My problem,' Broucek said, 'it's the past I sometimes see coming round a second time. That man and woman who paid a visit.' He nodded his head through the window at the band of street beyond the village and a track curving uphill to the seminary. 'I heard what you told Jiri.'

Mirek wriggled his backside into a more comfortable position. He was happy to talk. 'The man I didn't pay much attention to. He's the sort of middle-aged man you picture walking with a limp, even when he doesn't. Fuck him. But the woman . . . Well, that's a different story. Fuck her, actually.'

This time when he grinned he ran his tongue over his bottom lip.

'Anyway, she arrived first, off the bus from the station. I watched her walk past the old church and up the path to the priest's house. When I say "watched", I mean it. Never mind the tits, you judge a woman's potential better from behind. Right?'

He drank again and topped up his glass.

'She's a good mover. Her ankles, her calves, her legs all the way up. Her bum sort of winks at you, just like an eye closing, first one side, then the other.'

'She was wearing a coat, wasn't she?'

'My point. Even wearing a coat. Imagine when she takes that off and then her dress, imagine what she'd be like then.'

'How old is she?'

'Mid-forties, in there somewhere. Listen, I don't go chasing after fifteen-year-old schoolgirls who know nothing. You could tell this one knew a thing or two, which is what I appreciate.'

This time Broucek joined him in a grin. So the man was a pig. But in this village he wouldn't see many attractive women and a grin costs nothing.

'She went to see the priest?'

'The church is closed but he's still called the priest. He's really ancient, been here since before I was born. She was with him fifteen or twenty minutes. Out she came—'

'You're watching all the time? Waiting for her?'

'She drops something. Must have. Anyway she bends down to pick something up, then she sort of straightens her shoulders and makes her way up the hill. Yes, I was waiting to have another look at her. The track she took only leads to the seminary. Then a little later, like from the next train, the man arrives.'

'The limping man who doesn't limp?'

'That's the one. At first I thought he was lost because he stood and looked around him. Then I thought: he's been here before, he's looking for old landmarks. See, I'm like that. Psychotic, my friends call me. He disappears inside the café and stays there about ten minutes. Then up the hill he goes, out of sight. They're lovers, I decided, escaping for the afternoon from their nearest and dearest. Good luck to them. I wouldn't mind being in his shoes. Except he'll be taking his shoes off if they're having an afternoon at it.'

His throat was dry from the talking and he drank

again. He's more than a witness, Broucek decided, he's a bloody peeping tom.

'A bit later it struck me. The seminary is locked but the old priest has a key and that's why she saw him. Get the key. And the seminary, after the state took it over, had another use altogether. Big secret it was meant to be. Of course in the Party we got to know. So I said to myself, Hello, Mirek, just a minute, this needs looking into. So I ducked into the café and they said, Yes, he was asking questions about the old seminary, was it empty, when did They leave. Right, he must be a snooper, one of the new ones, bloody trouble-makers. I went and fetched Jan and the lad from the repair shop and we drove up there. Have another beer.'

Broucek's stomach had been settled by the first beer. A pain still nagged behind his right eye.

He said, 'Gets rid of the taste of toothpaste.'

'Right you are.' Mirek returned with two more bottles. 'Now the strange thing is . . . You been up in the old days? No, you don't have to tell me. Strange thing is there's this big double gate and let into the gate is this door and the door is locked. So right away I'm convinced they're in there and wanting to keep anybody else out. But Jan and I searched and searched and we didn't catch a sniff of them except for a little bunch of snowdrops on a hump of earth that could be a grave. That's what I thought it was, anyway. Vanished into thin air. Strange. Weird. Cheers.' He clinked his glass with Broucek's and drank. 'Unless they'd opened up one of the tombs and were in there doing it. Some people like doing it in coffins, I've heard. Christ, it would make me shrivel right up. So I guess they left while I was fetching Jan.'

'You searched everywhere?'

'Had a good look round. I told you, they must have gone already.'

He had another pull at his beer and then gazed at the froth. He gave it the close examination of someone who was lying. He was not lying in any significant way, to protect anything more important than his own self-esteem. Wasn't Wednesday the day of the European Cup semis? Some big match on TV to get away to. Broucek felt he'd had enough of Mirek. Psychotic, indeed. Jesus.

'The priest will have a key if she gave it back. But I don't want to trouble him. I'll take yours.'

'Yes?'

'I'm going to look around, see where they might have been.'

What's the point? Mirek was about to ask. Then a sickening doubt sneaked into his head.

'Don't tell me it's your missus?' God, what had he said about her? About her bum winking as she walked? Her experienced ways? One man's bawdy was another man's insult.

Broucek was standing, his hand held out. 'The key.'

It had been the Seminary of the Holy Name before the state octopus embraced it. After a tussle it was the Finance Ministry that established a lasting hold on it. They said they had a definite need for somewhere the latest research techniques could be applied and people lost their inhibitions about public speaking, a place away from Prague with its wagging tongues and prying eyes and sharp ears. A sort of Think Tank among

Elysian fields, the Finance supremos made it sound. Or, as their rivals put about, their very own Lubyanka-in-the-hills, or a Bohemian version of the Serbsky Institute. Officially it became the Treasury Research Facility.

The Security Police had offered specialists in research techniques but the Finance Ministry preferred to recruit its own. It was a way of ensuring research findings were kept for the benefit of those who had worked so hard obtaining them. Enter Broucek.

He had a background in military intelligence, the American target, but had found the Army hierarchy inhibiting. He had gone freelance, doing jobs even the Security Police found not to their taste, selling information to whoever would buy, taking a little pay-off from a former informant in the American embassy whom he threatened to expose. Finding out about the scandal Bodnar was going to expose was his good fortune. Pepa Radl had sent for him and he was on his way.

Broucek had not been a fulltime member of the research staff but he enjoyed a regular visitor's privileges. In fact he came more frequently in his early years when he was a forceful young man with a lot of surplus energy. As time passed he distanced himself from what came to seem mere manual labour.

Standing inside the Facility on this late winter morning, a lot of memories flooded back. The years when he'd come regularly had been vivid ones. The changes he noted were unsettling, as they are to anyone revisiting early haunts. The smell used to insinuate itself everywhere: cabbage, urine, cigarette smoke, and the sort of maleness you get in a sports changing room. Does testosterone smell? Or is it just unwashed armpits? Broucek lit a cigarette, frowning. The smell had gone. A thief had crept in and made off with a piece of his life.

And the sound. He could hear crows but he listened for the other sound. He could not think of this place without the voicing of dogs. German Shepherds had been favoured for their bark as well as their bite. Obedient, too: sit, heel, kill. They didn't patrol the ground on a regular basis, only their barking did. That was enough. The inmates of the cells could hear and imagine. There had been no attempts to reach the wall.

Yes, the wall. Broucek decided the two beers he had drunk provided him with pressing business. He unzipped and let loose. Was it only yesterday he'd been with Pepa? Well, now he was fertilizing the wall. There'd been some who'd argued the wall wasn't high enough to defeat escape. 'Grow taller,' he breathed as the puddle grew.

It was older than the Berlin Wall, was still standing, and so far as Broucek knew nobody escaped over it. The Berlin Wall had been protected by searchlights and watch towers and barbed wire and dogs and landmines and automatic-fire machine-guns and still people escaped over it. Where did the Germans get their reputation for efficiency? They should have given it to the Treasury Research Facility to guard.

If nobody had ever got out, two people had got in. Mirek protested they had gone away again while he was fetching Jan. First he thought they'd come to screw for the afternoon, then he swore they'd left after half an hour. Had they agreed to meet here or were they strangers with a common interest? The gate had been locked but Broucek couldn't believe they'd left after such a short time. They were inside, they'd heard the car, they'd gone into hiding.

He walked first to the grave of Vaclav Bodnar. Broucek had been the one to insist the body was buried there and the X painted on the wall. In truth he could not remember why he had been so stubborn about it. Perhaps, as Pepa suggested, your first corpse was like your first woman. For ever after they might be so much meat but the first was unique. The body had long ago decomposed and the hump of earth nearly flattened out.

Ignoring the chapel, Broucek made his way to the building at the rear which had housed the priests when it had been a seminary, and the prisoners when it had been the Facility. A cell was a cell. Both lots prayed for salvation. There'd been new locks and sliding spyholes added to the doors. The walls were stone blocks that provided good sound insulation. This wasn't where the real research took place. Yet another building beyond the refectory had been for the hard work. Prisoners spent weeks or even years here: black marketeers, currency dealers, factory managers with careless bookkeeping habits, economic criminals of all kinds whom it might be unsettling to put on open trial. The cells had encouraged solitary reflection on their misdeeds.

He entered cell number 4. He stood in the centre absorbing the atmosphere through his pores and felt . . . nothing. He must feel something. He'd been in a rage all those years ago, a rage to find out what Bodnar knew, then a rage to make use of his hard-won knowledge. Pepa had said that some had wanted to have him killed because of what he found out, and he understood that. Perfectly natural reaction. What had happened to the rage he had felt? Shouldn't it throw a shadow down the years? Did the rage burn itself out completely? Was it middle-aged softening?

Shit, he told himself, I need that hardness now. Look, remember, feel. That was the reason for coming. He didn't expect to find the man and woman hiding. He needed to find himself as he had been then.

There was the bunk. There was the tall narrow window with the iron bars in the form of a cross. There was the pisspot in the corner. There was the table. Late August 1968. Day and night had meant little because there was so much to do. In his recollection it flickered between light and dark like an old movie. But this particular memory was fixed around dawn or possibly dusk. All hours had been worked. Research efforts had been redoubled with the arrival of Soviet steel in the capital.

No, it had been dawn, the details were growing clearer. He'd looked in through the spyhole and seen the bunk empty. He remembered unlocking the door and making out the figure crouched beside the table. The light was dim, the man naked and his bodily existence already seemed to be fading. Broucek had taken a step into the room and seen the man holding the nail between thumb and forefinger. With infinite pain he must have extracted the nail from a table leg. Resting his pistol between the man's eyes, Broucek had disarmed him. Then he realized it was not a weapon, or rather it was a weapon of a rather different kind. The man had been using it to scratch words in the wood of the table. A scream for help, a scream at any rate. It was his message in a bottle that he hoped would be washed ashore years later.

Broucek crossed to the table now and felt with his fingers. The words were still there. He had to bend to inspect them for the light in here was always dawn or dusk. He read:

A. BROUCEK IS

That was as far as the prisoner had got before being discovered.

Is what? Is a bastard? A torturer? Is hungry for power? Is the person who knows the truth? Is the person to whom I have confessed everything?

Had he? Were there no secrets left to be squeezed out? Broucek had to satisfy himself he had found out all there was to know. Then Bodnar with impeccable timing went and died.

Not a great many people had died because of the great socialist experiment. Broucek had heard a figure of ten thousand. It might be only nine thousand. Put another way, 15,670,000 didn't die. Rats in a medical laboratory would be overjoyed at such figures. But Bodnar had been one of those who had pushed the socialist system too far, and the system had pushed right back. All systems had to defend themselves. Even the current system was setting up its own lines of defence.

I, too, have a right – no, a duty – to defend my life. Broucek told himself so.

He looked round the refectory, the games room, the staff bar where his searches uncovered no forgotten bottles. Finally he went to the other low building. The ground floor was where the staff had slept, the upstairs rooms had been unused.

What he was really after, he decided, was a sign. Some kind of sign.

Suppose I were hiding – for whatever reason – from Mirek and Jan conducting a search, where would I go? Up. Delay the moment of discovery. Perhaps they will grow bored with searching and leave. As they had.

He climbed the stairs and moved from doorway to doorway. What constitutes a sign? You only know it when you find it. In one room he saw a closet gaping and on the floor a handkerchief. It was small and white, a woman's handkerchief by the frilly edging. Such a gift made him immediately suspicious.

A suspicious person needs a rationale.

The non-limping man and the sexually alluring woman retreated into the closet. It was not to make love, for the closet was too cramped, but to hide. The door was closed. It was dark, airless, claustrophobic. Sweat sprang from her pores. She used the handkerchief to dab at the secret rain on her face. In the release of tension after they were free to come out, her grip relaxed and the handkerchief dropped.

Satisfied, Broucek picked it up and raised it to his nose. There was a hint of perfume still, but he didn't know what. He stuffed the handkerchief in his coat pocket. I have my sign, he thought. In himself he felt a change, as if the wind had veered and made the flags flutter in a new direction.

He had left his car down in the village so as not to draw attention to his visit to the Facility. In fact his name was advertised to anybody who bent over to look at the spiky letters gouged in wood.

A. BROUCEK IS

Is what?

It troubled him still, irritated, itched. He had never found out. There was a gap in his knowledge of Bodnar. The man had kept one secret after all. Well, shrug that off. Move forward.

Prague beckoned.

From the window Broucek watched gulls wheeling above the river. The Vltava flowed into the Elbe and eventually into the North Sea, four hundred kilometres away. What business had seagulls here in the heart of Europe?

He swivelled the chair round so he was at his desk, looking again at the sheet of paper ranged so squarely in the centre. It was signed M. Filipova, in full, very formal, very unbending. Familiarity was not in her nature. Her job was to hold the office when Broucek was out. He needed an office person because it raised him several levels above the men who worked from hotel lobbies, bars and – the lowest – the street. If he needed work doing that was heavy, he could hire one of those.

Filipova hadn't been able to contact the English banker Challoner before she went off at lunchtime for the weekend. She'd left a message at his hotel blah

blah. He supposed Challoner had come to see the sights over the weekend, do business next week. All right, Challoner was a problem for Monday.

It was the second part of her memo he read again and again. 'Someone called on behalf of Mr Radl. He wanted a progress report.' Two sentences. Not much in them but Broucek sensed a pressure behind the words.

He went to a cupboard and got out his office bottle to pour himself a whisky. He took it back to his desk and swivelled his chair to look out of the window. On the other side of the river, a half kilometre away, was the Finance Ministry annexe where he'd had an office before he cleared out at the collapse of the old system. He could see a corner of the building but not quite the window of his former office.

Pepa wanted a progress report. He had been with Pepa yesterday afternoon but even by this morning he was expecting progress. He was pushing. When Pepa pushed . . . Broucek stared out of the window, not finishing the thought. He watched the gulls and drank his whisky and turned the problem over in his mind.

Pulling the telephone to him across the desk, he dialled the number of a pal in the Interior Ministry. It was Saturday afternoon but his pal often worked on Saturday afternoons on private matters.

'Are you receiving me well?'

A joke, a bit of gossip, a nod in the direction of Radl. Yes, Pepa drinks a little more but he still hears all the whispers. So to business.

'It means your going back to nineteen sixty-eight,' Broucek said. 'There was a trouble-maker called Bodnar, first name Vaclav, who deceased without an official certificate. He had a female friend whose name I cannot for the life of me recall. Am I growing old, do you think? I can still get it up but sometimes I forget the name of the woman I'm getting it up into. I did meet her once only. But her name will be in Bodnar's file. And the address where she was living at that time. Maybe she's still there.'

He watched the gulls soaring and swooping. Out in the North Sea were there Prague pigeons shitting on ships' captains just as the gulls whitened the heads of statues on Charles Bridge?

He read Filipova's note again. Her handwriting was so even it was like italic printing. 'Someone called on behalf . . .' There was no warmth in her writing, no eccentricities, you could say no humanness. Why don't you get another assistant, plenty out there looking for a job, someone blonde and pert and bouncy? Because. Because why, Tonda? Because it was rock certain no one would ever seduce Filipova and get her to betray secrets. That had been important in the old days and the old habits of thought had not left Broucek.

Nor had they left Pepa. He shouldn't be pushing so hard.

Waiting to be rung back, he smoked three cigarettes.

Chapter Seven

From the living-room window Prerova could see the spire that topped the TV mast. In the old days They used this to jam Western broadcasts full of imperialist lies and ads for glossy consumer products unavailable in the socialistic republic. People moaned the jamming waves were bad for their health, causing headaches, nausea, giddiness. The authorities paid no attention. Possibly the waves were also the cause of absenteeism from work, alcoholism, fornication and hooliganism. This was Zizkov. Thieves and gypsies. And Prerova. There was no jamming any longer. The drunks, adulterers, layabouts and hooligans were no better.

It was late afternoon, the light fading, evening rising up from the city streets. For an actress, a special time. For a seller of fruit juice and programmes at the Palace of Culture, not so very special. But in the last days she had felt a stirring in her life. The discovery of Venca's grave, the priest with his unpriestly eyes, the men who came searching while they pressed together in the closet . . . Her life had turned an unexpected corner. As an actress at this special hour she would bestow one final lingering kiss before rolling off the mattress, stand naked, raise her arms above her head and stretch.

Stretch her limbs, stretch her emotions, stretch her imagination. She would stand in front of the window and stretch her eyes wide, again, again. Let in more light, see more clearly. Just like this.

And she saw the car glide to a stop at the kerb. Other cars were parked down the street but none so glossy and sleek as this one dressed in Henry Ford black. It was an ocean liner while the Ladas and Wartburgs and Skodas were barges. It had drawn up in a space reserved for invalids, but who wasn't an invalid here? If you weren't an invalid in body, you were an invalid in spirit.

Prerova's eyes wandered down the street, which was unnaturally deserted for this hour. Nobody was stumbling out of the hostinec. The windows of the Supraphon office showed empty desks. No one operated the cement-mixer by the apartment block supported by crutches of wooden scaffolding. She liked to see people doing ordinary everyday things.

If she turned her eyes back to the car again, it was because nobody had got out. Was he waiting for somebody? Watching a door? Was he early for an appointment? Did he want to catch the end of a concert on the radio? Did he – or why shouldn't it be a couple? Saying goodbye before she went up to her domestic chores? A final final final kiss? A Zizkov affair.

The car door opened and the man stepped on to the pavement. He was of a certain age, well dressed, with a stocky body, his face shadowed by the dusk. He peered down the street at the dozen metal rubbish bins ready for tomorrow's pick-up. His attention switched to a window opposite. Prerova heard nothing behind her double glazing but she knew he could catch the sound of the violin lesson Votruba was giving. Finally he turned to her building and his head began a slow tilt upwards.

Prerova took a step back. She would not be caught at the window mooning down at him like a lovelorn schoolgirl. Her pulse had quickened, though.

She knew from the methodical way he checked the street and the building opposite and raised his eyes to search out whether windows showed light that he was going to climb the stairs and ring her bell. She absolutely knew it as she knew when a man was going to speak to her in the theatre and suggest a drink after the play; but that was when certainty ceased. Should she say yes or no to the man in the theatre? Should she let this man in? Should she pretend she was not at home even though the lights were on?

She had stepped back before his face was fully turned up and didn't recognize him from what she'd seen. If she were an actress still, a famous one, the darling of critics and audiences, she might be agreeable to an unknown admirer calling in a Mercedes as glossy as a sable. The famous actress could give him no time now but might be agreeable to a glass of Krug after curtain-fall. Or she might not. But when you sold programmes . . . It was to do with Venca. She knew that as she knew the blood that flowed in her own body. She hadn't seen the man's expression, his eyes. She had seen his body, the way he held himself. The actress in her had noted his stance. He stood as if he was looking

down at you. That was the way They always used to
stand.

'Prerova, Milena?' he asked.

'And you?'

It was dusk or worse in the stairwell. The plastered
walls were cave grey. The air pushed like a hand in the
face. Sounds were all within her body: heartbeats,
breath rasping. Stepping forward uninvited into the
doorway Broucek saw the shock of recognition drain
the blood from around her eyes. For an instant there
was an expression between fear and disgust on her face
and then determination as she made to slam the door.
It was what he had been expecting and his knee was
already against the panel and then the bulk of him rode
her back into her own apartment and kicked the door
shut behind him.

'Are you going to scream for the neighbours or are
you going to listen to what I have to say?'

'Get out.'

'I will. Do you imagine I want to move in here?' A
door from the entrance hall showed an empty kitchen
with unwashed cups and glasses on the draining-board.
Another door was open to a bedroom with a double bed.
A short corridor lay ahead. Broucek pushed forward,
Prerova stepped back. Two closed doors. Bedroom?
Bathroom? Ahead was the sitting-room and it was here
they stopped. His eyes skipped round the room, its worn
carpet, boxy chairs, TV, telephone on a low table, vase of
dead roses. Broucek detested slovenliness.

'You should throw them out. They start to rot and
then they stink.'

Prerova looked from the flowers to Broucek. 'And you would notice, would you?'

He ignored her, pondering the heavy old desk that was so out of place. A man could install himself at a desk like that, with a bottle of ink, an old-fashioned fountain pen, a blotter. He could draft a report for Challoner on Joint Venture Opportunities in the Heavy Industrial Sector. That had a more dignified ring to it than Taking a Gamble on Rustbelt Factories. In the deep bottom drawer that was always kept locked would be a well-thumbed copy of *The Delta of Venus*, with illustrations.

'Leave me alone.' Prerova didn't want to know why he'd come. 'Get out this minute.'

Above the desk was a poster for the Laterna Magika company appearing at the Palace of Culture. It was not some framed historic poster, it was the current production *Odysseus* tacked to the wall. Silhouettes of Odysseus and Penelope faced each other, superimposed on a montage of modern war destruction. Odysseus had all the adventures while Penelope had no fun at all. Which was her own fault, Broucek felt, because she had suitors enough.

'And who are you? Penelope?' Despite her years she looked striking enough, and anyway make-up performed miracles. But the Laterna Magika's style demanded the energy of youth.

'Leave me alone. Don't you understand what I'm saying?'

'Calypso, maybe?'

'I'm Miss Orange Juice. Oscar nomination performance when I pour. Critics rave. The last drop is like a

full stop. Quote unquote. Now get out. I'll call the
police. At last I can do that. He forced his way in and
tried to rape me. Why not? It's in your blood. Are you
getting out or—'

Her hands gripped the front of her blouse ready to
rip the buttons off. With each deep breath her breasts
pressed against the cloth. Broucek ran a finger along
his chin, wondering about her. Would she scream and
rip her clothing and expose herself before she rang the
police? Would we sit around and wait for them to
come? Would we make small talk? How did you come
by that razor slash on your right breast? No, really?
You don't say. It had slipped my mind completely. But
he did remember she had high firm breasts all those
years ago. And now?

'You think I've come to molest you, isn't that so?'

Her mouth was shut tight.

'Prerova, I came to give you some advice and to get
a piece of information. I'll start with the advice, which
is short and simple. Forget about Bodnar. Don't go on
pilgrimages to his grave. You understand? No more
visits. No talking about him. Don't raise any kind of
fuss. Don't go round making a public spectacle of yourself like you did once before. That was a long time ago.
The world has turned quite a lot since then. Just drop
it. I'm advising you for your own good.'

He stopped, waiting for her to speak, asking what
would happen if she didn't do as he told her. She said
nothing. She watched him, her eyes never wavering
from his face.

'If you ignore my advice, things will go badly for
you. Very badly. Don't think you'll be dealing with me,

calling on you in my business suit. I know men who are totally ruthless and will do to you what I tell them. After all, they had years of practice under the old system. They have no emotions about things like this. It will just be a job. This is the only warning I'll give you. Keep whatever you know about Bodnar locked inside you.'

'No.'

His chin lifted a fraction. 'All right, I'm going to have to be quite explicit.'

'No. It makes no difference what threats you make. You're too late. Bodnar will live again. And in bringing him alive, you will be destroyed.'

He stared at her. Yes, that's what Pepa had said. She still stood with a hand straining at the blouse.

'I'm not talking about rape,' he began. She cut him short.

'Good. Now get out.'

She seemed to have erected a barrier in her mind that he couldn't penetrate. He said, 'That other time, if I gave you a shock, it was a necessary shock. You were out of control. I had sex with you and I calmed you down. Those were hard times and very possibly I saved your life.'

She opened her mouth as if to scream. In the end she did no more than whisper, 'I don't believe what I'm hearing. You were my saviour?'

'It's not a question of belief but of understanding. This time it is more serious. This time you are right on the edge.'

'Maybe you've come to kill me. Maybe you'll succeed. But you'll fail because it's not just me.'

'Exactly. That's what I've come to find out. There was a man with you, or at least at the same time as you, and I need to know about him.'

'So they were your men at the cemetery.'

'I had no men there.'

'Something alerted them. They reported to somebody. That somebody told you. What difference is there? I saw one kick the posy of flowers on Venca's grave. They were your men. Maybe you never met them, maybe you don't even know their names. But they were your men. Your kind. The ones you said did things without emotion. They are rotten now and they stink but you don't notice.'

She had let go of her blouse and was gesturing, hands, shoulders, nose. Broucek saw the actress in her. She came forward, she turned, she stepped away. Movement brought her to the window and she looked down to the street where the car was parked.

'There are no men waiting,' Broucek said, 'but it only takes a telephone call.'

A shoulder twitched, a shrug, indifference.

'You were seen going to the old priest's house,' Broucek went on. 'That's where you got the key. You went to the seminary, to Bodnar's grave. That's where you were joined by the man I'm interested in. Then the men who'd observed you getting the key came to check who you were. It could be you were working for a gang. In these new liberal times there are criminals who steal silver and paintings from churches, even huge chandeliers.'

'Don't be absurd. You and your type stole everything worth stealing years ago.'

'You gave no account of yourselves. Instead you went upstairs and hid in a closet.'

'If you say so.'

'I say so.' Broucek was standing quite close to Prerova. He took the small frilly handkerchief from his pocket. 'You dropped this. It's got your perfume in it still, the one you're wearing now. Did he give the perfume to you?'

Prerova had turned her head to examine the hand- kerchief. She supposed it was hers. She raised her eyes to his face. 'He's a priest. Priests don't give perfume to women.'

'Priest?'

Prerova wanted to call her words back. She shouldn't be saying anything. It was just that there was so much hate for this man inside her and words kept forcing their way out.

'Not the old priest from Benevice?'

She said nothing.

'No,' Broucek said, 'not him. Of course not. But he wasn't wearing priest's clothes. He went to the café and asked questions about the past. Why?'

She couldn't hold things inside her. A taunt forced its way out. 'You know why and it frightens you. You try to be tough to hide your fear. The past isn't over. Not any more. You see, it's not just me.'

'What's his name?'

'Correction.' Prerova shook her head. 'That part of the past is over. You can't interrogate me any more. You no longer have that power.'

'Where is he living?'

'I never asked. Now get out. Out.'

They both turned at the sound of the front door of the apartment opening, then clicking shut.

'Is that you?' Prerova called out.

There was a patter of shoes across the linoleum. They were light footfalls and Broucek pictured a hollow-cheeked ascetic priest taking humble steps.

'Olina . . .'

Olga stopped in the doorway, an eyebrow arching at her mother with another strange man. They stood quite close together. Had they been kissing and broken apart?

'Ciao,' Olga said. She wore Cuban boots and blue jeans. An Afghan jacket was open on a Frank Zappa T-shirt. A diamond winked in one nostril – well, a diamond in intent. Silver loop earrings enclosed dollar signs. Purple eyeshadow was echoed in dabs of purple in her dark hair. Her lips were silver. She had stepped from an alien spacecraft. 'Sorry to intrude.'

'You're not intruding. This man is going,' Prerova said, 'now.'

'And this is . . . ?' Broucek prompted.

When Prerova ignored the question, Olga said, 'I'm her daughter.' She came forward with her hand out to shake. 'Olga. She calls me Olina. Olinka when I was a baby. But I'm grown up now, make my own way. And you are . . .?'

Broucek took her hand. The fingernails too were silver. They were talons that could scratch your back, except for one thumbnail bitten to the quick. It was the thumbnail that caught his eye, a small thing like that, as if it was the last of Olinka's habits. The hardness he had put on with Prerova disappeared with her daughter. The thumbnail was a detail, a hint of the little girl thrust into the adult world. The eyes were certainly not a young girl's. They had taken in Broucek's frank appraisal and now showed a hint of mockery as Broucek held onto her hand.

'You could say an old acquaintance,' he told her.

She raised an eyebrow at his reluctance to give his name then let her gaze drop to her hand still grasped by his. The feel of her skin was a disappointment to Broucek, who expected beautiful girls to have the texture of a silk sheet. Was beautiful the way to describe her? Striking, definitely. She seemed made for the stage, like her mother. Her face had the same bone structure, the same full lips, the same expressive eyes.

'Are you an actress as well?' he asked.

'As well as my mother?' She nodded to Prerova. 'Would you say I'm an actress?'

'You're acting now.' Prerova's frown was for both but then favoured Broucek. 'Are you planning to steal her hand? Let it go and get out.'

Olga drew a deep breath as if for the first time smelling the atmosphere. Not a lovers' spat – she'd never seen the man here before. Not some artistic difference – the man had no look of the theatre about him. Not some political argument – her mother wasn't interested. What else was there? Definitely something personal. She'd winkle the secret out of her mother later. She took a cigarette from her shoulder-bag.

'You have a match?'

Broucek lit her cigarette. She steadied his hand with her own while her eyes looked up into his face. It was a cheap sexual gesture learnt from a bad film, except her eyes said she was mocking him.

'What do you do?' he asked. 'Are you a student?'

'She sells,' Prerova said.

'But not myself.' The mockery was still in Olga's eyes.

'What then?'

'Jewellery. Rings and things. Bracelets, pendants, all original designs and hand made.'

'Junk for tourists,' Prerova said. 'From a tray on Charles Bridge.'

'It pays.' Olga drew on her cigarette until its tip was a fierce glow. 'It pays better than selling fruit juice from a tray.'

'Where do you live? Do you live here with your mother?' Broucek nodded towards one of the closed doors.

'No.'

'Where do you live?'

'I have my own place. That's where I live.'

'My car's below. I can give you a lift.'

'That black bathtub parked outside?'

Olga drew fiercely on the cigarette again. She held the smoke in while she gave this offer mature consideration. She pursed her lips as if to blow a kiss and let out a stream of smoke in Broucek's face.

Broucek stopped at the front door of the apartment. It had taken more sharp words, the battering of Prerova's will and a certain amount of shoving to get him there.

'Don't come back. If you come back I'll get a knife from the kitchen.'

Her? Did she think trimming a pork chop made her an expert with a knife?

'Remember what I told you. Leave the past buried.'

'Out.'

Where had his hardness gone? Olga had stolen it temporarily. He took a fistful of Prerova's blouse, bunched it up so it dragged tight across her breasts. 'Listen to me and understand what I say. Maybe you don't care for yourself but remember – now I know you have a daughter. Think about it.'

The shock came into her face as if he'd hit her. He saw it and knew she understood. She was remembering another time when he'd said: 'You or your mother.'

'Leave her alone. Don't you dare touch my daughter. You of all people.' Prerova had been angry with Olga for talking too much. Towards Broucek she displayed fury.

Broucek lurched but grabbed the doorframe. He didn't know where Olga lived but he knew where she hung out and worked. On the bridge along with the sellers of postcards, guidebooks, souvenir ashtrays, T-shirts reading 'Prague – Czech It Out', CDs, barely dry paintings of the Old Town Hall clock and all the other stuff. One day some capitalist millionaire would boast of having started there.

'Strange the twists in life,' Broucek began. Perhaps he intended to give another warning but Prerova bent forward and made to bite the hand that held the door-frame. He snatched the hand away and found himself heaved on to the landing and the door locked in his face.

On the other side Prerova closed her eyes and pushed with her back against the door for good measure.

CHAPTER EIGHT

In the summer it would be different. Trees would be leafed, the cover thicker, sounds deadened.

Broucek, crouching, heard a twig snap ahead of him. He was sure of it, absolutely sure of it. He listened to it again in his head. It had been a twig snapping, a sound like a knuckle being cracked. Or a pine cone hitting the ground. There was a stand of fir trees there making their own patch of darkness. Nothing moved. Nothing moved that he could see. The revolver in his hand was heavy but he didn't lower it. It was a long-barrelled Colt .45, a perfect copy, locally made.

In summer the woods could hide a whole platoon of attackers but now the only ambush positions were a pile of sawn logs and that stand of firs. Still crouching, Broucek took half a dozen steps to his right. He could feel his pulse beating faster. The shine of sweat on his forehead felt cold. Another thing, he had a sudden conviction that he was in someone's sights, somebody among the fir trees he couldn't see was lining up a shot on his forehead. Drop to the ground? Sprint for the shelter of the beech trunk? You're not a panicky schoolkid, he scolded himself, though he could feel muscles tightening round his windpipe and there was a burning like acid in his throat. He raised a hand to his forehead to wipe away the moisture.

From some distance away floated the sound of gun-fire. Broucek had come from there, strolling casually at first as if to answer a call of nature, moving more purposefully, finally, when he was among scrub along the bank of a stream, breaking into a trot, ignoring the shouts. He had dodged across ploughed land and into these woods. Old snow lay in patches and Broucek felt vulnerable as he crossed it, gaudy against its whiteness.

The city was Broucek's territory. He was at home among the rush of cars, the crowd waiting for the lights to change, the men who stood in doorways. Country brought unease, forests and fields. Look on it as a woman, its slopes and contours and swellings. It can be bought, lived with, made to bear crops, hunted over, fought over. He told himself this as he stood and wasn't made any easier. The land was beyond his control. It stretched out to the horizon where he was peering, and behind his back where he couldn't see. It couldn't be seduced or manipulated or terrorized.

Country as a woman was a stupid fancy.

He was jumpy this morning, no doubt of it. The telephone call still reverberated. He'd rung Pepa from the office in the evening. He'd stood by the window holding the receiver pressed to his face. The river showed reflected lamps and he could see a floodlit corner of Hradcany Castle. Are you receiving me well? The usual. And Pepa had said: What progress have you made? Is it finished yet? He'd told Pepa about Prerova and he'd asked: In what state did you leave her? So it's not finished yet. And her daughter's seen you. And there's a priest involved. You haven't got much time before it's spiralled beyond your reach.

When he'd had lunch in the country there'd been two Pepas: the generous host and the sharp operator. And two tones of voice. Last night on the telephone there had been no generosity in the voice.

From a distant field came an explosion. A horse neighed, a man cried out. Broucek wanted a cigarette, a beer, but above all a piss. Fertilize the roses? He'd be fertilizing his pants if he didn't go. He holstered the revolver, unzipped and loosened himself, and let fly. And this was the moment.

'You there!'

Not from the fir trees. The voice was from behind him. Broucek swung round, splashing his trouser legs, at the very instant of an explosive pop. He was struck in the chest, missing the heart, though not by much. On his coat a starburst of vivid red spread and dripped.

Where the land rose up a gentle hill, the chainsaws had been, felling the old chestnut trees for furniture. The smaller branches were stacked for firewood and it was against one of these piles that Broucek and Novacek squatted. Their backs were to the sound of battle. Red had run down Broucek's uniform from the paintball.

'Why are you dressed in that?' Novacek asked.

'Why? How should I know? I'm a Lieutenant, a Captain, I didn't ask. I just told the organizer I was thinking of joining and he pulled this uniform out of a box and told me to get stuck in, see how I liked it.'

'You see,' Novacek said, 'you're on the wrong side.'

'What are you getting at?'

'You're a Confederate.'

'A Confederate?' Broucek repeated. Bloody country-side, beyond comprehension.

'A reb. Basically rebels are there to be killed.'

'Sounds familiar.' Broucek brought out his cigarettes and they both lit up. 'What are you?'

'Sherman's Militia. We're the winners. We get to march through Georgia, burning and pillaging. Bit of rape on the side.'

'Rape? Are you serious? I didn't see the raw material for that.'

'They turn up towards midday with the food and beer.'

'You do it for real? Rape?'

'Tonda, this is the new Czechoslovakia. We've all got to learn how to be democrats and liberals. Rape is the old Czechoslovakia. We must respect women.'

'And do women respect you?'

'Men and women must learn to be partners, sharing in the future.'

'Sounds to me much like the old propaganda,' Broucek said. He licked one broad finger and rubbed at the paint on the uniform. His fingertip turned red.

'It sponges clean away,' Novacek said. 'More than you can say for the real stuff.'

A bugle sounded, thinned by distance. Broucek nodded his head backwards.

'You really enjoy all this? Dressing up, hide-and-seek, toy guns, fake blood?'

Novacek frowned. 'It gets me out of the apartment.'

'What's the problem? Too much sharing? Missus showing no respect? So leave her.'

'If I leave her, I lose the kids.'

'I know a lawyer who could fix things,' Broucek said, one eyelid drooping, a finger tapping against his nose.

'Looks like someone gave you a bloody nose.'

Broucek's face wore a scowl. 'Your wife's got you by the balls. So you come here and play bang-bangs. Perhaps you should listen to this idea I've had. What does this outfit call itself?'

'The American Civil War Club.'

'All right. You start the Nineteen Sixty-Eight Club. It belongs right here in our own homeland, none of your imports. There's something in it for everyone. You've got your rebels, your dissidents, your students with long hair, your girls with no underwear on, your actors, your hotheads with cobblestones. On the other side you've got your cops, your leatherjackets, your fraternal socialist forces. You can dig up all the authentic stuff, caps, uniforms, riot gear, even some old Russian tanks around I could help you with. Save on fake blood – use real bullets. Everybody can break everyone else's head. Everybody can have a good time.'

Broucek seemed to have finished. He'd certainly stopped talking. Novacek didn't know how to take what he'd just said. He seemed dead serious about it.

Novacek cleared this throat and said, 'Great.'

There was silence between them while they finished their cigarettes and listened to horses' hooves and a booming cannon.

'Nineteen sixty-eight, you say. Do you see a part for yourself in this?' Novacek asked.

'I'll be right there, standing in the fir trees, back in the shadows.'

'Where you think no one can see you.'

They paused again. It was Novacek's turn to get out his packet and they lit fresh cigarettes. There was the clump of boots coming round the wood pile. A uniformed man came into view, a rifle raised at them.

'What are you doing?' the soldier asked. 'Why aren't you fighting?'

'I've captured this Yankee officer,' Novacek said. 'He's wounded but he could still be dangerous, so I'm guarding him.'

'We're not taking prisoners today. I'll finish him off and then you can get back to the battle.'

The soldier moved his rifle to aim between Broucek's eyes.

Broucek never raised his voice. 'You do that and I'll kick you in the balls.'

'Hey now, whoa.'

'You heard what I said.'

The rifle held steady a moment longer, wavered and drooped.

'Excuse me, friend,' the soldier said. 'What's steamed you up? Only a bit of fun.'

'Piss off.'

'You see why I have to guard him,' Novacek said. 'He's got a vicious streak.'

The soldier looked from one to the other. He shrugged and shambled off in search of more sporting players. They watched him out of earshot.

'Back in nineteen sixty-eight,' Novacek said, 'you were standing in the shadows where you were invisible. That's what you believed. But now it's nineteen ninety-one and someone's feeling around in the dark for you. Everyone else's balls are in danger today, so why not yours? Someone's going to be squeezing very hard. It's what I telephoned you about. You never got back to me.'

'I had a full day,' Broucek said. 'It went on late.'

'And a full night before that? At your age.'

Franta Novacek didn't like him. It was in his voice, the shadow of a sneer. Broucek wouldn't cry in his beer over that. To be sneered at by someone who played toy soldiers was nothing. So long as they watched each other's backs.

'Tremor. Isn't that the word you used?'

'Probably.'

'A tremor in the Prague District Party?'

Novacek was General Liaison Officer, a title that lowered a cloud over his functions. In the past he'd worked with the ministries and his liaison had consisted in smoothing difficulties in the way of senior Party men. What sort of difficulties? All sorts. It could be a problem with the foreign press, a bank account, a pregnant girl. Now, like a cloud, his job had largely evaporated.

'It's like this. One area in which I've kept my influence is the Party files. Weed them out. Lose some, burn some, keep some. I mean, those files are ours, they're not for some new minister to look at, or the mustard new police chief, or a journalist with a sharp nose.'

Files were knowledge, knowledge was power. Broucek nodded agreement. 'So?'

'An oddball request for a very old, very dusty file. Back to nineteen sixty-eight. A specific piece of information was requested, though the request was all dolled up. A certain car was registered to the Party. Number given: CS.02.48. Question: name of the person who had the use of the car.'

Broucek was nodding again, but slower. He was not a member of the Party. Novacek had weeded the files so that he never had been a member. But there was always some forgotten detail that tripped you up. That damned car, that stupid joke of a number.

'What did you do about the request?'

'That information is definitely lost. If it ever existed.'

'Thank you, Franta. Really good of you.' It was not so much that he felt grateful as that he didn't want to be in Novacek's debt. An effusive 'Thank you' could settle the score. 'Tell me, was it a priest asking?'

'Priest? Are you growing mushy in your middle age? It was someone in your own ministry, your ex-ministry I should say.'

'Does this person have a name?'

Novacek handed him a scrap of paper. Weiser, first name not given but initial M. The name meant nothing to Broucek. He tucked the paper inside his cigarette packet.

'So.'

So the past was not over, Broucek acknowledged. That's what Prerova had said and was proved right again. But now it is we who seek out open spaces where no microphone can eavesdrop. We sit on a pile of wood in the open air passing secret messages without speaking names. We are the dissidents now.

It was Sunday and the annexe to the Finance Ministry was empty except for Broucek and the security guard.

The guard was just inside the entrance door in something like a glass-fronted sentry box. He'd gone straight back into it after unlocking the door so he could sit in front of a one-bar electric fire. The heating in the building was off and he wore overcoat, scarf and cap. He held Broucek's pass in a gloved hand, tilting it back and forth under the lamp, looking from the photo up to Broucek's face. Did he think it was forged?

'I can't accept this. It's out of date. New passes have been issued.'

'Well done,' Broucek said. 'I'll tell the Deputy Minister how alert you are. Is he in yet?'

The guard straightened in his chair. 'The Deputy Minister? Nobody told me to expect him.' Then, thinking about Broucek knowing the Deputy Minister, he added, 'He's not arrived yet, sir.'

'It's an emergency meeting,' Broucek said. 'Something unexpected came up. You know how it is. I hope he's dressed like you or his brain will freeze up.'

'Economy measure, they said.'

'I'll wait for him upstairs. Be warmer.'

'About this pass.' The guard was uneasy. He was new, someone Broucek didn't know. What had become of the old guards? Some had been retired. Others were suspended while their pasts were looked into. Had they perhaps performed special duties?

'Stupid mistake,' Broucek said. 'I was in a hurry and picked up the wrong pass from my desk. It's at home. I'll show it to you next time.'

If it had been one of the old guards he wouldn't have to put on this act. He wasn't smiling but he was keeping his expression pleasant. He could feel the muscles in his cheeks stiffening. The new democratic Prague was a pain.

The guard turned the pass over and inspected the reverse. He was frowning as he handed it back. 'I'll have to tell the Deputy Minister when he arrives.'

'Good idea. Then it's his responsibility.'

'Yes,' the guard said. He thought about it and nodded. 'Yes, that's right.'

Broucek slipped the pass back in his pocket, climbed the three steps to the lobby and set off. The security guard's eyes were on his back. He could feel them. Ahead was the lift.

'The current to the lift is switched off on Sunday. It's the economy measures.'

Broucek had been right: the guard was watching him every step of the way. If no one came in on Sunday, why bother to switch the current off? Broucek wanted to ask, but it would only disturb him. He made for the staircase and began to climb. The information he needed wasn't much and he supposed he could get it in just about any office. Call it nostalgia, call it curiosity about who had it now, but he went to his old office. Four flights of stairs left him puffing. Once this business was over he'd exercise more, cut down on the beers, lose five kilos.

The door had a visiting card tacked to it, a Doctor Somebody, a name that meant nothing. His office on this Sunday felt familiar and strange both at once. He stood just inside the door, looking round, trying to explain the feeling to himself. Like waking up in someone else's bed after she's already left to go to work. Yes, that would do. Who inhabited this space now? A doctor

of medicine, a doctor of economics, a doctor of philosophy? A sportsman of some kind – a tennis racquet
stood against a wall. A doctor who appreciated
Broucek's choice of art: a pair of lovingly detailed
Schiele drawings still faced the desk.

The absence of noise was uncanny. The muffled
sounds of telephones, footsteps, whistles, voices, coffee
cups, lift, doors had vanished. The office was holding
its breath to see what he would do.

So. He moved to the desk. Weiser. M stood for
Milan. The departmental directory gave it to him. Head
of the transport section. Head of bloody transport. He
felt anger renewing itself that some little prick in his
old ministry was stirring up trouble, asking questions.

Prague had become a city of questions. Everybody
demanded to know where the answers lay. Under the
ground, some of them, up the chimney, in filing cabinets, in the shadows, in the woodwork, in memories
that were locked tight.

Coming along the path to the annexe Broucek had
heard a step behind him and whirled. It could have
been someone with a question and demanding an
answer. It could have been Weiser or Prerova or Olga.
There was a growing army of questioners, more each
day. Was it you who killed Bodnar? In what manner?
What corruption had he uncovered?

When he whirled round, there'd been no one. It had
been a footfall in his head.

The question that Weiser had been asking had no
answer now. The file had been destroyed. But there
were always other questions.

Restless, pacing his old room just as he used to, he

stopped by the window. Bare branches, roofs, an expanse of sky with a couple of gulls lifting, banking, swooping down to land on the river. It was very like the view from his new office, which was probably why he had chosen it.

'See those gulls,' Broucek remembered telling some pen-pusher from the accounts department. This was in the old days, not the democratic question-asking days. They'd been standing on this very spot and he'd put an arm round the shoulders of the pen-pusher as if it was a friendly chat. 'You're in accounts, new there, and you're not sure of the rules yet. I appreciate that. So let me tell you.' Broucek had started off with his voice quiet but the tone hardened. 'Rule number one: when my expenses sheet comes to your department your job is to pay it, not query it. Because if you don't, you'll be saying hello to the gulls on the way past. Remember Masaryk.' Broucek had applied gentle pressure until the clerk's face was pushed hard against the glass, nose flattened, eyes wide as they took in the drop from the window. 'And rule number two is make sure you always remember rule number one.'

He reached for the internal directory again. Weiser, Milan, home address in the suburb of Nusle. Next century they'd be running coach tours to Nusle. It would be a historic quarter to rival Old Town Square, with Japanese tripping over their video cameras. You want to see the triumph of the planned economy? Special two-hour tour in air-conditioned luxury. Gasp at the distressed concrete, the reeking chimneys, the weed-grown yards. Marvel at the patina of centuries of picturesque decay achieved in a mere twenty-five years.

Have your photo taken – only ten dollars, US, cash – in front of an authentic poster celebrating the great achievements of the socialist age.

He went to the cupboard where he used to keep glasses and a bottle of Scotch but it stored stationery now. He needed a stiffener. It already seemed a long day because of the early telephone call.

'Are you receiving me well?'

If it had been Pepa he would have had to talk to him, or listen to him. But this was one of his men, going to ask about progress since last night.

Broucek had said, 'Who do you want to speak to?' The telephone had gone dead at once.

He tried the deep bottom drawer of the desk but there was no bottle there either. For the third time he looked at the internal directory. He wanted a name from the transport section that he recognized, someone whose Sunday he could disrupt.

CHAPTER NINE

Side by side they contemplated the naked flesh. A buttock was turned, a face glimpsed over a half-lifted shoulder. Fulnek's eyes shifted from kicking legs to yearning arms. These were children's bodies, young boys presenting a rear view, undeniably flirting.

Milan Weiser ran his tongue over dry lips. Excitement took some people that way. So did fear.

'This is the most . . . convenient place I could think of,' Weiser murmured.

Convenient? Fulnek noted the hesitation in choosing the word. It was not convenient for either of them. The pause and the paleness of Weiser's face showed his meaning. The place was safe. Fulnek murmured in his turn: 'It is perfect.'

You must absent yourself for a while. That had been the command, and yet on the very next Sunday he was back in church, this time in the congregation. Why hadn't he anticipated how disturbing it would be? It could be him by the altar rail, robed in purple and cream and red, declaiming from the huge Bible held open by an acolyte. 'And there shall come forth a rod out of the stem of Jesse, and a branch shall grow out of his roots.' Fulnek's nose twitched to the hints of candle wax, incense, unwashed clothes, ancient dust, fumes of beer from Weiser. 'And the spirit of the Lord shall rest upon him, the spirit of wisdom and understanding, the spirit of counsel and might, the spirit of knowledge and of the fear of the Lord. And shall make him quick of understanding . . .' But understanding slipped beyond his grasp. They were words, just words.

'In the morning, at the Slovak service, it is barely half full. But now at the Czech service . . .'

Now it was crowded and a crowd offered protection. There were middle-aged couples, whole families with young children, young men in army uniform, the black shadows of old widows. Was there a young widow with frank eyes?

'And the leopard shall lie down with the kid . . .'

'You never know when They may be watching.'

'It is not like that any more,' said Fulnek. 'They are no longer in power.'

'They are Their own power. They are not the state any more, They have privatized Themselves. People talk about the mafia.'

'Mafia is just a word,' Fulnek said. 'Even where I live people talk of the mafia. Somebody only has to lose a coat from a hook in a café and it is the mafia. This is Czechoslovakia. There is no Italian connection.'

'It's a good short word to describe Them.'

Weiser was very serious about it. And Fulnek remembered how he and Prerova had hidden in the closet. Mafia or not, They existed.

This was the second time they had met. The first time Weiser had been full of fun. Of course I'll help, he'd said, I'll do it for love of her. Fulnek wondered if he too called her Prerova or used some more familiar name. Weiser had given a conspirator's wink: Maybe we both do it for love of her.

Weiser had smiled at Fulnek, but Fulnek hadn't smiled back. He didn't want the complicity of a smile. For him Prerova was . . . was . . . special. Beautiful still, certainly. That scar only scratched the surface of her beauty. Radiating a female allure that even a man of the cloth had to acknowledge. Speaking to him not just with her voice but with her eyes, her gestures, her whole body. Trying to shock him as a priest and succeeding only in drawing him closer. She tempts me, Fulnek acknowledged, though is she aware of doing so? Is any woman not aware of her power? Or maybe the magnetism starts in me and draws the temptation out of her. Does this make sense? Or just make an excuse? Dear God, do you know what you have wrought with this clay?

'. . . and the lion shall eat straw like the ox . . .'

'Tell me what happened.'

'Nothing happened, nothing or everything.'

Weiser's voice had not risen above a murmur. There should be a screen between us, Fulnek decided. It is like confession.

'The car you are interested in was one of a number at that time used by the Party – allotted to people with a certain power. I know that because the licence falls within the serial the Prague Party used in nineteen sixty-eight. That much is easy for me to verify because of my position. The next stage requires me to go further, to enquire at the Party itself. Or what remains of the Party, the skeleton of the Party. So I put in what appears to be a formal request from the Finance Ministry, saying that we are investigating the possibility of fraudulent use of state property.' For a moment there was a little rascal grin on Weiser's lips, thinking of all the big words he had used. 'Investigation is widespread at the moment though usually applied to real estate, not cars. After all the car is long ago on the scrapheap. I asked about three vehicles licensed in nineteen sixty-seven.'

'Nineteen sixty-seven?' Fulnek said a little too loudly. A head turned, a meaningful glare was given. He was quiet.

'I needed to establish records were kept. Also in such a matter I thought it wise to circle round the true objective. I established that files have been kept. Then I repeated the exercise for nineteen sixty-eight. CS.02.48 was one of the numbers. I thought I was taking every precaution but I tripped over some alarm wire. Somebody became suspicious. Who was I? What was my authorization? What was the purpose? It was part of a sample, I said, to see if there was evidence worth pursuing. This was late Friday afternoon, after hours, the beginning of the sacred weekend. It must be urgent to be pursuing such information at irregular hours. Suspicion in the tone of voice, a hint of accusing. It is a way of talking They cannot lose. At this stage it was official but unofficial, I replied. I was quite pleased with that. This was a telephone conversation, you understand, but I didn't know who I was speaking to. Acting Duty Secretary, some title without substance. They were being official but unofficial too. He rang back in a quarter of an hour. CS.02.48 was not listed. The files didn't go back that far.'

'They went back to the year before.'

'Exactly.'

The acolyte carrying the Bible paused as he crossed in front of the altar, turned and genuflected before continuing.

'Exactly,' Weiser repeated. 'There are lines of defence and tripwires and I'm the one who blundered into them.'

Fulnek closed his eyes. There was nowhere restful in the church for him to look. This was not Gothic gloom, this was Baroque frenzy. Putti were everywhere, plump little cherubim disporting themselves in poses of innocence, coyness or open-armed welcome. Winged angels threatened from the ceiling. Walls were painted pastel blue and pink with framed slabs of veined marble. Blank spaces were a vacuum to be filled. There was a riot of gilt: picture frames, scrolls, leaves, vines, sunbursts, mitres, chandeliers, saints.

Fulnek felt movement beside him. Weiser was going to take communion. Fulnek felt unable to follow this good example. Even a priest must confess. Particularly a priest. His face sank into the darkness of his hands. Lord, are you guiding me? Were you guiding me before? What do I do now? Am I pursuing a long-ago murderer and rapist for justice? For personal reasons? Because of Prerova? As an act of atonement, something to drop in the other pan of the scales of judgement?

The questions dried up and he had no answers. He remained kneeling with his hands shielding his face even after Weiser had returned to his seat.

The desire to do wrong and afterwards to be forgiven, that was what it was to be a man. Fulnek sighed.

*

'You know about St Ursula?'

They were standing outside the church. Fulnek let Weiser tell him.

'She was the daughter of a British chieftain, a princess who was betrothed to a pagan prince. She begged for a three-year delay before her marriage and she went cruising with ten other ladies. Each of them had a ship with a thousand companions, all unmarried maids. They sailed up the Rhine as far as Basel, went on foot on a pilgrimage to Rome and then returned to Cologne where they were martyred by the Huns because of their Christianity. Every last one massacred – enough to make Stalin jealous. But eleven thousand virgins, what a waste, eh?'

It is a faulty translation, Fulnek wanted to say. In the Latin there were eleven virgins, no more.

Weiser looked away from St Ursula's church down the street to the golden crown on top of the National Theatre. A cold wind was blowing off the river. Fulnek looked the other way towards Maj, a hulk of a department store. We checked each way without thinking, Fulnek realized. We are conditioned. They initiated us and we can never be virgins again.

No one was watching.

It was Fulnek's idea they should go for a drink. Slav gloom sat poorly on Weiser's face. Chase away the shadows, the skirmish with the Party, the eleven thousand lost chances.

'Ummm,' Weiser said. His resistance didn't last long. 'I'd better see Eva first.'

Eva was his wife. Before taking the tram out to see

her, Weiser went to a florist's kiosk in Wenceslas Square for a bunch of flowers wrapped in cellophane. Tiger lilies.

'I'll wait outside,' Fulnek suggested as they walked from the tram stop. 'That will be better.'

'No, no, come with me.'

Flowers from an errant husband. The scene was clear to Fulnek. His own presence was required as support.

There was no surprise to the block of flats in Nusle. It was five storeys high, concrete, with neighbouring blocks identical in every detail. In the entrance there were rows of letter boxes, a fire hose on a red reel and a sign warning No Bicycles Here. Who rode a bicycle in Prague? The sign was just a bureaucratic prod into people's everyday lives. The apartment was on the top floor, which made them both out of breath. Weiser unlocked the door which opened and came to an abrupt stop on the security chain.

'Eva,' he called. 'Eva, it's me.'

She released the chain to let them in. She was blonde and younger than Weiser by some ten years. She wore a thin dressing-gown which she clutched together at her neck. Her lips were pressed bloodless, no welcoming smile or words.

Weiser unwisely chose a bantering tone, which Fulnek had sometimes noticed in guilty husbands. 'Why are you keeping me from you, my poppet? Why the chain?'

'In case of rapists, since you are never here to protect me.'

'My wife Eva,' Weiser made a ceremony of the introduction, 'my friend Alois Fulnek. For you, my precious.'

With a flourish Weiser produced the bouquet from behind his back. Eva Weiserova accepted it, though not for long. She tossed it on to a table beside a vase of fading blooms.

'How kind,' she said, 'how thoughtful, what a generous provider. The lot you brought last time are very nearly dead.'

'Pretty flowers for a pretty lady.'

Weiser seemed incapable of taking the situation or his wife or possibly himself seriously. This is the man, Fulnek reminded himself, who was buying frilly underclothes in Kotva for some mistress, this is the lover of Prerova, this is the adulterer who takes the body of Christ in the church of the virgin St Ursula. Also this is the man whose career was blighted because he refused to join the Party, whose life was diminished, was reduced to this concrete box with its veneers, where the plastic-covered sofa squeaks when you lower your body on to it, where the television rests like an altar in the centre of a wall. This is the man who at some risk to himself enquired about the car of a rapist and murderer.

'I suppose I could ask where you've been,' she said, 'or who you've been with.'

'With Alois,' Weiser replied. 'We've just come from church. Isn't that so?'

'Yes. St Ursula's, actually.'

Fulnek found himself thrust into the front line. Eva inspected him for some moments, which made him uncomfortable. Her expression moved between disbelief, scorn, boredom, impatience, resignation, dislike – Fulnek could not make it out.

'Really?' she said to Fulnek. 'On your knees all last night, too? Well, he's developed a new taste then.' She turned to go through an open door into the bathroom.

'It was to do with my work,' Weiser said.

She swung back in fury. 'Don't lie to me. Just don't bloody lie to me. You, the exalted head of the transport section of the Finance Ministry, are out all Saturday night and most of Sunday too, and you say it's to do with your work?'

It was a domestic war and Fulnek had in the past found himself as peacemaker in such situations. Or sometimes a negotiator. This evening he felt wearied of it all.

'I think I should be going.'

'Yes,' Eva agreed.

'You're not going on your own,' Weiser said. 'I'm coming with you. We'll go for that drink. Somewhere friendlier.'

'Run away, both of you,' Eva said, 'why don't you?'

She stared after them, frowning, expecting the door to be slammed. She was not disappointed.

The frown faded slowly. She shivered. A draught snaked round her ankles and climbed her legs. Behind her the curtains twitched and parted to show french windows opening. A man dressed in a black leather jacket stepped into the room from the balcony. He brought the cold with him.

There was a bar at the corner but at the last moment Weiser veered away to cross the road. The rumble of male voices didn't suit his mood. Or he didn't like the

look of the man who pushed open the door with his
back before facing the street; in each hand he carried a
two-litre glass jug of beer.

'You wouldn't like it in there,' Weiser said.

'They sell beer.'

'Nothing but men getting drunk. Then they want to
fight.'

Nothing but angry husbands, Fulnek interpreted,
cuckolds.

In the next block double doors were open to a
vestibule with a coat-check counter. A painted sign
announced the K Salon, Dancing Wednesday 5–9,
Sunday 3–7. Was this K for Kultur or K for Kafka?

'It's hardly worth going in,' Fulnek said, checking his
watch.

'Don't worry. It never finishes on time or there'd be
trouble. And there's always afterwards.'

Afterwards? A hint, a promise that moved uneasily
inside Fulnek. He should come straight out and say:
I'm not the man you think I am, I'm a priest. But he
owed Weiser a drink for the questions he'd asked. A
drink at the very least.

Formica-topped tables lined the walls of the K
Salon. A five-piece band performed on a platform at
one end with a woman vocalist in a flouncy dress and
a man in puffed shirtsleeves and waistcoat. On the
dance floor were a dozen couples. A bar at the end
opposite the band had a clump of serious drinkers.
Weiser saluted a friend across the room and they
weaved between the dancers to join his table. Fulnek
ordered beers from a waitress. His attention switched
to the stage. The man and the woman sang a duet,

taking alternate lines. It was not a song of the 'nineties, at least not of the nineteen nineties. Beside Fulnek a woman clinging on to her forties had her face tilted, her eyes raised, her lips parted. It was a form of ecstasy he recognized from certain religious subjects. St Teresa of Avila in her pre-Carmelite days. In some painting by some artist in some church somewhere. Details had vanished from his head. Only the duet remained.

'Do you remember when you first met me?'

'At the corner of the village square.'

'Do you remember where you first kissed me?'

'At the corner of your cherry lips.'

'Do you remember where you first said you loved me?'

'Where the apple blossom made a blanket on the ground.'

'Do you remember where you first held my hand?'

From across the floor a hoarser male voice broke in:

'Do you remember where you put it?'

It was Weiser who had wandered over to join the drinkers at the bar.

Eva Weiserova slid the security chain into place on the door.

'Don't bother,' the man in the black leather jacket said. 'I'm going.'

She turned to face him. Her hands were behind her, resting on the door. In this position her breasts were very prominent, thrusting forward against the thin rayon dressing-gown. She cocked one foot behind her so her knee showed. It was a pose she had picked up from old films, a girl on the streets of Paris.

'He won't be back,' Eva said. 'Not for hours. Maybe not all night.'

'I can't stay.'

'Why not?'

'Because I must go,' he said with some irritation. He had something to say first but she wouldn't give him a chance.

'Kiss me, Karel.'

When she reached out to him, her gown fell open. As they embraced his hands slipped inside her gown, as she knew they would. They moved over her shoulders, down the rutted lane of her spine, ending up on the curve of her buttocks. She felt fingers working their way deeper into the cleft while his tongue was in her mouth.

'Bitch,' Karel said, breaking loose. But her hand had caught the belt of his trousers. Fingers worked at the buckle. 'I have to go.'

'No,' she said. 'Not yet.' She shook her shoulders and her breasts swung in the gap of her open gown. 'Isn't this enough for any man? So why does he stay out?'

Karel gathered a fistful of her blonde hair. As his grip tightened, the roots darkened. He stared into her eyes. 'I can't stay long.'

'We don't have to go anywhere. We can do it right here.'

'In the hall?'

'Yes.'

'Where – on the floor?'

'Yes.'

'Like animals?'

'Like animals,' she breathed in his ear.

The woman who had possibly the face of St Teresa had the arms and legs of someone brought up on a farm. One arm encircled Fulnek's waist. The other arm stuck out at shoulder height with his own, their hands locked. Sturdy legs had a pump action that bumped him.

'You have no idea how to dance. You have no rhythm in your body. Follow my lead. No, your right hip should be in line with your elbow.'

Fulnek made the mistake of watching his feet, trying to avoid stepping on her toes. A brisk movement of her arm, as if humping a bale of hay, snapped his head up.

'What's interesting about your feet? A man who is any kind of a man should look in a woman's eyes when they dance. Unless she has her cheek against his.'

Were her eyes laughing at him? Was it her way of flirting? Was it her beatific look? Was it the last gasp before the working week? Was it the drink? Only beer was on sale but someone had come round slipping Borovicka gin into the glasses. 'Turns it into a Dog's Nose because it's cold, wet and has a bite underneath.' As they circled the dance floor Fulnek could feel the drink marching through his body, his knees, his elbows, his cheeks, his ears. He was unused to much alcohol and was uncertain if he found the effect pleasant. The room revolved round them, other couples, Weiser in a close embrace with a woman on the dance floor, the female singer seated on the platform swinging her legs over the edge and smoking a cigarette, men at the bar, Teresa's face just in front of his.

'Do you know,' Fulnek said, 'your face reminds me of a painting. It was of St Teresa.'

'Oh yes? You think I'm a saint?'

'She was Spanish. General Franco used to keep her mummified hand beside his bed.'

'Charming. Are you feeling all right? Do you fancy some fresh air?'

She steered him out of the dance salon but near the coat-rack in the vestibule she stopped.

'Kiss me.'

Without waiting she pulled him close and glued her mouth to his. Her lips were flaky and chafed by winter weather, her tongue as vigorous as a small animal. Appalled, Fulnek's eyes widened. She tired of working at the kiss and pulled back.

'What's the matter?'

'I'm sorry,' Fulnek said.

'Are you missing a hormone?'

Now her mouth had gone he felt the imprint of other lips, soft and pliant. In his imagination these lips moved and pressed and moulded and explored. 'Lojza, Lojza,' his name more urgent the second time, 'give me your tongue.' His tongue was taken, manipulated, pulled deeper and himself with it.

Fulnek raised his hand to his mouth. The alcohol must have reached there. Burning.

'I can't make you out,' Teresa said. 'You don't dance, you drink like a sparrow, what else don't you do?' She jiggled the top of her body and her breasts heaved like a wave out to sea. 'Tell you what – kissing you is like kissing my father.'

*

'Wearing that makes you look like . . .' Karel searched his mind, which was not richly furnished. Eva Weiserova was naked except for his black leather jacket. It was unbuttoned and her pubic ruff showed dark and generous.

'Yes?' An eyebrow rose in expectation. She put a hand on her hip.

'I don't know. A peaked cap on that blonde hair and jackboots on your feet and you could play one of Heydrich's outriders.'

Heydrich had been the Nazi appointed to run Czechoslovakia. His assassination led to furious reprisals, the razing of Lidice.

'Thank you very much,' she said. 'Was that meant to be a compliment? Some kind of joke?'

Karel sighed. 'I need the jacket. I have to go.'

'You said that before.' Eva shivered without the jacket and shivered even with the dressing-gown. 'When do I see you again?'

It was clinical, like making a dental appointment. Love had nothing to do with it. They had met at a pre-Christmas party of the Ministry's transport pool where Karel was a driver. In a sense Weiser was his boss. Perhaps revenge had something to do with it.

'I don't know next week's roster yet.'

She frowned. She didn't appreciate being part of the roster. Maybe other women were too.

Karel was buttoning his jacket and paused. 'Eva, listen to me. There is gossip going round the car pool.'

'They're just jealous. What are they saying about us?'

'No, listen.' He shook his head. 'About . . .' He nodded towards the matrimonial bedroom.

'Him and one of his fucking women,' she said.

'About his past.'

'Some little vixen digging for money.' Eva's mind ran down the broad path of her husband's misdeeds.

'No.' He was loud and emphatic. He concentrated on getting it right. 'Someone is asking questions about what he did. Work questions. You know, coming clean about the past. Some things can be forgiven, but some things never can.'

Eva felt a little twist in her stomach. There was something in everybody's past, but what was so special in her husband's? 'What sort of things?'

'Terrible things.'

'Terrible things in a car pool?'

'Organizing transport for prisoners to be taken to illegal places.'

'Illegal places of what?'

Karel looked stern. He shook his head. Better not to enquire, he seemed to be saying. In fact Broucek, who had rehearsed him, hadn't given him the answer to that question.

'This is grotesque.' Abruptly Eva switched to the side of her husband. 'He never got promotion because he wouldn't join the Party. Never mind his faults, he was a man of principles. Suddenly he's turning into Their hatchet man.'

Karel was not a subtle man but he did his best. 'That man he came with tonight – who is he? You told me he is to do with your husband's work but I know nothing of him. What is his name?'

'I didn't pay any attention.'

Karel, on the balcony, observed through a crack in

the curtains but double-glazing had made eavesdropping impossible. 'If you find out, let me know. Anything, well, suspicious, you must tell me. Where he lives, tell me. I want to help you.'

Eva gaped at this man. How could telling him these things help her? But he was so earnest she felt a clenching inside her. Not fear, exactly. Nerves. Something out of the past. Half a century of war, dictatorship, invasion and secrecy cast a long shadow.

Outside on the landing, the door closed again. Karel drew a deep breath. Yes? All right? Broucek would be pleased? In the years he'd known Broucek he could never recall seeing him smile as he had. You mean you know Weiser's wife, actually visit her? A piece of luck at last in his swirling nightmare. Karel didn't know what it was all about and didn't want to know. If the woman came to him with anything, he'd pass it on to Broucek.

On the bloody hall rug. His elbows were sore.

The dance salon was locked and dark but a party had taken hold in the cloakroom off the vestibule.

'Welcome to the Salon K Free Republic,' Weiser announced to the world at large. A dozen or so coats still hung from a rail. People leaned against walls or each other, glasses and cigarettes to hand. 'Everybody is President, nobody is a streetsweeper. Everybody is a student of life, you can talk philosophy or flirting or fetishes, there is no boss glowering at eight in the morning, no husbands and no wives exist, all bills are paid by God, all hangovers cured by the devil, all politicians lose their tongues, all enemies lose their balls, all spinsters lose the chains round their thighs. Are you feeling all right?'

Fulnek had his eyes closed. When he looked again he saw St Teresa of the Chapped Lips gazing. She stood with another woman. They seemed to have been discussing him and there was a speculative look to their faces. Teresa had a twinkle in her eyes: Go on, I dare you to . . . Her companion was biting her lower lip: Shall I . . .?

'It's the dancing,' Fulnek said, 'the heat, the noise.'

'Lovely,' Weiser said. 'Have another drink.'

This was how Weiser lost his weekends. How much did he remember on Monday mornings?

Fulnek turned to the counter on which someone had dropped a cloakroom ticket pad. He wrote down his name and the telephone number of the house he was staying at. A noise beyond the hanging coats puzzled him. Staring into the gloom, he recognized the female vocalist lying on the floor with her skirt pulled up to her waist and the pianist riding her. Hastily he drew the coats together. Across the room came shrieks from two women.

'I have to go,' Fulnek said.

'That's absurd. It's only . . .' Weiser raised his wrist and peered at his watch. 'This little window – does it say Sat or Sun?'

'You know our bit of business?' Fulnek tucked the paper in Weiser's pocket. 'If you find anything out, telephone me here. Or you can leave a message.'

'Alois – I may call you that?' It had been later he turned into Lojza. 'You seem to avoid me, pull back, as if I alarm you.' I assure you not, Fulnek had tried to say. 'Disturb you, then, because of what I am.' A human being, Fulnek had said, but already feeling the argument slipping away from him. He stumbled on: unique, of course, and like all human beings, with a unique human value. 'You talk of my human value as if I'm an abstraction. Which I'm not. Alois, I am a woman and we make up half the human race. I have a bodily existence. I am present right now in this room with you.'

Sometimes a memory slipped unasked into his mind, dug its claws in and had to be forced out, pressed back into the box, the lid nailed down.

Borovicka and beer lifted him above the pavement. Walking westward he felt a world of women was walking with him. St Teresa of the Chapped Lips, her friend of the mocking eyes, the singer who made a nest behind the coats, Eva Weiserova, the ogress who rented him his room and patrolled his morals, Prerova, her daughter Olina. Even the church was St Ursula's. And her, of course, who exploded a face full of rage out of the box until he jammed the lid shut again. Of men, only Weiser.

At the metro station he ran to catch a train standing at the platform. The doors slid shut and the train moved off towards the city centre. He was still puffing as the train slowed for the next station. The metro ran above ground along this stretch and he stared at the looming Palace of Culture, a 'gift of the Soviet people'. The Soviet people must have had a production line for these gifts, dropping them like monstrous dog turds across their slice of Europe. When they were at last persuaded to go home they neglected to take their concrete gifts with them.

The monster disappeared from sight as the train stopped in the station. She's in there, Fulnek thought. If she hadn't been Bodnar's lover twenty-three years ago, if he hadn't been a crusader, if Bodnar hadn't been murdered, if she hadn't been raped and disfigured and threatened . . . How many ifs make a dream? If all that, she wouldn't be selling fruit juice at the Palace of Culture, she'd be Hedda Gabler at the National Theatre.

Not many people got on. As the train left the station Fulnek saw again the concrete hulk, darkened.

Of course. It's Sunday. She's not working.

He never questioned the impulse that made him get off at the next station.

'It's Alois,' he said.

Fulnek had bent forward to mouth his name, not speak too loudly. That was how Prerova found him, leaning close to her, when she unlocked the door. Fulnek saw it was an evening of dressing-gowned women. As before, Prerova's eyes slipped away beyond his shoulders. Satisfied, she let Fulnek in and closed the door. She had to speak at once.

'He came here.'

'What is his name?'

She shook her head.

'Well, who is he? What is he?'

She shook her head again. There was no need to say who they were talking about.

'When?'

'Yesterday.'

'Did he threaten you?'

'I threatened him.' She gripped the lapels of her gown with both hands. 'I told him I'd accuse him of attempted rape. He's done it for real, after all.'

'What did he want?'

'You.'

'Ahhh.'

Fulnek let out a long breath. He felt excitement running in him. Two people wanted each other. The desire was there, it was simply that they could not find each other. And when they did meet? Fulnek could not picture the scene.

'What does he look like?'

Prerova considered her answer. 'He's larger than life.'

Fulnek was little wiser. In his mind he was looking up and up, boots, legs, belt, torso. His opponent was a giant who lived in a cave in the mountains, one of those mythic figures that mothers say will carry off boys who continue being naughty. Or mothers used to say that. Fairytale giants lost their power to frighten when real ones marched into the country.

In the sitting-room Prerova lit a cigarette and drew in smoke in rapid puffs. She was too much on edge to sit. Behind her were the roses with their drooping heads, petals scattered round the vase. Like Weiser, he should have brought a fresh bunch.

'Tell me . . .' Fulnek began.

'Tell me, tell me.' Prerova was impatient. 'I'll tell you everything. He didn't give his name, or his occupation, or how he heard about me or this address. He came in a big car and I couldn't see the number plate. He knows you are a priest – I was caught off-balance and let that slip. He doesn't know your name or where you live. But he wants to meet you very much because you asked questions at the café at Benevice. You are guilty by association with me. He is certain you are concerned about Venca's death. There. That's it.'

The facts. The most interesting fact was still that he and the murderer were looking for each other. Fulnek should advertise.

'You let him in here.' Fulnek tried to picture this larger than life person behind the desk or beside the dead flowers. 'He talks, asks for me, says his farewells and leaves.'

The cigarette tip brightened. 'I'm supposed to keep him here amused in case you turn up? Or I telephone the police?'

'That's a possibility.'

'Accuse him of rape twenty-three years after the event? I don't know his name but he's a powerful rich man. What evidence do I have? Tell him to pull his trousers down and I look at his cock. That's the one – the guilty member.'

She stopped. She considered Fulnek's face, which had a glow.

'I'm sorry, Father. I shouldn't have said that.'

He shook his head. What did the words matter?

'So what are you going to do?' she asked. 'Now you know he's after you.'

'What I intended all along: find the identity of the man who murdered Bodnar, raped and mutilated you, and see justice done.'

'Just like that. You imagine it's like church – he'll confess?'

She sat down and fell silent. Her head was angled as if listening for a sound. Was someone else in the apartment? A man? Was that why she came to the door in a dressing-gown?

'Is Olga here?' he finally asked.

'No, I'm alone. She lives with her boyfriend in a slum of a flat across the river. She only sleeps here if she's had a fight with him. Once or twice she's brought another man for the night. Vary the diet.' Prerova shrugged that off. 'He'll kill you if he finds you. Don't you understand that? He killed Venca and he'll kill you to protect himself.'

'He didn't kill you.'

'No need. With me it's different. He's got a hold on me to ensure silence. Olina. You could see them sniffing round each other. It was disgusting. I protected my mother from him, now I protect my daughter.'

Fulnek was quiet. He couldn't picture the future. The man was evil and evil must be punished. That was justice in the abstract. But how?

'Alois, can't you see the danger you're in? He comes from the old Czechoslovakia. You can smell the money and the power. He has a network of people from the past. He wouldn't kill you himself. Someone else would do it, a job, while he had a perfect alibi.'

Fulnek took his time, trying to picture this ogre. He said, 'If anyone's in danger, it's you. You're the one who's linked with the past.'

'Is that why you came?'

'It was,' Fulnek thought about it, 'an impulse.'

'Ah yes, an impulse.' Prerova glanced down at her dressing-gown, how it parted at the knee when she sat with her legs crossed. Impulses I have known. Impulses I have followed. Impulses of the men I have known. 'You had the impulse to protect me and that's why you came tonight – even though you didn't know he'd called.'

Divorce him, kill him, lock him out. To Eva Weiserova these courses of action seemed equally valid. Her husband Milan was a soak, a toady, a creep, a skirt-chaser, a failure, a small prick in large trousers. She hadn't always seen him like that. She was just one more woman he had bullshitted. Or he'd changed. Or she had.

He was stretched out along her flank. One arm flopped over her breasts and she flung it back. Those were her breasts, those were not his breasts. Possibly they were Karel's breasts, squeezed, pinched, teased, kissed, scratched by his unshaven Sunday chin.

Eva had turned away from her husband but the smell of beer wafted over her. This had always been his get-out. A drink after work with the lads, part of the job, part of being a man. Booze would blot out the smell of another woman.

Well, I am another woman. She hugged herself with that thought. I have my lover. Karel. She cradled his name to her. Karlicek, my own baby. Granted Karel had no style and was forgetful about bathing. Getting basic about it, was washing what you looked for in a lover? She looked elsewhere. Her body held a memory of him, hard and vigorous.

Her husband snorted and turned. How long had he had his little ladies? For ever, maybe. Only recently had his caution slipped. In her imagination she saw him tomcatting down every alley. Did these flings start about the time of the car pool gossip?

Concentrating on it, brooding on it, there seemed whole areas of her husband's life she knew nothing of. What did he do at work now? After work? Where did he go? What lies did he tell his other women? Did he honestly expect her to believe he was going to church? Or was there some huge sin he was atoning for? Who was the stranger he brought home? What dishonesty was he hiding? What dirt was in his past?

When she got out of bed, the pattern of his breathing was unchanged. Coins, keys, cigarettes, a soiled handkerchief were dumped on a chest of drawers. Cast-off shirt, socks, underwear were on a chair. She tripped over his shoes as she made for the closet, paused, listened to the sawing of his breath. His trousers and jacket were on a hanger. Dipping in pockets she found a comb, a lighter, two pieces of paper.

She closed the bedroom door and switched on the hall light. The rug was askew. Was that Milan's lurching feet? Or Karel's and her lovemaking? The pattern of the rug could best be described as Debased Oriental: curlicues, lozenges, ovals, twirls. Had another pattern been imposed on the first? It would be a hollow, like a depression in the grass caused by two animals rutting.

Eva sank to the floor to bury her nose in the rug. Dust and mould. It should smell of sex, of sweat, of juices. Ah well. On the rug she spread the two pieces of paper. One was a small page with a printed number torn from a pad. It simply said ALOIS FULNEK together with a telephone number. Yes, the name had a faint echo in her memory, the man introduced to her. The other was a folded sheet of writing paper. She smoothed it open. It was in her husband's handwriting, undated, started, never finished. Boredom, forgetfulness, caution, a quarrel had cut it short. *My sugarfancy*, she read, *You give your ball-and-chain the slip and I'll get clear of mine. Loose, lighthearted, free, we'll let joy soar in our hearts.*

Furious all over again, she laid her head in the depression of the rug and cried over her husband's many betrayals.

She asked for Karel. She gave no name. It was a personal matter. When an anonymous woman telephones on a personal matter, a man is wary.

'Yes?'

'Karel?'

There was a hesitation, as if even to agree was compromising. 'What is it?'

'I have a name for you.'

'A name. Oh, a name. Just a minute.'

It was mid-morning and the curtains were open. She looked through the french windows at the block opposite. The buildings were cut to an identical pattern. The french windows opposite allowed a view of an identical living-room. Identical lives, identical fears, tears, desires. Once she saw a man staring back at her. They were neighbours in a way but had never met. He'd blown her a kiss from five metres away. In response she'd wiggled her hips. God knows why. He'd grinned and raised an eyebrow.

'I've got a pen and paper.'

'The name is Alois Fulnek. Do you want me to spell it?'

'I went to school. Is there an address?'

'There's a telephone number. You can get the address from that.'

Her eyes focused on the french windows opposite again. She had gone on staring at the stranger but when he had beckoned her with a finger she had jerked the curtains closed. She had never found out about him. That was in the old days, before she was open to suggestions.

She read Fulnek's telephone number from the bit of paper. She repeated it to make certain there was no mistake. There, had she not proved herself?

'Karlicek, see how much I love you.'

'Hey, what's this Karlicek shit?'

CHAPTER TEN

Two gentlemen meet for lunch. One is an English banker, a prince among capitalists. The other is a former high official in the Finance Ministry, a former communist party member even if the records deny it. And now? Well, an adviser to help the uninitiated travel the uncharted road to the new Czech future. Is it possible to tell them apart? Both wear suits of that deep dark blue which gleams like coal, shoes that are polished to points of light, white shirts that blind. Both wear striped ties: one the striped tie of a privileged school; the other a striped tie in purest silk which in this country denoted privilege. Gold winks at their cuffs. Omega and Rolex are on their wrists, though you might lose a bet on who wore which.

'It's not the best restaurant in Prague,' Broucek said, 'but it is the best restaurant within strolling distance of the British embassy.'

'Oh dear, Czech,' Challoner said with a baffled shake of his head. 'How is it pronounced again?'

'U Tri Pstrosu.'

Lifting his napkin, Challoner inspected the motif on his plate.

'Always a first time. I've never eaten ostrich before.'

'Here we eat duck. Are you disappointed?'

'To the contrary.' Challoner patted his stomach. 'Any sound you hear is my digestion applauding in relief.'

Is it possible to tell their smiles apart? Perfectly formed though small, fleeting and with no depth.

Unbidden, a waiter placed a cocktail glass in front of each man. Challoner reached for his, raised it to inspect. It had the colour of a Pink Gin. He thought of Sunday mornings, the golf clubhouse, Spikes Bar. Broucek in turn raised his glass, a toast.

'*Nazdravi.*'

'Cheers.'

It is Pink Gin, Challoner decided, without the gin.

'Let me apologize again that Mr Radl isn't able to see you. He is very disappointed. He collects bankers, you know, like other people collect Picassos. You would have been his Picasso in his blue period. He has no one from your bank – or rather not recently, not since the change to the market economy was begun.'

'His illness is not serious?'

'I think his illness comes from too much healthy living in the country. When he meets a germ he has less resistance than us city folk.'

'I'm impressed by your English,' Challoner said. 'You don't mind my saying so?'

'But to be able to speak English now is crucial, particularly in the financial field. When we get people from the IMF or bankers from Zurich or indeed from London, we can hardly expect them to speak Czech. I made a point of learning English. It makes all this much easier.' Broucek waved both hands like a Latin, embracing the room, the table, the pair of them. 'I hate that business of waiting for an interpreter.'

'And the Finance Minister? He's the one in the front line with the IMF, all those people, me even.'

'I would say the Minister is learning.' Even to Broucek that sounded evasive, like massaging the truth. 'He has so much to learn, so little time.' Not much better. Challoner was watching him. Test the famous British sense of humour. 'A while ago I passed him in the corridor waiting for the lift. His eyes were closed and he was reciting something. Passing close I heard him murmuring to himself in English: "The pound was found on the ground. The pound was . . ."'

'His three month forward rate forecast?'

Challoner smiled. Broucek smiled. This mutual stroking, the soixante-neuf of business, was interrupted by a waiter with a bottle. Broucek stopped him as he was about to pour and inspected the label. There was a sharp exchange of views and the waiter departed.

'Vavrinecke, I ask you,' Broucek said. 'They keep some perfectly decent burgundy under lock and key in the cellar so we'll be all right.'

The waiter returned with a dusty bottle that met with Broucek's approval. He raised his glass.

'*Nazdravi*.'

'Cheers.'

There was pâté, vol-au-vent with puréed salami and cream cheese, pickled mushrooms.

'I imagined Russian would be the second language at the top.'

'Pepa – that's Pepa Radl – has some Russian. It was necessary for the Deputy Minister to show willing.'

'But you . . . What were you exactly?'

'I was designated special assistant to the Deputy Minister.'

'Wasn't Russian necessary for you?'

'I refused to learn it.'

'Was that wise?'

'Very. The prospect of interminable trade negotiations, stuck in some Moscow hotel where the whores swarm over you until they find you're not a Westerner – I couldn't stomach that. If I had English, I reasoned, I would be sent to Washington and London.'

'*Nazdravi*,' Challoner said, raising his glass.

'Cheers.'

'Robin sends his regards to Mr Radl. Perhaps you could pass them on.'

For a moment Broucek's whole body was completely still before his face relaxed. 'Of course. I'd forgotten they'd met.'

Robin equalled Leigh-Pemberton, Governor of the Bank of England. Challoner had dropped his name casually to show his closeness with the authorities. Broucek's reaction impressed itself on Challoner. He had a snapshot of it in his mind: how Broucek froze like a wild animal in the presence of an unknown danger. Or as if Broucek was searching for a hidden significance. Or as if Challoner was introducing himself with a code.

Come, come, altogether too fanciful. Challoner brought himself back to this lunch.

'He hopes to visit Prague soon,' Challoner said, 'but he has to choose his time.'

'He will be given a warm welcome.'

'Precisely. A visit will be seen by his political masters in London as a political gesture.'

'You're saying that in a democracy one must avoid politics?' Broucek asked.

'Be wary.'

'It seems our discredited old system and our brave new system have something in common.'

'All systems have politicians in common. Which is why I value this lunch and making your acquaintance. You and I, we share . . .'

Challoner could not bring himself to finish the sentence with words. Words were too substantial. With one hand he made a rounded gesture, drawing the two of them together in common ground or in a common situation or even in the face of a common opponent.

There was a pause while two waiters appeared bearing trays covered with silver domes, and the head waiter fussed over the serving of the duck.

There was an etiquette to such fleshy occasions that the main course of business should not be broached until the main course of the meal was served. First impressions, clothes, handshake, eye contact, were the aperitif. Then with the first course, the first taste of the other man, his style, the 'how' of him: how he drank, how he ignored, thanked or clicked his fingers at the waiters, how he made small talk, how he saw the world, how he saw himself.

Challoner had had experience of men of Broucek's type. At least that was what he thought. He would come down hard on people he felt to be below him. With equals he would be chary, would banter to deflect any direct contest of will. Later, out of sight, the stab in the back. He would acknowledge no superiors: but when he met one he would obey. Hitler would have made him a *gauleiter*. Challoner was confident he had met many Brouceks before in the boardrooms of troubled British companies.

The duck was perfect, its fat melted away, its skin crisp. Sauerkraut cut through the richness. But three kinds of dumpling? The Czechs needed the security of a tight belly.

This was the main course, the time for serious business. But Broucek held back. His business was very different from Challoner's. He would let the other man talk first. And . . . there was something about Challoner that made Broucek hesitate, reach for his glass and take a long pull. Could he define the something? Was it to do with the century and a half tradition of his London bank? His class? There was effortless superiority about Challoner. He had never had to fight with fist and metal, never extracted information, never killed to achieve success. That didn't make him weaker. He could be ruthless in a more devious way.

Challoner had a pitch to make because he needed a friend at court, or at least someone who knew the ways of the court. He ate, then talked, and then ate some more. He explained his merchant bank had a narrow focus in its investment search through the former communist countries. Germany was right in the forefront of the race for machine tool and car factories and construction companies and mines. Broucek ate and nodded. Challoner said America and France and even Italy were panting up in the rear. Not forgetting the Japanese, Broucek said. Never forgetting the Japanese, Challoner agreed. This reflected their own countries' strengths. Challoner's bank's special interest lay in the service industries. Not, of course, in the sense of the waiter who had just been despatched for another bottle of Chambolle Musigny. Banking, insurance, accountancy, investment advice, international law and patents, intellectual properties, social trends, the medical sector, consumer credit . . .

He broke off as the waiter poured from the fresh bottle. It was a lot of alcohol for lunch. Challoner saw it as a rite of passage with the man who had been Special Assistant to the Deputy Finance Minister and still could open doors.

'These are the areas in which we have expertise. We can compete here and win. We have money to spend. Czechoslovakia needs both money and expertise.'

'Just so,' Broucek said.

'And to help us we need to find someone locally with experience of government, of local conditions and laws and customs, with contacts at a high level.'

There. Enough, Challoner judged. Let Broucek make his own connections.

'Cheers.'

'*Nazdravi*.'

A waiter whispered in Broucek's ear and he excused himself.

'We have no mobile telephones here yet.'

Challoner said, 'You can eat in peace.'

Standing, Broucek took a moment to regard the room, the vaulted ceiling, the solid oak furniture, the stone walls, the candles. He could be a sergeant-major viewing new recruits, gawky peasant boys who had to be bawled into shape. He shook his head. The lunch guests had briefcases but no mobile phones.

At the desk in the hall Broucek picked up the telephone and walked as far as the flex would let him. He was frowning. The telephone was not mobile enough for privacy.

'Hello.'

'Are you receiving me well?'

He recognized the smugness in Karel's voice. He was a dull man who believed he was shining brightly. Broucek turned his back on the receptionist.

'Well, thank you.'

'I can give you his name, his telephone number and his address.'

Karel paused, waiting for a pat on the back.

'Just a minute.'

Broucek got paper from the receptionist. The telephone tucked under his chin, he used the wall as a desk to write down the details.

'You want me to take care of it?' Karel asked.

'No,' Broucek said. He'd talked to Prerova about people who would do a job, but he felt personal involvement, as if there was a score to settle. 'No, this one is mine.'

He walked along the corridor and down the steps to the men's room. He unzipped and let fly at the porcelain. Fulnek, I piss on your face. It trickles down your cheeks like tears. Your priest's eyes overflow too late. You should never have asked questions, begun prying, getting in my way. With the priest dead and Prerova cowed into silence, it could be he would have done enough. No need to put pressure on Challoner. At the basin Broucek splashed water up into his face to take the heat out. In the mirror his eyes looked angry and in the palm of his hand he cupped water to bathe them. In the mirror he inspected himself once more.

So?

There was really no choice.

Well then, how to?

He had never killed a priest. There had never been any need to. Priests had never been a threat. It had not been like Poland. Priests had kept their protests to a whisper. Or joined Pacem in Terris and kept quiet altogether. Would a priest expect special treatment? Did he have to pray for his soul? Or for that of his killer? The hell with the priest. He wasn't going to be on his knees side by side with him.

He splashed more water in his face.

At his house he kept a Luger, an old one taken from the corpse of a Wehrmacht officer. Beautiful weapon, smooth action, perfect condition. As Challoner noted, engineering was a German strength. At the office, locked away in the bottom drawer of his desk, was a Colt .38. The Colt was snub-nosed, slipped with ease into a jacket pocket.

But no. He dried his hands under the hot air blower. Guns left evidence. Perhaps, after all, a priest was deserving of special consideration. He looked at his hands, joining them together, marvelling how the fingers and thumbs formed a circle exactly the size of a man's neck.

Challoner had divided what was left of the burgundy and Broucek drained his glass. He summoned the waiter and issued orders.

'I've been giving some thought to what you said,' Broucek said to Challoner as if he had to explain his absence. 'I would very much like to help.'

Challoner let a smile cross his face.

'Let me tell you about our revolution,' Broucek said. 'You know how it is?'

'Tell me.'

'Take me, for instance. I used to be employed by the state. Always had been. Nearly everybody was until eighteen months ago. About the only exceptions were prostitutes, thieves and black market dealers.'

Broucek was not concerned with absolute truth. He was an impressionist. Challoner was relaxed, another smile chasing across his face.

'The free enterprise system in embryo.'

'Then came all the revolutions rippling through the old Soviet bloc. Poland, Germany, our turn next. All those images. Crowds, candles, flowers. A few heads broken by the police. And who gave the order for that? The hardliners wanting to show who was boss? Maybe the reformers wanting martyrs to provoke more street action? As if a hidden hand is pulling the strings, the old guard steals away and we get a political prisoner as President. He has a sense of humour, which makes a change up there, so he must have had a good chuckle at the irony of it. The Velvet Revolution is declared – not the old model with bullets and tanks, the new softer, kinder model.'

Broucek broke off to let the waiter serve coffee and brandy. Broucek stirred sugar round and round in his cup.

'Socialism is abandoned as the state religion,' Broucek said. 'Red stars come tumbling down from the sky. The new President has the uniforms of his Guard redesigned to be more *opera buffa*. You see bananas in the shops, but who can afford to buy them? Prices rise. Then they rise again because the first rise wasn't enough. The Germans invade for the second time this century and marvel at how cheap the prices are. The filing cabinets of the last forty years are opened and the files are discovered to have walked away. Half the population was compromised but nobody can be certain which half. Was it my neighbour? Was it my lover? Could it even have been me? Memories are notoriously short. Where are the guilty men? Where are the informers, the spies, the jailers, the executioners, the phone-tappers, the state thugs, the bootlickers, the rich cream at the top of the classless society? Where are the people who gave the orders and signed the warrants? As midnight struck,' Broucek's voice dropped like a conspirator's and he leaned forward, 'all these players tiptoed off the stage. Now there is a whole new cast who have learned new lines and their make-up is so perfect you can peer and peer and never see the old faces underneath. That, in a nutshell, is the history of the Velvet Revolution.'

Did this seem to have strayed from the point? Broucek took half his coffee in a succession of sips. Challoner had gone still, waiting.

'As for me.' Broucek paused to draw together the threads of what he wanted to say. 'Nearly a quarter of a century spent in the Finance Ministry, through bad times, worse times and new times, holding a unique position of influence. Now, in the new democratic Czechoslovakia, working on my own account. But the network of contacts I used to have is still valid. Some have changed their titles but the country hasn't come to a standstill. Czechoslovakia needed those people. They run banks and insurance companies and accountancy offices – all those service industries that attract you.'

Broucek lifted the brandy glass to his nose, inhaled the fumes. Challoner imagined he had finished.

'What you're saying is you know where the bodies are buried.'

Broucek's brows were pinched together. 'You could say that. In a manner of speaking, yes. Or skeletons in closets. Twenty-five years of skeletons makes quite a crowd because everyone has a skeleton somewhere. You only have to know where to look.'

Broucek's eyes, full of darkness, focused on Challoner. For some reason Challoner felt not quite comfortable.

Broucek went on, 'When the big change came I decided it was my opportunity to set up on my own. A new word came into the Czech language: wheeler-dealer. I couldn't see myself trying to guide inexperienced politicians to some sort of understanding of the big world. Others – good colleagues of mine – stayed. They have initiated reforms, brought together overseas investors and local enterprises, identified the first sectors of commerce and industry to be pushed into the private sector. I'll introduce you to some of these people.'

Challoner raised his glass and touched Broucek's in a toast. 'Cheers' and '*Nazdravi*' were slurred together.

'There has been some talk at head office,' Challoner said, 'of opening a branch here. Early days yet. I'll have to form a judgement on the potential.'

There was no offer of a job but it was in the air between them. Another time, another restaurant. U Maliru even had a van that made a weekly trip to France for supplies.

Broucek drew a breath and opened his mouth and then closed it. There was the other affair, the business that Pepa was demanding progress on. He still felt it was not yet time to broach it. Challoner had to be drawn closer. And it might not be necessary. Leave it for today.

'You were going to say something?'

Broucek said, 'Your meeting with the Minister is . . .?'

'Tomorrow morning.'

'I'll fix it so you meet two or three other people. Useful contacts.'

Outside, in the gloom of an overcast afternoon, they exchanged a handshake. Broucek watched Challoner walk away. His dark overcoat with its astrakhan collar was smooth, a second skin. His back was straight, his head held high, his walk firm. Was his background military? He knew how to drink. Another thing bankers and the army had in common: they got pissed and then they pissed all over the rest of the world.

Thinking of which made Broucek feel the need again. He went back inside the restaurant to relieve himself and then, on his way out, felt that possibly one final brandy was called for. It had been a good lunch, a useful lunch, a solid foundation had been laid.

Broucek felt the afternoon was forfeit.

He stood in the tiny forecourt of U Tri Pstrosu, his face turned up to drifting snowflakes.

Maybe it had been forfeit since the first sip of that pink concoction that demanded a chunky burgundy to take away the taste.

Was the snow serious?

Then a second bottle to keep the first company.

Or was it just a tease? Could you have a snow-tease like a prick-tease? Nothing come of it?

And the brandy to lubricate his transfer to be the bank's far-flung sentinel. Nothing had been actually offered but Challoner had it in mind. No doubt. A deal hung in the air between them and it only needed a hand to reach out and grab hold of it.

Broucek stretched up and swatted at a snowflake and when he opened his hand there was nothing in the palm. Snow was like a woman, he thought, cold at first, melts . . . The rest of the thought slipped away.

Possibly the final brandy had been a mistake but one brandy did not feel like celebrating. One brandy deserved another.

Broucek had only to cross Mostecka, and ten minutes' stroll would take him past the annexe. Then over the river to his new office. He could telephone a report to Radl. Yes, Pepa, I had lunch with the British banker, yes I made progress. Pepa, he is on the brink of offering me a job. He thinks I shall be useful to him, but nothing like as useful as he will be to us. We shall be able to guide his bank into making all kinds of investments, joint ventures, good legitimate deals. Why, we shall all end up with invitations to shake the President's hand and ask if he has any time for writing plays any more. As to the other business, Pepa, about Bodnar and the one-time actress and the priest – no, it wasn't the moment to raise that. And it may not be necessary. There are other ways . . .

Thinking about Prerova, thinking about her daughter, he found instinct or impulse persuaded him to take a different route. He turned left on to Charles Bridge. It was mid-afternoon, the clouds low, a snow flurry cutting visibility. He could barely see across the Vltava to the tower at the end of the bridge. By the statue of St Francis he stopped to stare upstream. He could see the annexe with his own former office. On the other side, upstream, his new office was obscured by a building. Further still, beyond the National Theatre, beyond Slovansky Island, was Rasinovo Embankment. At number 78, on the top floor, was the apartment that Havel kept. The snow flurry got in the way. What he could see were the rivergulls, the same ones he watched from his window. He took in their flight patterns, the long glides, the reined-in turns, the swoops. Nothing flew with the elegance of gulls. They had the manners of street gypsies but the delicacy of ballerinas. Trapped by some boring farts in his old office he had been saved from screaming by a fine fantasy: he would swing open the double casements, spread his arms and join the gulls, swooping and gliding. He'd catch the air currents and escape. The screams of the people left behind would be echoed by the calls of the gulls.

People complained the bridge was no better than a souk. But Broucek liked to see budding capitalists sharpening their claws. He had in mind the man who set up a telescope at the far end of the bridge. See Hradcany Castle, St Vitus Cathedral, the Presidential palace. How much do you charge? For you, dear citizen, it is free. Once a crowd had gathered the story changed: This is a magic telescope. It can penetrate walls and show you President Havel hard at work on our future. Only ten korunas and you can actually see the future that's being created. When you put coins in the slot, the view through the telescope turned to black.

Turning to gaze at the castle on the hill, Broucek came face to face with Olga. A wooden case and a collapsible stool leaned against her leg. One hand cupped the other elbow. Her face was scrubbed clean of any expression. She took the cigarette from her lips to blow a stream of smoke.

'It was written in the stars,' she said. 'Sooner or later you would come.'

CHAPTER ELEVEN

S he wore the same cowboy boots, jeans and Afghan coat which was unbuttoned, never mind the snow. Under the coat was a cardigan of indigo blue. Under that he caught a glimpse of a T-shirt from the Hard Rock Café in Los Angeles. And under that?

'I wait around all day,' Olga said, 'with my tray and I hear the tourists come and read from their guidebooks. I'm the expert now. This statue here is St Francis. You know about him? Everybody knows about St Francis. See how the birds love him still, perch on his head. His hair is quite white.'

'You've packed up for the afternoon?' Broucek asked.

She drew on her cigarette again. 'It was nearly eight centuries ago. Francis took all his clothes off in the square in Assisi. He gave them to beggars but the locals thought he'd gone mad. Naked man in the market square. They hurled stones at him.'

'I mean you've finished,' Broucek said.

'Well, it's all I remember about him. He must have been cold if it was winter. I read somewhere you lose fifty per cent of your body heat through your head. Does that mean that if I jammed a Russian fur hat down on my head and took the rest of my clothes off and stood in the snow, I'd be just as warm?'

'They wouldn't throw stones at you,' Broucek said.

Olga drew fiercely on her cigarette. She handed him the collapsible stool and started to walk with the wooden case under one arm, gripped tight. With her free hand she gestured.

'Over there St Jude Thaddeus, and here Procopius and Vincent Ferrarius, saints both. Everybody is a saint on the bridge. I mean the statues. The people, the actual living people . . .' She looked at Broucek. 'Would you say you were a saint?'

'It's early to stop work,' Broucek said.

'Really? How about you? Oh, back a little way was where people who were not saints were ducked.'

'They didn't drown them,' Broucek said.

'They kept them under long enough to make them repent. If they didn't look sorry for what they'd done – or at any rate sorry for themselves – they went into the river again. What do you think of that?'

Broucek was thinking the human race had not changed much. In the Research Facility, five centuries later, they'd used the toilet bowl to duck the prisoners' heads in. Sometimes the bowl had not been flushed. It was like flotsam drifting down the Vltava. Prisoners had repented.

'Well, it seems you don't think,' Olga said. She flicked ash over the wall. 'I forget who these next saints are. Do you know? No, you aren't speaking. You wandered on to the bridge where I was but now you've lost your tongue. Over here are some Christians who have been arrested and are being guarded by a Turk. The Christians don't look happy. Well, the Turks did have a reputation. Like certain people of recent times in our own country.' When she drew hard on the cigarette, the diamond stud in her nostril reflected the glowing tip. 'There, that is Petr.'

'St Peter?'

'No, the man with the Red Army medals and caps. Amazing the stuff the soldiers have been selling. Petr's got two boxes of Soviet grenades. Certain criminal types from Germany are making him interesting offers and Petr is leaning towards selling to them. You know why? He told me: "Provided they use the grenades in Hamburg or Berlin, it will be Germans who get killed. That is a Czech's revenge for nineteen thirty-eight." Isn't that beautiful? Do you think Petr is a great patriotic hero? One of those stupid romantics who start wars? Or just one of those dirty shits who never washes between his toes? What do you think?'

Broucek saw a man with undernourished cheeks and quick street dealer's eyes. He wore a military greatcoat and a fur hat on which flakes of snow had settled. Where did he keep the boxes of grenades? He had a suitcase with him.

'But of course,' Olga went on, 'you're not someone who thinks. Petr wants me to sleep with him. He says we should go away for the weekend somewhere. But,' she flicked the cigarette away and gave Petr a hard stare, 'I don't know. I'd ask your opinion except you don't think.'

Petr was returning the stare. He looked from Olga to Broucek.

'Don't go with him to Berlin,' Broucek said. 'Not if he's carrying that suitcase.'

'Good,' she said, one purple-shadowed eyebrow raised. 'Very good.'

Broucek found he was close to U Tri Pstrosu again. 'We'll go and have a drink here.'

'No.'

'No? What do you mean?'

'No.'

Such a simple, direct, emphatic and unapologetic refusal baffled Broucek. No explanation softened it.

'Why not?'

'I'm on my way.'

'Where to?'

'The tramstop.'

'And then?'

'You're drunk, aren't you? Getting on a tram obviously. What a silly question.'

'To your mother's?'

'No. Give me the stool now. Carrying it seems to have exhausted you. You've gone red in the face.'

Broucek gripped it tighter. She could see his knuckles whiten. Over Broucek's shoulder Petr was watching.

'Where is the tramstop?'

'In the square.'

He set off and she followed after her stool. Half of Mostecka seemed to be up because of roadworks. She had to walk behind him, studying his back. Certainly the back was broad enough. You would have said he could heft a crate of beer or a kicking struggling woman. But he was not used to fetching and carrying. The stool was awkward in his hand.

In the square they joined a cluster of people waiting at the tramstop. The afternoon was closing down early but the street lamps weren't on yet. Through the café windows the people at the tables looked set for the day. Broucek and Olga stood a little apart. Olga knew exactly what was going to happen but made no effort to prevent it. What would the man do if she screamed? It was almost worth it to see his face. But the police would ask dumb questions. Why did you call for help? That man won't give me my stool. Did he grab it from you? No, I pushed it in his hands. And now he's following me home. But several eye-witnesses will swear it was you following him up Mostecka . . .

'What tram do you catch?'

She paused. 'Number twelve.'

'Where to?'

The silence was longer. 'Near Soviet Tank Square.'

On the tram Broucek said, 'I have no ticket.'

She gave him one to punch in the machine. 'I expect you've never travelled on a tram.'

'Yes,' he said. 'Yes, I have.'

They stood squeezed together by home-going workers. Olga could smell the drink on his breath, and something else. He had a male animal aura. She could smell power.

There was no place in Broucek's thoughts for Fulnek or Challoner or Pepa. He had known Olga's mother once. There was an excitement in having the daughter so close.

He stared at the purple patches in her hair, at her ears which had little brightly coloured cockatoos today, at the curve of her cheeks, at the stud in one nostril. When she kissed, did it scratch her partner's nose? What other bodily adornments were hidden? Rings through her nipples? Tattoos? For a moment his mind jumped to a fraternal visit to Bucharest: a woman with a snake tattooed round her waist, her pubic hair shaved and the snake with flickering tongue disappearing out of sight. A disturbed people, Romanians.

At the stop just before the tank Olga got off, Broucek behind her. He fumbled with the folded stool, clutched it to him. Olga turned away but his eyes went to the tank. How could you pretend something like that wasn't there?

A nation was made from martyrs, heros and lies. The Soviet tank was one of the lies They tried to build a new Czech nation from. Comrades, this is the tank, the actual tank, that was the first to liberate Prague from the Nazis. It sounded like a huckster's cry but They didn't hear it that way. There wasn't, of course, a real bloody battle for the city like there had been the Battle of Berlin. Not many bullet-pocked buildings, not many Resistance martyrs, not many Red Army heroes. But the tank would do. It had a plaque. It is the actual tank, comrades. On my mother's grave it is.

At this time it was still its drab military colour. Olga detested it. She had an idea it would be better painted pink, more striking, making its point. An artist friend had asked her: But what is its point? She had replied: It has no point any more, that is the point. Pink, eh? At this moment her artist friend was still brooding on this but later in the spring, much to Olga's joy, he finally did it: painted the tank a glorious pointless surrealist pink.

The buildings were five storeys, city grey, reminders of the Annexe. He followed her across the road to an alley. At the end it swelled into a cobbled area jammed with dustbins and a couple of cars. An ornate lamp jutted out from a wall. On one side iron gates guarded a grand apartment block. Broucek stared through the bars.

'No, over here,' Olga said. 'This is the end of the line.'

She was standing at the entrance to a crumbling tenement. It had ten doorbells on a panel and a view to a diminutive courtyard hardly more than an airshaft. In Montmartre, in nineteenth-century Paris, an artist would have starved in a place like this. He would have lived on day-old baguettes and eleven-degree rouge. A sulky model would have flopped nude on top of the bed until the cold made her cough too distracting. Under the blankets, the artist would warm her up. It looked picturesque in the Hollywood version but Broucek, smelling the communal lavatories and hearing the shouts of a warring couple, hesitated.

'Which is your place?'

'The very top.' She pointed. 'Understudy to God. Give me the stool.'

The window at the gable end was dark, uncurtained, unshuttered. Broucek stared up, the stool clutched tight, and seemed to be assessing the number of stairs.

'I don't know your name,' Olga said. 'You kept it a big secret.'

He looked back to her, opened his mouth and drew a breath before speaking. 'Antonin. You can call me Tonda.'

'May I? Oh thank you.' She shook her head to herself. 'And thank you for carrying the stool, Tonda. I'll take it now.'

'I'll bring it upstairs for you.'

'Don't bother. I'm not letting you in.'

'Why not?'

'My lover is up there. Life is complicated enough. You were seeing my mother.'

'Did she talk about me?'

'Well, now.' Olga had to stop to think about this. There had certainly been an exchange of views but when she analyzed it it was mostly angry words. 'She refused. If she doesn't talk, I have to use my imagination. Now . . .' She reached for the stool.

'I don't think anyone's up there. There's no light on.'

'My lover's up there waiting for me to come back. I just told you. He's probably reading.'

Broucek took another look. 'Don't be absurd. Your room's pitch black.'

'You think you need to have light to read a book, Tonda? Hmm?' She paused for effect. 'A braille book?'

Broucek took a moment to think about it. He wanted a cigarette but to get at the packet he'd have to put down the stool and Olga would snatch it.

He said, 'What a waste.'

'A waste?'

'Being blind. He'll never be able to see you. Have you ever tried what you were talking about – put a fur hat on and stood naked? Perhaps in the woods? Wouldn't that be something?'

She stared at him. In the cobbled area the dusk had deepened but he caught a glint in her eyes. The errant eyebrow was hoisted again.

'Tonda, you believe you are paying me some kind of compliment and I'll swoon at your fine words and beg you to come up. Tonda, you have a male perspective on love. You are blinkered but how could you not be? You are sorry for a blind man who cannot enjoy looking at my body, never mind what the woman's concern is. Let me straighten your thinking with the real version. Are you listening, Tonda? You're not picturing me in the woods? Right. A blind man makes the best lover because of learning braille.' Olga's hand touched her cheek, slid down her throat, stroked across a breast until a finger traced a circle round a nipple. 'Do you understand? His fingers read my body just as if it was a book. He takes his time. No cheating and skipping to the end. Each chapter, each page, each line. His fingers go everywhere so he can build up an image of me in his mind. He creates an erotic masterpiece.'

Broucek swallowed. He wanted her to continue. She played tricks with her voice, whispered, hesitated, swooped like the rivergulls. She was taunting him, teasing him and he was enthralled. Now her voice didn't claim his attention he was aware of other sounds: the mutter of traffic passing at the end of the alley, scratching sounds like rats beyond one of the cars, even snowflakes seemed to touch the cobbles with a sigh.

The lamp high on the wall above their heads flickered and came on. Broucek twitched at the unexpected brightness. Olga glanced up and smiled.

'Do you want to hear how I met him?' Olga knew the answer and went straight on. 'That lamp that's fixed to the wall is awfully bright and shines through the bedroom window, so late at night I cover it with a curtain.'

She stopped. Broucek was puzzled. 'What's so unusual? At night everybody draws the curtains.'

'No! In summer I like to sleep with the window wide open, no curtains, to let the air come in. What I do is lower the curtain to cover the streetlamp. In summer when it is warm I sleep naked. It's important you should know that. Now you can picture the scene: a warm summer night, I am at the window leaning out naked, lowering the curtain over the streetlamp when I hear a wolf howl. Looking down I see Jan – who was not my lover yet because I had never met him before – and he sobs out: "Lovely lady, I am howling because you are covering the moon. Take pity on me and let me come up." So he did and I comforted him and that's how we became lovers.'

Broucek stared at the lamp, then at the window and finally at Olga.

'He howled –'

'Pitifully.'

'– because he could not see the moon?'

'Yes, exactly.'

'But he could see you.'

'Yes, yes.'

'But how could he see either you or the moon if he is blind?'

'Oh, you are Tonda the Dull.' In one brisk move-ment she banged the wooden case sharply on the toes of his shoes. Crying out in pain, he dropped the stool. She gathered that up and retreated to the entrance. She paused long enough to say, 'You expect consistency in me? How boring. I tell stories and that is much more interesting. You must choose the one you are most comfortable with and let that be the truth.'

'Olga . . .'

But she had vanished.

Broucek leaned against the wall holding a foot. His toes were on fire. He raised his head to look at the lamp-moon. Perhaps if he were to howl . . . From behind one of the cars came the sound of soft clapping.

'I think she was not receiving you well. But what a performance.'

CHAPTER TWELVE

B ehind the cars the two men looked at each other.
'I'm from Pepa.'

Broucek nodded.

'Name is Rudy.'

The lamp bracketed high on the wall cast a down-light on Rudy's face, making pits of his eyes. Broucek thought he had seen Rudy before but it took him a few seconds to place him. Afternoon had dissolved into early evening and he was no longer certain of anything. But Rudy, he suspected, in another life functioned as a gardener at Pepa's estate. Or at least patrolled the garden.

'I feel a pressing need,' Broucek said, unbuttoning his coat and unzipping his fly. 'Got to take a leak.'

Broucek aimed at the wheel of the car, as a dog does. He felt relief as the pressure eased. Rudy was waiting, not talking. He should take a leak too. Sharing not waiting. Stand up, be a man and piss. Olga could tell stories but she couldn't do this. Simple male accomplishment.

The pleasure Broucek felt in his emptying bladder faded. Rudy hadn't been waiting here in the cobbled area all the time, Rudy had to have been following him. Rudy must have been on the tram, and before that on the bridge, before that at the restaurant. How had he known about the restaurant? Maybe he'd been following all day, right from his office. Being followed, being checked on, there was not much between them.

'Bloody winter,' Broucek said. 'In summer the booze evaporates. In cold weather I'm like a tap you can't turn off.'

'Pepa wants to see you.'

'I don't have time.'

'He said I was to tell you he wants to see you.'

'How is he?'

'He is concerned you haven't telephoned.'

'Was I supposed to?'

'He is concerned about why you haven't spoken to him after your lunch with the banker and certain other things.'

Broucek jerked round towards Rudy, spattering his trousers. 'Rudy, there are big things happening in this country that you know nothing about. Why should you, stuck out in the country? There are opportunities opening up that would make your mouth water. Big money is going to be made. Do you want to spend the next years bodyguarding an old man? Pepa is not the future. I don't think he even understands the future. Having lunch with the banker – that is the future.'

'That is why he wanted you to telephone. That and other matters – that girl's mother, the priest, certain discoveries about the past, your involvement, links with Pepa and others.' He paused to check he'd remembered it all. 'That's why he is concerned.'

Broucek took time to zip up his fly and button his

coat. Pepa did not understand. He wanted Broucek to go back to the past with the banker, not plan for the future. But there was no point arguing with Rudy. Rudy was not the future. Rudy's future basically was as a man with a gun. One day he'd meet another man with a quicker gun and then he'd have no future.

'All right, I know. Tell Pepa everything is being taken care of.'

In the old days police of one kind or another would have tracked Fulnek down and picked him up for 'behaviour liable to disturb public order'. This was a marvellous catch-all. Anything could disturb public order from throwing a bomb to farting on May Day. The authorities called it 'the rubber paragraph' and loved it because it bounced trouble-makers into cells. Now Fulnek was something he must take care of personally.

'That matter he worries about,' Broucek went on, 'tell him the problem will no longer exist. Very, very soon. Rudy, do you understand what I am saying?'

Rudy and Broucek stared at each other. Maybe Rudy understood, maybe he didn't. Principally he looked as if he didn't give a shit what Broucek said. But there was a drop of charity in Rudy.

He said, 'I heard Pepa talking after your last lunch with him. He is concerned you are drinking too much.'

'Concerned.' Broucek mimicked Rudy's speak-your-weight machine accent. He kept using the word as if he'd just learned it.

Broucek was staring into the glass. This was no Chambolle Musigny. Nor Vavrinecke. Lunch with

Challoner was history now. This wine was not even
Gracie. Lunch with Pepa was ancient history. This was
Moravian fall-down-under-the-table wine. And if you
were under the table here your cheek would be pil-
lowed by squashed cigarette butts, discarded metro
tickets and mud. This was a café for people in distress.

Pepa saying that he – Antonin Broucek – drank too
much was rich. The faults we accuse others of are the
ones we cannot see in ourselves. Pepa had been the one
who poured the whisky, called for another bottle of
Gracie and dug out that Hungarian firewater. Yes. Yes,
indeed.

Broucek swallowed more of his wine.

'Life is a struggle, friend,' a voice at his side said.
'You look like I feel. Shall I tell you what my trouble
is? You want to know? It's not my wife – God bless
her – but the woman who wants to be my wife. Or
thinks she wants to be my wife. Why does she think
that? Don't go away – listen to this. Because I showed
her how to do it doggy fashion. She calls me her little
puppy dog. Don't laugh, friend, it's no joke. "Puppy,"
she says, "do you want a biscuit? How about a bone?
Oh, naughty Puppy, you've got a bone down there
again." Well, now she says she's going to tell her husband. Here is the part that will make you want to suck
in your cheeks and say ouch. Her husband is a train
driver and he is due in from Budapest,' there was a
pause, 'in two hours and twelve minutes. He is a big
man. If the train ever broke down, I think he could
push it himself. The woman who wants to be my wife
says she is going to tell him when he gets home
tonight. She says she doesn't want to stay with him

any more because he is violent. She's going to pack a
bag and come round to my place. She doesn't know
about my wife, see. I can see this big man coming with
her, carrying her suitcase. Then I can see him taking
off his coat and rolling up his sleeves. Then I can't see
any more. So there is my problem and I think the only
way to solve it is for us to have another glass. A glass
shared is a problem shared – that is my philosophy.
What do you say?'

Broucek looked at the man. He was dumpy with a
straggly moustache. A worn blue cap sat on big ears.
This was the great philosopher and lover. This puppy
was going to be wetting himself soon. Broucek drained
his glass and made a face.

'What I say is that in Moravia the cats piss red.'

Outside in the dark the snow had stopped. It had been
a snow-tease, vanished except where it drifted against
walls. Broucek followed Kafkova round a dog-leg curve
looking at the numbers on the doors. What he saw
first was the sign in the window: ZIMMER FREI. He hammered on the door with his knuckles before he noticed
the bell, so he rang that too for good measure. Hurry
them up in there.

'Ja?'

Turning from looking down the street Broucek was
confronted by a woman with grey hair in a bun. Pulling
the hair back made her features severe. No smell of
cooking came with her though she wore an apron. She
was the kind of woman who always wore an apron,
Broucek understood. Had she ever been pretty? Had her
eyes ever flirted? Had she one summer night covered the

moon and made a man howl? Had she ever done it doggy fashion?

'*Ja?*' she repeated.

'This is still Prague, isn't it? We speak Czech here. You have a notice in the window *Zimmer Frei*—'

'I have no rooms.'

When she closed the door she found Broucek's knee in the gap. He rode her back into the hall the way he once had Prerova.

'I think you have a room for me. Who am I doing business with?'

She hesitated.

'Your name.'

'Hasslerova.'

'Hassler,' Broucek paused, 'ova.' He made two words of it. He stressed the German origin of the name. He thought of the German exiles – von Waldersomethings – who had bothered Pepa, but not more than once. In the silence and the way he stared he seemed to suggest a whole existence that the woman had left: a widow without doubt, stretching her pension by letting rooms, Germans preferred so they could bring first-hand news of the Fatherland, her husband very likely deceased during the war, a volunteer who committed a pointless act of bravery lobbing a grenade at a Soviet tank that now liberated a square away in the south of the city. Broucek was nodding, as if he understood all this. 'Hassler, yes,' he said.

She wiped her hands on the apron. 'I have one room but it is not large.'

'Do I look large? Powerful, yes. But a giant, I think not.'

There the name was, written in the book she made him sign. FULNEK Alois. For an address he had written: Travelling. Well, that was true enough. We were all travelling through life trying to avoid the potholes and the big train drivers.

'But you live in Prague.'

She was looking down at the address he had written.

Broucek nodded. 'I had bad news this evening. My wife is leaving me. That is why I don't want to stay at home tonight.'

'The price is two hundred and fifty korunas a night. No visitors are allowed in the rooms.'

Broucek had a story of an international express train driver stealing his wife's affections but Hasslerova was uninterested. She led him to a small room, cold and narrow, and left him. Broucek smoked a cigarette while he stood at the window and stared at dustbins in the courtyard. He should have brought a bottle with him, even Moravian cat's piss.

He stretched out on the single bed and closed his eyes, just for a moment, to collect his thoughts.

Broucek had told Challoner that Yes, he knew where the bodies were buried, where the skeletons were in the closets. But this was not quite true. Nobody could know all the graves. Nobody could be certain if that was a skeleton in the closet or somebody hiding. The old system had been a secret society, a freemasonry whose members knew each other by signs and words and handshakes. The old system was kept going by fear. But it wasn't ordinary men and women who were afraid: it was the oppressors. The government and the

Party and the police and the special investigators and agents and all the placemen and the widening circle of tell-tales and curtain-watchers were glued together by fear of their own citizens. When the system fell, it shattered. What good were the pieces?

I am a piece, Broucek thought. Novacek is a piece. There are hundreds of pieces in television and radio and parliament, thousands in the ministries, millions in offices and factories and shops. Some pieces are fragments, dust, like Mirek and Karel and Rudy. Other pieces bulk large: Pepa, certain ministers, police chiefs who have put on new faces. They are big pieces. Some big pieces were stamped on, crushed under a heel into smaller pieces. Not too many. Sacrificial big pieces. Other big pieces kept their value, were worth picking up and preserving.

What a piece of work is man. How noble . . .

At something past one in the morning Broucek woke shivering. The sweat on his body had chilled him. The dream was fading but it was the same as the one the night before. He is chasing a butterfly that flits up out of reach, then swoops low and dances in the air. He runs after it through the conservatory of a grand eighteenth-century château. A window is open and like a hurdler he leaps the sill after the butterfly. Now he is in the graveyard of the private chapel where statues have tumbled, arms amputated, noses chipped off. There is a yawning, waiting grave. The headstone reads A BROUCEK 1939–199 . The inscription is unfinished but a chisel lies on the ground as if the mason was interrupted and will return at any instant to finish the job. A footfall alerts Broucek but as he turns he wakes up.

Standing by the basin in the corner relieving himself, he looked out of the window. The dustbins were prisoners crowding together in the exercise yard: this one is for release, that one is due for special questioning, the last one will not see another sunrise. The lid on this third bin was tipped forward. It was a head bowed in prayer. Broucek laced his fingers together, twisted his hands palm out and forced his arms straight until his knuckles cracked. Fulnek, the priest, must have prayed enough already in his life. One more time would make no difference.

In the passage it was black. No crack of light outlined any of the doors. Bathroom and kitchen on the opposite side, Fulnek's room next to his, sitting-room at the end, Hasslerova's room beside it. It was a big apartment for one old woman.

If Fulnek had not yet returned – gone one in the morning there was no good reason for a priest to be out – still, if Fulnek had not returned, Broucek determined he would wait for him, surprise him as he closed the door to his room.

Broucek took small steps, feeling his way along the wall in the darkness. He froze at the sound of something scrabbling near his feet. Mice? There was the sound of little claws scratching at polished wood, a patter of feet retreating down the passage, a slither through the doorway, silence on the sitting-room carpet. The bubbly yowl of an angry feline came softly.

His fingers found the handle and closed round it. Strange that the handle should be slippery. He wiped his palm on his trousers and tried again. The handle turned, the door eased open. He listened and heard breathing, his own.

It was the approach that was something of a puzzle. In former times a prisoner would be delivered like a sack of coal: throw it on the ground, dump it through a hole in the cellar. Suppose Fulnek sat up in bed. Lull him with apologies about going to the bathroom, mistaking the door coming back. Draw closer. Reach out.

He stepped in. The curtains were open, the window was an oblong of the night sky of Prague. The bed appeared empty. Broucek closed the door and went to the bed. Fulnek was not under the covers, nor under the bed, nor crouching by the dresser. Broucek switched on the bedside light. Had he made some mistake? It had to be the right room. He doubted the priest was visiting Hasslerova in her room. On a chair were a pink nylon shopping bag, a crumpled shirt and discarded socks. On the shelf above the basin were a man's toiletries. On the dresser was a scrap of paper on which was written:

> PRAGUE 10.00
> KOLIN 11.11
> ×
> KOLIN 11.40
> KUTNA HORA 11.52

Kutna Hora was the station closest to Benevice. It was the right room. Broucek walked to the window and closed the curtains.

'Damn you, Fulnek, where are you?'

Fulnek had made minimal impact on this room. It was his cell. How many nights in that narrow bed? How many mornings frowning at the face in the mirror as he shaved? What did he do in this room? No books, no radio, no TV, no newspapers. Did he make notes about Bodnar? About what Bodnar had found out? About the car back in 1968? About other pointers to Broucek that Broucek had overlooked? Broucek opened the drawers of the dresser, all four, even the bottom one that jammed, knocked them shut again. Nothing. Fulnek only came here to sleep.

There was a sound from the passage. In three steps Broucek was by the bed, switching off the light. Three more steps and he was by the door. He chose the hinge side to give him the element of surprise. He wiped his hands down his trousers again. In the Research Facility twenty-three years ago there had been a guard name of . . . He forgot. Never mind. The guard had instructed him, demonstrated on a prisoner, the difference between a choke and a strangle. See, with your choke you block off the air supply by applying fingers and thumbs to the windpipe. Now your actual strangle is more interesting. With your strangle you shift these muscles – can you feel? – so you can apply pressure to the carotid arteries behind and below the ears. Now watch – it only takes seconds. See – the prisoner faints. Sometimes the heels shudder on the floor. Then ease the pressure to let the blood reach the brain again. If you want to make it final, the guard said, just keep the pressure on.

There was a faint click from the handle as it turned.

The door opened a fraction and paused. This was a
wily old priest who could smell trouble. He could sense
Broucek's hands raised, feel the warmth of him through
the wooden panels, hear the uneven breaths through
an open mouth. The door opened fully and Broucek
heard shoes shuffling. He kicked the door shut and
grabbed for the throat, stifling any cry. There was a
jerk, a convulsion, and he felt an elbow in his stomach.
Broucek's thumbs dug and searched at the side of the
neck. Had he lost the skill? Should he go for the windpipe like some common murderer in an alley? His
thumbs probed and shifted until at last they came to
rest in the lank and oily hair of the bun at the back of
Hasslerova's neck.

Dejvicka metro station had started life as Leninova.
   'I killed her,' Broucek said.
   'You mean the old lady's dead?'
   It was a mistake naming roads and towns and sta-
tions after politicians. The wind changed and the
names were blown away.
   'If I killed her,' Broucek said, 'obviously she's dead. I
had to. She knew me.'
   'You want me to make arrangements about the
body? I can get an ambulance, load—'
   'Leave the body. Karel, this is the problem. I wiped
my fingerprints off everything I think I touched. I
straightened my bed and that. Emptied the ashtray.'
All these details. There was too much to think about.
'There is one thing I overlooked before I got out. I
signed her register.'
   'You used your own name?'

What could Broucek say? Must have been drunk? He said nothing.

'I'll tear out the page,' Karel said. 'Give me the address.'

'You already know the address.'

'Oh, right.'

Damn names. Even writers' names glowed and faded. Hasek's name had been in and out of favour, *The Good Soldier Svejk* on and off the shelves, all through the great socialist experiment.

'Take the whole book, Karel. They've got some new method they can read the impression a pen makes through ten pages now.'

'That's all? Just take the book? Shouldn't I mess the place up like she disturbed robbers?'

Now branded the great socialist disaster.

'All right. Take any money you can find. Nothing that can be traced to her.'

'I know it's late.'

Broucek leaned against the wall talking into the telephone. When he opened his eyes the steps down to Dejvicka station were very close. The concertina gate shut them off and the entrance was dark.

'Late?' Challoner's voice was vague. Broucek could hear the sound of a body heaving in a bed. He assumed it was Challoner's body turning over. 'It is late, right.'

'I need to see you in the morning before you go to see the Minister.'

'You mean something has come up in the middle of the night that is so vitally . . .' Challoner thought better of finishing the sentence. He made a conscious effort to lighten his tone. 'You've just come across another skeleton in a closet.'

'I'll come to your hotel at nine.'

'Are you receiving me well?'

There was a moment's pause. 'Yes. But you pick your times.'

'I understand, Petr. Can she overhear you?'

'No.'

'There's no extension she could be listening to?'

'No. Tonda, are you all right? You sound . . . disturbed.'

'What's her name?'

'Is that why you called – to get her name?'

Names were important. You couldn't have Mendelssohnstrasse in Hitler's time. In Tel Aviv Wagner Avenue would be fouled with graffiti. He was talking to Petr, though not the Petr that Olga knew with the hand grenades.

'I have a name for you. Fulnek, first name Alois. A priest. Tell me, Petr, we have a contact in the church administration, the ecclesiastical whatnot, I don't know what their bureaucracy is called?'

'What do you want?'

A bunch of traffic passed, released by traffic lights across the square. A police car cruised slowly. The cop who wasn't driving stared at Broucek.

Broucek passed a hand across his eyes. More than tired, he felt shattered. His head ached from the drink, from Olga's tease, from Hasslerova. He had to find Fulnek but he had to plan for Fulnek having gone into hiding. Hence Challoner first thing. But if he could track down Fulnek, that was still the way to close this thing. Pepa, here's the progress report, so stop pressuring me.

'Where is Fulnek priest of?' Broucek said. 'What is his background? His history? Look, Petr, even a priest can have something in his past.'

CHAPTER THIRTEEN

The Monastery of the Knights of the Cross had a fine position overlooking the Vltava. When They had been the power in the land, the Monastery had no longer been devoted to the greater glory of God but to the greater security of the state. It had been the operational centre of the STB. There was a neatness in the reversal. One creed promised heaven hereafter. The other boasted: Why wait? Heaven can be right here on earth. We just have to clean a bit of trash out of the way and we can start building.

Fulnek pondered this and other matters as he walked down Kafkova. Such as why monks should elect to live in something very much like a prison. And why bishops and commissars displayed such similar traits. And why priests in Poland expressed the collective will of their flock, whereas here . . .

As he rounded the dog-leg in Kafkova the early sun struck him. He paused to scan the faces of the shop assistants, bank clerks, office workers, waitresses, bureaucrats, students, street-sweepers, builders, doctors of philosophy, bakers, lawyers, whoever, whatever. The Party used to have one million six hundred thousand members. One in every seven adults belonged. Where had they all gone now the Party was over? He counted off the passers-by, stared into their faces. You, sir? You, madame? Every seventh person should be like a seventh wave: bigger, more dangerous, with a powerful undertow, capable of drowning you. The faces hid their secrets.

At the Monastery of the Knights of the Cross the security bosses must have rubbed their hands and chuckled and finally thrown back their heads and roared with laughter. Let us – They decided – use the domed chapel as a conference room. In the old days it was conferring with God. In the communist era it was for conferring with the visiting chieftains of the KGB. What a wonderful joke. What a sense of irony.

God, Moscow, the principle was the same. You bowed your head, you bent your knee.

But now a miracle had occurred and maybe God really did have something to do with it. The old régime had crumbled, the godless had been smitten, the lies and evasions and double-speak had evaporated. The new system was in place, open and free, with all the wonderful possibilities that men were capable of. Truth was the new power, truth rewarded the good, truth punished the evil. People spoke of the Velvet Revolution but there was nothing soft about the power it could wield. When Fulnek told the truth about what had happened in the August of 1968, justice would be done. The truth was an invincible force for good.

Fulnek knew all this. So did his adversary. It made no difference what power he wielded, who his influential contacts were, what bribes and threats he made, Fulnek would expose him to the bright light of the new Czechoslovakia and he would be finished.

Fulnek dabbed at his forehead with a woollen-gloved hand. There was dampness there despite the frosty air. His hand trembled. It had been a bad twenty-four hours.

He knew the building by the ZIMMER FREI sign in the window. This time he checked the number because the oblong of cardboard was gone. Hasslerova must have let her other room. The window was clean, the glass showing no outline of dust. Well, she was a fastidious woman, obsessive that her world should be clean physically and morally. Fulnek surprised himself letting out a sigh.

Hasslerova was not summoned by the bell nor by his knocking. At this hour she might be having a bath. Or have gone out to buy breakfast rolls. Fulnek decided on a walk round the block. He hammered with his fist one final time, in case she had a tap running. His hand dropped and came to rest on the handle. He didn't command his hand, not exactly. But nor was he much puzzled to find the door opening.

A cat was advancing towards the gap so he entered swiftly and closed the door. Why not? I've taken a room, he reassured himself. But he felt a tingle up his spine, a quickening of breath. A sneak thief must feel like this. Silly.

'Hello, are you home? It's only me.' Remembering the other room had most likely been let he added, 'Fulnek.'

There was no reply except from the second cat that appeared from Hasslerova's sitting-room. Both cats stared at him and one – the female, he thought – rubbed itself against his ankle. They had never shown signs of friendliness before.

'Where is she? Gone out for your milk?'

When he reached his hand out, the cat – the one he thought was female – hissed.

The apartment was silent. His room, as he shut the door behind him, was also silent but had a violated air. Someone had been in. A faint aroma of smoke lingered. Plus something he couldn't place. He raised a hand to his eyes because the something had brought Anna to mind. *I'm your Anicka, aren't I? For ever and ever.* Why had he been reminded? A woman's smell? A smell of violence? *I hate you, Lojza, hate you.* Was there a smell of hospital, of life amid death? *You're not a priest, you're not a man, you're not an animal. Do you know what you are?* Yes, Anicka, I know what I am: I am what God made me. *Hypocrite. I'll tell you what you are: a zero. The outline of a man with nothing inside.*

Not nothing. Sorrow, regret, loneliness, but above all pain.

He came here to shave, to wash, to change his shirt. He stripped to the waist as he ran water in the basin. Soaping his face, rinsing it in warm water, because soaping it a second time made the bristles softer. Simple actions were a comfort. There was a noise from the passage, a rat-tat-tat. He stared at the door in the mirror but he decided it was cat's claws on the wooden floor.

Then he saw.

His eyes flicked from looking back over his left shoulder at the door to looking over his right shoulder at the bed. Beside his right ear but on the other side of the room a foot jutted out beyond the bed. He saw a slipper, an ankle, the calf of a woman's leg. She was lying on the floor and the bed hid the rest of her.

There was a scratching, as of fingernails on wood, but it came from the door. The cats wanted food or their mistress who was stretched out on the floor. Fulnek knew it was her without needing to see her face. He knew she was dead. He knew she had not suffered a heart attack or slipped and struck her head. He knew she had been murdered. He knew all this with a certainty that left no room for doubt.

'Oh Lord,' he said and clapped a hand over his mouth. Oh Lord, have mercy on her soul. Oh Lord, what is going on? Oh Lord, what am I to do?

He went across the room and knelt by the body. She lay on her stomach with her head twisted to one side. He could see an eye open, bulging. Bruise marks stained her throat. An arm was bent under her, the hand reaching out at an awkward angle. He touched her wrist gently. The skin felt cold. She was beyond help. Lord grant her rest.

Slowly he rose to his feet. Why was she in his room? She wore slippers, a long nightdress and a bathrobe. Had she heard some noise and come to investigate? No visitors allowed, Mr Fulnek, I warned you. So had she disturbed someone ransacking his room? He had nothing to steal. Was it, then, someone lying in wait for him?

He should call the police. He should tell them he'd been out all night and when he returned he found the front door unlocked and her dead. He should tell them he was a priest and all about the synod deliberating his future and what it was about. He should tell them to question the other guest who was staying.

He tiptoed down the passage and eased open the door to the other bedroom. Just a crack, then wider. Nobody else was staying. But somebody had been in. The room was as immaculate as Hasslerova had kept things, even the ashtray empty, but a smell of stale cigarette smoke was in the air.

He went to the entrance hall where the registration book was to see who had checked in after him. The book was gone. No clue to the departed guest. Or, come to think of it, to him.

He went back to his room, wiped the soap off his face and dressed. He stood looking at Hasslerova, then closed his eyes to concentrate. He concentrated his mind down to a point of light but when he tried to pray the point of light spread and other thoughts got in the way.

He had been the intended victim. Fulnek was persuaded of that. He gathered his few belongings and put them in the nylon shopping bag. The piece of paper on the dresser caught his eye. It was the note he'd made of the train times to Kutna Hora. At the top was written in a careful anonymous script: FOR MR ALOIS FULNEK.

If he couldn't be the victim, he could be the murderer.

At a stand-up café in Kafkova Fulnek had coffee and an egg-mayonnaise roll. He had left Hasslerova's body, closed the front door and walked away with his pink nylon shopping bag.

God, what choice did I have, someone in my situation?

God, who did this deed? Who wrote my name on the paper?

God, what punishment will you inflict? Who will be your instrument?

But God was otherwise occupied and made no reply. A police car passed with its light flashing. It was headed in the direction of Hasslerova's apartment. Someone would have telephoned. The anonymous caller, the honest citizen. It would have been his name found on a scrap of paper at the murder scene, but for the grace of God.

Lord, have mercy on her soul.

He was speaking to himself. No, he said it inwardly but God was party to his thoughts so it was not just to himself. Lord, he prayed, what do I do? Where do I go from here?

'Mrs Bodnarova?'

'Yes? Do I know you? I don't think so.'

Bodnarova stood four-square in the front door of her apartment in a peeling Biedermeier block towards the south of Nove Mesto district. She was not fat but she had spread across the hips and bust. She was dressed in a navy blue skirt and a deep gold top. Her lips were glossy, her eyes shadowed, her black hair falling loose across her forehead and swept back into a knot. She tilted her head to one side to inspect Fulnek. She took a pull at her cigarette, then brushed non-existent ash off her bosom.

'I don't think we are acquainted. Fulnek, Alois Fulnek.'

'No.' She gave a tiny shake of her head. 'But you have sought me out.'

'I wanted to see you. If you have the time, that is. You're not just going out, are you?'

She drew on her cigarette again. Her eyes slipped beyond Fulnek's shoulder for that Prague probe into the shadows.

'You're not a tax inspector, by any chance?'

'Well, no, I'm not.' Fulnek frowned.

'No offence intended. Come in.'

The sitting-room had furniture that was solid but well used. Heavy curtains were drawn back in swags. Potted plants led an unhealthy life. A large dark canvas depicted a bowl of walnuts and a brace of dead cock pheasants. An overflowing ashtray, an open book, an empty cup and a lighted lamp showed where Bodnarova had been sitting. But she stood and faced Fulnek.

'Who recommended me to you?'

'Recommended?'

'You had to find me some way or another. The birds twittered my name, you heard it in the wind, your wife's second cousin told you.'

'Simple.' Fulnek smiled at the simplicity. 'I looked up your name in the telephone directory.'

The idea popped into his head as he was leaving the café in Kafkova. Why hadn't he thought of it earlier? The directory listed just one Bodnarova but he didn't want to question her on the phone. He couldn't say: Are you the widow of a certain Vaclav Bodnar, last heard of in the late summer of 1968? Splendid! Now I want you to turn your mind back to the time of the murder.

'But somebody had to tell you my name. Oh well.'

She shrugged. 'Give me your coat. Don't forget it when you leave. They say there's more snow coming – the Poles are exporting it.'

When she returned from hanging up his coat she pointed to two chairs at a square table. Fulnek sat with his hands on the table while she stood inspecting him.

'There are one or two questions I want to ask which I hope will not be too painful,' Fulnek began.

'No questions,' she interrupted with firmness. 'I have learned two things in this life and one of them is that questions lead to problems. Will Seles win Wimbledon? Will Jan come back to me? When will grandad die? Difficulties, misunderstandings, recriminations. No specifics of that nature.'

Baffled, Fulnek said, 'It's your husband I want to talk about.'

'That bastard. Is this some dirty trick he's put you up to?'

They stared at each other and for a period of time there was silence.

'Vaclav Bodnar was your husband?'

'Oh my, oh Lord,' she muttered. Her gaze turned inward, rummaging in the past. 'It's Venca you're interested in. That's part of history. No, it's practically pre-history. Venca is another matter altogether. Not that he didn't do me wrong. That's the other thing I have learned in my life: that Venca was a bastard. Like husband Number Two. Like all men. Probably you.' Her eyes had a rekindled fire in them. 'But at least it was with another woman. It turned out I was sharing Number Two with boys. I got rid of him. Out. Pack your bags and go. This is my place, you see, so I stayed put and gave him the toe of my shoe. And threw his name out after him. I'm back to Bodnarova. You know where you are with a dead man for a husband. At least I thought so. Though knowing Venca as I came to, he's most likely up there chasing female angels behind the clouds.'

She found something out of the window to interest her for a few moments. The Polish snow had not arrived yet. On a table that caught the pale sun was a dark wooden box.

'Once or twice I've said to myself that if I knew where his grave was,' she gave her attention to the box, lifting its lid and fiddling inside, 'I would carve on his headstone: *Venca, vidi, vici*. Venca saw a girl, Venca had to conquer her. Hilarious and erudite at the same time, yes? Screamingly funny, don't you think?' She turned to face Fulnek. 'No, I don't think so either. But then I was his wife.'

'Venca used to say there was gypsy in my blood. That must be what attracted him: a bit of wildness. After he'd gone and I needed to make something of the rest of my life I turned to this.'

She picked something out of the box and carried it in both hands. She unfolded a large purple silk square on the table, smoothing it with her hands. In the centre she placed a pack of cards, face down. She laid both hands over it in the form of an X.

'Bodnarova, given name Miroslava, professional name Madame Mirka, clairvoyante. I don't do horoscopes or palms or crystal balls or Ouija or bumps on the head or things that go bump in the night. I do

Tarot. You don't believe? You shrink for some reason?'

Fulnek had been prepared for a sorrowful widow, even an angry one, not this. 'Tarot cards – I confess ignorance.'

'Good. People are usually full of opinions. Tarot originates in China, they say, the emperor used the cards to keep his concubines amused. Maybe it was India. Surely it was Egypt say the scholars because Tarot is a corruption of the Egyptian word *Ta-rosh*, the royal way. *Ta-rosh* tosh, say other scholars who on a wet Sunday afternoon with nothing better to amuse themselves made an anagram of the Latin word *Rota*, the wheel, the circle of life from birth to death. Nonsense and double-nonsense, comes a voice from the dark, think of the Hebrew *Torah*, the law. And there's more, so better keep your ignorance. Simply put your trust in the practice.' She drew her hands away. 'You must shuffle the pack, shuffle well.'

Fulnek hesitated.

'It needs to have your imprint. Your future is in your hands.'

He said, 'Only God knows the future.'

'Then God will influence the cards in your hands.'

Fulnek was shaking his head. 'You need God's fortitude to be able to bear knowing the future.'

'You refuse to? You're a stubborn man.'

Bodnarova fanned the pack out on the table. Running her finger along she slowed and stopped, drew out a card and flipped it face up. It was the Hanged Man.

'You didn't shrink when you saw that. Good. Most people do. But the Hanged Man isn't a death foretold.

It's a symbol of salvation. He has taken his life in his hands and jumped into the void. Now he is suspended upside down by one ankle. See that serene smile? His faith in a greater power saves him.'

She drew another card. It was the Fool, a small bundle of his possessions over one shoulder, grinning, oblivious to the precipice so close to his feet.

'Oh Lord, the cards are confused today.'

The cards are confused . . . Fulnek regretted following his impulse to seek the woman out. All right, he would be the Fool, jumping off the precipice.

'Do you know Milena Prerova?'

'Know her? Milena Prerova?' Bodnarova gathered the pack together and squared it off. 'Oh, sure. We're bosom friends. We have a coffee and a chat every week. We swop recipes and knitting patterns. Why not? We swopped men. Or rather, it was a one-way swop because I got nothing in return. What do you think? She only took my husband away from me. Do you imagine I embrace her and call her my darling Mila? Are you married?'

'No.'

'Ever been?'

'No.'

'You've been in love though?'

Fulnek put a hand over his eyes at this questioning.

'Don't tell me it's boys, like—'

'No.'

'All right,' Bodnarova said. 'You're a man, you're another bastard. A bachelor at your time of life will have known quite a number of women. You eye us in the street. We're pressed close to you on the bus. We

take our clothes off for you in films, and in the flesh. I
mean, we're all round you. Lots of us. Is there any need
to go after a married one? Same thing applies the other
way round. A woman can take her pick of the men who
are not committed. Not Prerova. If she'd stolen a coat or
a car she'd have gone to jail. Is stealing my husband less
than that? She's your friend? She put you up to this?'

'I met her for the first time last week. It was at the
place where Venca is buried. She'd brought flowers.'

Once again they'd reached a block in the conversation and there was a hush. It was Fulnek who went on.

'Because Prerova was at Venca's grave she's been
visited by a man from that time back in nineteen sixty-
eight who had raped her, slashed her body and most
likely killed Venca. Because I've been trying to find out
his identity, he's been trying to silence me.'

'Silence you?'

Fulnek simply let her think about it. She lit a cigarette and shook her head.

'Those were bad times,' she said, 'bad, bad, bad, bad.
The situation in the country, the Russians invading,
my husband deserting me, then his disappearance and
death. It's not a time I like to reminisce about.' She
concentrated on the glowing tip of her cigarette.
Finally she gave a shrug. 'Well, it was a long time ago.
After I'd lost Venca, after I found out he hadn't just left
me for that woman but had most likely died, I went a
little crazy, turned into a bit of a bastard myself. Of
course it's men who invent language and give us names
so I was a slut, a whore, a nympho. I was pretty in
those days, good figure, good legs that you could see
men's eyes travelling up. A pretty girl has no trouble

getting a man. I could go into a room and snap my fingers and every man would look my way. Truly. I could have my pick. So why couldn't I keep Venca? What tricks did that bitch know that I didn't? Why did he leave me for her?'

'I don't know,' Fulnek said. 'Love is a mystery.'

'Love? Well, I loved him. Oh, how I loved him, you have no idea. I learned my lesson the hard way: love is for youth when we make our mistakes.'

Oh, Fulnek wanted to ask, and what are the mistakes of middle age?

She stabbed out her cigarette. 'Venca was here part of the time. This is the summer of 'sixty-eight I'm talking about. He was looking terrible. The big one – that's what he called the story he was working on. Overworking on. Following leads, tracking people down. Too much coffee, too little food. Not enough sleep. Seeing her, of course. I doubt he got any sleep there. Sometimes I'd wake up in the morning and he hadn't slept in our bed. But he'd be standing in the doorway looking at me in my half of the bed. His face was haggard, drawn. There were times when he gave the impression he knew about everything in the world but this was something he couldn't work out. "I care for you," he said. "But you'd rather be with her," I finished for him. He looked as if I'd slapped his face but he nodded. He was honest, you see. I'm not sure that honest people lead happy lives. Are you?'

She looked at Fulnek. Did she mean: Are you honest? Did she mean: Are you sure whether honest people are happy? He made a vague gesture as if the question was too profound to answer.

'You told me some bad person had been trying to silence you. Frankly, you don't seem much of a talker at the best of times. You mean someone has been trying to kill you?'

'I think so.' Or have him framed for murder. But Fulnek didn't say that.

'You could always go and live somewhere else.'

'Possibly I have a personal interest in the matter.'

'A personal interest in her, you mean?'

He didn't deny that in words but he shook his head. 'They took over the seminary where I trained and used it as an interrogation centre. It's where Venca is buried.'

'You?' She poked her head forward as if she could see right inside him. 'You mean to tell me you are a priest?'

'Yes.'

'And you've been hiding it from me?'

'I haven't been hiding anything. I just told you.'

'And you have that woman as a friend?'

'I count her as a friend.'

'And what is she? An actress, a woman who flaunted herself naked on a public stage, someone who stole my husband, who got into trouble with the authorities and then shut up. You, a priest, are happy to know her?'

'Some people would say that a woman such as you describe needs a priest more than anyone.'

Fulnek shut his mouth and stared at her, stared hard until he saw her blink.

'Well, Father Fulnek,' Bodnarova said. 'Or is it Father Alois? I'm not a churchgoer myself.'

'Call me Alois, if you find it easier.'

'Because you're here for personal reasons, you mean? This is not church business.'

'It could be.'

'It could be? Does that mean you don't want to think about it, examine your motives?' When he didn't answer she raised her eyebrows. 'Well, your motives are your own. I don't know – why am I talking so much today?'

'Sometimes you need to.'

'Like confession?'

'If you're not a believer you have nothing to atone for.'

'Really? That lets her off the hook too, I suppose. It wasn't me who committed the sin. I think you should go and tell your friend to get down on her knees and say a few thousand Aves for what she did to me.'

Fulnek had lost count of the number of cigarettes she'd lighted. The smoke in the room was like the haze of battle. She wandered round touching familiar objects, straightening the straight painting, prodding the soil of an African violet with yellowing leaves. She stuck a taper into the pot and put a match to it. The smell of joss drifted round Fulnek. It hinted at church incense.

'I don't like thinking about it,' she said. 'Inside, right here in my belly, it churns me up and it takes time to calm me down. Even after all these years. Sometimes I brood over it, can't help myself. Venca, my Venca, gone. Is that love or is it wounded pride because I lost him to that woman?'

'I should counsel forgiveness.' Fulnek hesitated. 'But

personally I believe there are some hurts we never recover from.'

'Well, well,' she said, staring at him for some time. 'I was expecting a sermon. I think you may be my kind of priest.'

'Does that mean it's safe for me to ask my question?'

'I won't know until you ask it.' She flashed a nervous smile.

'Did Venca make notes about the story he was investigating? Perhaps he typed things up, kept a notebook. Journalists do.'

'Venca did.' She nodded. 'He had cartons jammed with files. He had a desk over in that corner – I got rid of it – with drawers packed with stuff he was working on. Then on the day he disappeared for ever certain men in leather jackets came and took it all away – everything he'd written, his notebooks, his typewriter, his address book, his newspaper cuttings, his file of foreign correspondence, even his used carbon paper. I was a hero. I was angry. I was stupid. I yelled at Them: You can't take that – it belongs to my husband. One of Them turned and gave me the stare. You know it? The face as hard as January. He asked: "What husband?" That was the moment I understood. Here.' She drove a fist into her stomach. 'Then he began to grin and that was worse than his dead eyes. "You want sex?" he asked. "Then go fuck yourself."' She drew on her cigarette and the glowing tip reflected in her eyes. 'Where did They come from? How did we breed Them? Where have They gone now?'

'Some of Them haven't gone. Did They take—'

'Everything.'

'Everything?' Fulnek looked at her frown and the set of her mouth and waited.

'Everything, I said. Everything – don't you understand?'

Fulnek kept his eyes steady on her. He noticed how she smoked in quick puffs, furious at him or Venca or Prerova or the men in leather jackets or herself. He'd asked his question and she'd answered and he said no more. He watched. Perhaps the silence was a form of questioning. At length she jabbed out her cigarette. She went to the wooden box that held the Tarot pack and pressing underneath she swung open a hidden drawer. 'Except this.' She tossed a sheet of paper on the table.

My darling grey squirrel, it began.

'It's a love letter,' Fulnek said, lifting his eyes.

'And not to me. To the bitch.'

'No.' He put it down. 'It's private.'

'He had been writing to her the day he disappeared. I found the letter in a drawer in his desk and hid it. I expect I was planning a big scene. "Give her up or I'll kill you." Except somebody else . . .' She took a minute to recover. 'All right. I'll spare you the part about her black jungle hair and her . . . her woman's thing. Turn the page over.'

The paragraph jumped out at Fulnek: *The long search is over, my darling, I swear it. The smell of corruption is in my nostrils. I have followed my nose until I have reached the source of rottenness. You know what they say: turds rise. He works in the Finance Ministry, in charge of certain international transactions, a position he has used well to his own advantage. More than that, he is at the centre of a web of corruption. His name, his name you cry. I'll be blazing it soon enough: JOSEF RADL. He is a hard man and I think he knows men who are even harder. He must be exposed to the light and stamped on.*

There the letter broke off, as if Bodnar had been interrupted. It was unsigned. There were no kisses or vows of love.

'This is what I want,' Fulnek said.

'What you want! Did you consider me? You forced me to go back, think about the absolutely worst time of my life, live all the hurt and humiliation again. Just for you. Wonderful! Fantastic! Typical bloody man!'

In a fury she picked up the Tarot pack and hurled it at Fulnek. Turning her back she stood with her face in her hands, shaking.

On his knees Fulnek gathered the cards from the carpet. Three of Cups, six of Coins, two cards face down, a brick tower being shattered by lightning. Radl, he said to himself, the end of my search too if I can track him down before he surprises me.

'Here.' He held out the pack to her.

'Put it on the table.' She turned to watch him. 'You're right-handed?'

'Yes.'

She stood a moment at the table, looking down at the pack of cards, then sat on a chair. She touched her temples with the tips of two fingers.

'There are many different spreads,' she said. 'This one introduces the least complications.'

She laid out five cards, face down on the silk square, in the form of a pyramid. She tapped the card on the left.

'This card represents the important features of your situation.'

'Mine? I don't want my fortune told.'

'You gathered the cards. It was you who decided which order to pick them up. You directed your hand – this one here first, then that one. Imagine you went in a shop to buy a tie – wouldn't that reflect your taste? Every time you make a choice it shows what sort of man you are. Well, you chose this.' She turned over the eight of Coins. 'See the youth at the bench with the chisel and hammer. See the progress he is making in shaping the wood. The tide of fortune is with you and you can succeed.'

She turned the right hand card over. It was the seven of Cups.

'This card at the extreme right shows the limit of your achievement at this time. There are six cups beside the youth and the seventh cup is on a promontory. How are you going to reach it? Do it the direct way – hard swimming through the waves? The long way round following the shore? Use persuasion – beg a lift from a helicopter or an eagle? Wait for the tide to go out and stroll across? Use cunning – get someone to fetch the cup for you? A difficult decision to make and difficult to attain. Now this next card shows hidden factors which—' She broke off. 'Oh dear, oh Lord. The ace of clubs but reversed, upside down.'

'Is that bad?'

She paused a beat. 'So you are listening. I could have sworn I heard you say you weren't interested. I doubt you'll be pleased. You realize I'm giving you only the sketchiest of outlines of what the cards reveal and in this case it is sterility, barrenness, impotence. You laugh!'

'I'm not laughing. It's a rictus like you see on a corpse.'

'Heed it as a warning. Don't be proud.'

'I have nothing to be proud of.'

'Now let's see. The Female Pope, also reversed. You know her history?'

It must be the smell of joss that was overpowering. It clung to his nose and throat. He had a fit of coughing that squeezed moisture from his eyes.

'Maybe her life was too adventurous and you weren't exposed to it at your seminary. She was born in Mainz, fell in love with an Englishman and travelled across Europe with him disguised as a boy. In Rome she called herself Johannes Angelicus – some angel. She proved such a brilliant scholar that she rose to be Pope John VIII. This was the middle of the ninth century though I've forgotten the exact year. Still only her English lover suspected her sex. Then scandal struck, or at least care-lessness. She became pregnant and out popped a baby during a solemn procession.'

'That is an absolute myth. It has no historical—'

'Hah – some colour in your cheeks. Now listen closely. The meaning of the Female Pope reversed is quite clear: you must be on guard against the bad influ-ence of a woman. Yes, I can think of one. Are you in thrall to her, Father?'

Fulnek turned away. 'Where did you put my coat? I'm going now.'

'Curb your impatience. You should know the out-come.'

She turned over the card at the apex of the pyramid: the eight of Swords.

'I'm not interested.'

'Oh but you are, you haven't gone to fetch your coat. Everybody wants a peek at the future provided it's not bad.'

Fulnek looked down at the card. He saw a woman with long blonde tresses over one shoulder. Was she his fate? A tear was slipping down a cheek. Eight swords threatened her ribs. She was naked.

'Major difficulties, isolation, threatening circumstances – this is your future. Seems bad, doesn't it, but in fact it indicates a cycle of adversity is coming to an end and changes for the better are already operating.'

Fulnek waited but that appeared to be all. He went in search of his coat and when he returned he found Bodnarova frowning at the cards.

'I'll be going now. I must thank you for the name. I haven't decided what to do because I have no real evidence.'

Bodnarova shook her head. 'It's the Female Pope that worries me. That bitch, what does she mean to you?'

She looked up at Fulnek.

'You don't really expect me to put any trust in all that, do you?'

'You believe your magic, Father, I'll believe mine.'

The apartment door gave on to a landing grey with light from a never-washed window. There was an ancient lift with a concertina gate. Fulnek stabbed at the button.

Are you in thrall to her, Father?

Fulnek felt the acid of fury in his stomach. In thrall. Bodnarova had lived a life of bitterness towards a rival and it had eaten away at her judgement. She looked at others and saw only shattered pieces of her own life.

You believe your magic, Father, I'll . . .

Father This, Father That, Father Father.

He jabbed at the button again and again. There was no sound from the lift. A gate had been left open at another floor. He began to trudge down three flights of stairs that wound their way round the lift shaft.

Love is for youth, when we make our mistakes.

Really! Was that the wisdom she imparted to girls who wanted to know if their lovers would stay faithful? But no, of course, no questions, nothing specific, no future foretold, at least no real future, nothing one could come back to her and say: You were wrong.

The first floor landing was jammed with shiny metal ducts for some fancy ventilation system. There was no reason for it to be piled here. Fulnek felt this was a day without reasons.

And what else?

Oh Lord. She kept saying that. What lord was she invoking? Lord God? Lord of the underworld? Some dandy English milord she'd snapped her fingers at?

He stomped through the hall and stood at the entrance.

And what about: major difficulties, isolation, threatening circumstances?

Such garbage, such hokum, such platitudes. The poor and the lonely and the unhappy and the troubled went in search of reassurance and she spouted the lowest common denominator of human experience. What difficulty could not swell to be major by brooding? Who didn't in sleepless dark hours feel abandoned? Someone who knew the love of God would seek his priest out. If they had no belief in God, they believed in Bodnarova. Her magic. Threatening circumstances . . . Who couldn't summon up a threat or two? Health, marriage, money, family, job, future – only the dead left earthly problems behind.

Fulnek took a deep breath and concentrated on swallowing three times, as if Bodnarova was an attack of hiccups that could be defeated. All right, finished. The anger he'd had to suppress was all out now. He took a couple of steps when he heard a shout from above. Bodnarova's head jutted from an open window. She was yelling at him. It sounded like 'Fool', but traffic muffled her voice. She leaned further out, her dark hair falling forward to frame her face, and threw something. Her hand had a downward motion, sharp and angry, flicking whatever it was at Fulnek. It swooped, turned over, lunged to one side, a flash of white. An envelope.

Her head vanished. The window slammed. She had shut him out of her life.

The Fool? The Tarot card of the young man so close to the precipice?

Like a paper aeroplane it glided until some air current brought it up short. It became a shot pigeon, tumbling from the sky. It dropped to land in the road. Stepping out to retrieve it, Fulnek heard a screamed warning, felt a hand wrenching at the collar of his coat, was surprised to find himself flung on the pavement. A taxi disappeared up the street. The blurred face of a passenger appeared in the rear window but the taxi didn't so much as slow.

Half a dozen people had gathered round Fulnek and he stared up into their faces as he might from the bottom of a grave. Words washed over him but he was too shaken to tie voices to faces.

'Hit and run.'

'No, he didn't hit him.'

'He's a menace on the streets. Should have his licence taken away. He never even blew his horn.'

'Why didn't the passenger make him stop?'

'Did you get his number?'

'He was going too fast.'

'Are you hurt?'

'Here's your letter.'

'Fool' is what Bodnarova had been calling out from the window. It was what she'd scribbled on the envelope. *Bloody fool. You forgot to take this. I don't want to see it ever again.*

In the envelope was the love letter Bodnar had been writing on the day They drove him away to his death.

Chapter Fourteen

Waiting by the cemetery gate, Broucek had time to consider the matter of watchers. In the old days, before democracy, before Husak, before the false spring, way back in Gottwald's frozen 'fifties, there had been the last great show trial. And what a show it was. The prosecutors, naturally, knew their parts. But even the defendants had to learn their lines by heart from tape recordings. The charge: that they were Trotskyist-Titoist-Zionist-bourgeois-nationalist traitors and enemies of the state, imperialist spies and economic saboteurs. It was the first time that Zionism had been a charge. Of the fourteen charged, eleven were Jews, so it was natural to tack on that charge. Tactically it was a poor time to be a Jew. It made no difference whether you were born a Jew or not, you could always be made one. Slansky, sometime Party leader, was charged under the name Salzmann. He and ten others were hanged by the monster they had created.

The great growth industry of the era had been inform-ers, listeners and watchers. The hotels and restaurants and cafés provided the richest pickings and were prized for that reason and also because you kept warm and dry and had the chance of a beer. You might catch a Trotskyite thought on the wing there. Overhearing a

French journalist arrange a liaison with a Czech actress which she didn't report to the authorities could be a major career boost. Embassies, of course, were the reserved area of the STB. The Sixth Directorate would provide the maids, the drivers, the gardeners. The really hungry watcher had to scratch a living in places like this: the Jewish cemetery. Who came to mutter a prayer? Who escorted a foreign Jew on a pilgrimage? What did they discuss? Who was a closet Jew?

So who was a watcher now?

This question, this uncertainty, was assuming ever greater importance in Broucek's mind. He was followed, overheard, spied on by people he had taken to be his allies, his side. When he left his house this morning they were sitting in a car, waiting. It had happened so quickly that Broucek still could not come to terms with it. But perhaps it hadn't happened quickly. Perhaps he had ignored the signs of Radl's estrangement. He, Broucek, was making a career for himself, carving out a niche in the new Czechoslovakia. Radl, Pepa no longer, saw this as a rival muscling in. Broucek could be manoeuvred into doing one final service, cutting the link between Radl and a long-ago corruption. If Broucek killed Fulnek and Prerova, who would that leave who could endanger Radl? The English banker. If Broucek neutralized that danger, then who was left who could incriminate Radl? Only himself.

So once again, who was a watcher now?

There was no sign of Rudy but someone would be spying and reporting back. Broucek knew this. But who? That one there, ducking his head suddenly as he dipped his cigarette into the flame of a lighter? Or that one, face cut in half by a guide book? What was wrong with a girl? She had caught Broucek's eye, blonde and smiling, someone who would be a sunrise in Pepa's bed.

'German?' a voice suggested in Broucek's ear. 'One of those brazen beauties from Hamburg?'

Challoner had materialized while Broucek's mind had been wandering. Broucek glanced at him then back to the girl. She was attractive, alluring, no doubt of it, and not German. She giggled and ran a hand through her golden mane as a man hanging from a window called out to her in Czech. Democracy made women more beautiful and men speak their minds.

'One of ours,' Broucek said. 'There's nothing the West can teach our girls.'

'How are you this morning?' Challoner asked. He was giving Broucek's face a close scrutiny, noting the purple patches under his eyes and then dabs of white below the purple; and the lines of tension between his brows. 'You have the look of someone who didn't enjoy enough shut-eye.'

Broucek shook Challoner's hand. The banker had his aura intact this morning, as if he only had to snap his fingers and the Rolls-Royce would whisper its way down the alley, nosing the tables of souvenirs out of the way. Yes, it had been right to switch the meeting from the comfort and security of Challoner's hotel and walk him through the shadows.

'I appreciate your coming. Some stupid little crisis blew up and I had a meeting over there.' Broucek jerked his head back at the line of buildings that frowned down on the graveyard. 'Have you been to the Jewish cemetery yet?'

'I haven't had time.'

There was time now. The meeting with the Minister was scheduled for eleven-thirty. There was time to fill and things to say. For once, against the grain of his character, Broucek was undecided which way to go. He would like to make an appeal based on their future as partners, but that future had not been cemented. Failing that, buy him. There wasn't a man or a woman who couldn't be bought, if only you paid in the right currency. You could buy a woman with a pair of Italian boots; you could buy a Colonel with a military attaché posting to Paris; you could buy God himself with enough prayers. But what could he offer Challoner? Women? Boys? Transvestites? If Challoner wanted, he could satisfy the most bizarre appetites in London. What speciality had Prague made its own? Paranoia and persecution, and they were scarcely tempting. So that left the third possibility, the trickiest. Broucek took a deep breath. He was diving from the cliff top and could not change his mind halfway down if he saw he was heading straight at the rocks.

'It's worth the visit,' Broucek said, moving to the ticket window, 'though you have to pay to get in.'

'Unless you're dead.'

There was a special speed for walking in a cemetery, about the pace of four men with a coffin on their shoulders. The path meandered through a jumble of headstones. There were ten thousand graves, twelve thousand, Broucek wasn't certain. Jews had been for-bidden to buy more land for their cemetery so new

Broucek took time responding. In the end he did so with seeming reluctance. 'No, actually. No, I'm afraid the boilers had to wait for their next philosopher, some nihilist no doubt. It must be hard for you – coming from Britain, with your pragmatic tradition, your distrust of intellectuals – to think of philosophy as a high-risk occupation.'

'What happened to him?' Challoner insisted.

Broucek looked up at the sky which was grey with an unrelenting cloud cover.

'One could say that Maly was one of the broken eggs without which the socialist omelette could not be made.'

'But why did this chap go and stand in front of this particular grave?' Challoner was persistent.

'I think he did it solely to annoy. Because he knew the STB would be infuriated. Alas, fatally so. Some people signed Charter '77. Others acted suggestive versions of Hamlet. Still others – most of them in small ways, some in large ways – cheated the state.'

They walked a little.

Why has he brought me here? Why has he told me this?

The crowd of graves, the bare earth, the leafless trees created a sense of unease in Challoner.

He's thinking about it, Broucek decided. He's wondering: What's the point? What's it leading to?

Broucek's face had lost that slightly apologetic yet knowing air that Challoner had noted in Prague. Yes, that was our past; yes, we have survived it in our various ways; no, you cannot understand the little heroisms any more than you can understand the compromises or the betrayals.

Challoner stooped to pick up a scrap of paper balanced on a tombstone and weighted down with a pebble. The paper was a page torn from a spiral notepad. Unfolding it he read the message: Give peace a chance. Luigi.

'Luigi,' Broucek said. 'Now he sounds a dangerously philosophical sort of janitor.'

Many of the graves had little bits of paper held in place by stones or twigs or twenty-heller coins. Challoner picked up another: Costas loves Loula. A third read: God bless all the people. Kemal.

'They're all in English,' Challoner said.

'That's your gift to the world. It's the language everyone has to learn. It's the language Kemal speaks to God in because God is an English gentleman. Or these days God is very likely one of your American cousins. English is the language of business deals and airline pilots and conferences and terrorists and pop music and spies. We lesser nations speak it to each other. We organize our affairs to fit in with your view of the world. We watch your films and salute your military victories and applaud your politicians even when you have grown sick of them yourselves. We copy your economic blueprints and follow your ways. And occasionally, when things fuck up, we say: How did we get in this mess? Who can we ask to help out? Who else? There's only you.'

The buildings beyond the walls were six and seven storeys high. There were dozens, hundreds of windows gazing down on them. Broucek looked, then looked away. How could he pick out a watcher? This feeling of being overlooked and hemmed in would have reinforced the ghetto mentality of the Jews. It drove even Challoner and Broucek together. Broucek was relying on it.

Challoner seemed suddenly to feel the cold. It would be vulgar to shiver but he turned up the collar of his overcoat.

'There was a matter you wanted to discuss, something urgent. I assumed it was a matter of business.'

'Business, yes,' Broucek said. 'But not your regular business, not exactly. More in the nature of a private matter.'

'Following on from our talk at lunch yesterday?'

'I could answer yes or no to that. In truth really it pre-dates lunch, pre-dates it by a long time.'

'A piece of past history.'

'Ah, now in Czechoslovakia, you see, history is not necessarily past. In fact it is running hard to catch up with us.'

Challoner raised an eyebrow. I see, but I don't see. He waited for Broucek to go on.

'In fact, history is on our heels right now and anybody could be tripped up. Anybody at all. President Havel, maybe. The world holds him to be as clean as new snow but there must somewhere in the past have been a compromise, a principle that bent under an intolerable weight. Or the Minister you're going to see, who knows? Or me. Or you.'

Challoner looked hard at Broucek, looked hard into his eyes. The nod he gave was very slight and then he turned aside, lifting his hand and resting his chin on it.

He stared across the graves towards the entrance gate and waited. Broucek had introduced the personal element. Broucek was getting down to the real business. Let him make his pitch.

'People always say they remember what they were doing when they heard Kennedy was shot,' Broucek said. 'I remember what I was doing back in 'sixty-eight when I heard the Soviet tanks were rolling in. I was with a woman. The telephone rang and I got out of bed and went to answer it. "The Ivans are taking over. We've just got time to get out." I stood by the desk in my study, stark naked, holding the telephone. I knew the voice on the telephone. It was a colonel in the air force, someone I'd done a favour for. I asked him where he was calling from. "Ruzyne." That's the airport you flew into, you know?'

Challoner didn't answer. He was a statue.

'This is a true story. I'm standing there in the study which is across the passage from the bedroom. I'm bare-assed, as the Americans would say. My erection has shrivelled to nothing. And this air force colonel is telling me the country is being invaded and I must get out. My brain was overloaded. Get out? I asked him. How do you propose to get out? "I've got a MiG trainer, a two-seater. It's being fuelled up." I felt an arm round my waist. It was the woman who'd followed me in to see what was keeping me. I don't remember her name, I never saw her after that night. You actually mean to fly out? I asked. I was young then, I took risks, but this appeared stupid to me. If the Russians didn't shoot him out of the sky, the Americans would as soon as he crossed into Germany. The woman had begun exploring me with her hand and found my cock was about the size of an acorn. I'm wriggling, trying to punch her off with an elbow. The colonel is saying, "You've got to hurry." The woman is saying, "Who's that? Your wife? Your mother-in-law?" She's wrestling to get the telephone away from me. The colonel is saying, "What's going on? Someone's there, you're always running after women. Get rid of her, Tonda, pay her off. They've got cunts in the West." The woman is screaming into the mouthpiece, "Who are you calling a cunt?" Then she slams the phone down.'

Challoner had turned to look at him. 'So that's what you were doing when the Russians took over.'

'Wait,' Broucek said, 'it's not over yet. I slapped her face, teach her a lesson. She tried to knee me in the balls, ruin me. That kind of fight usually ends in a passionate clinch where you roll together on the carpet, but this time the telephone rang again. It wasn't the colonel but someone else whose voice I knew at once. He said, "Are you receiving me well?" I told him I was. He said, "I've heard from one of our friends that the Russians are leading a Warsaw Pact assault on our country." I've heard the same, I told him. The woman whose name I've forgotten – if I ever knew it – she'd sat herself down in the leather chair behind the desk. It's a big chair and she's sitting cross-legged on it – the lotus position – and she's pouting. I remember she was showing this thick pubic jungle and I thought: The Russians are invading and I'm not going to make it through the jungle. The telephone wasn't secure so the man simply said, "You know what your duty is." And he was gone.'

'And what was your duty?'

'Protecting our interests.'

'Our? Do you mean the interests of Czechoslovakia? Or some narrower our?'

'I'll get to that.'

A man and a woman were wandering arm in arm towards them. The man spoke to Broucek and handed him a camera. The couple posed together, smiling into each other's eyes against a backdrop of gravestones with inscriptions in Hebrew. Laughing, the man took back the camera and on impulse snapped a shot of Broucek and Challoner together.

'What was that all about?' Challoner asked.

'Honeymooners,' Broucek told him, 'from Brno.'

'Why did they take our picture?'

'To remind them of their happy day in the cemetery.' Though Broucek knew he had just met Radl's watchers and they'd wanted him to know it. Strange, to be talking about Pepa telephoning in the middle of the night and to feel his long arm reach out and touch him now.

'I had a choice,' Broucek said, picking up his story. 'On the one hand there was a so-called defender of the country preparing to flee, and I could go with him. On the other hand here was someone who could be described as an enemy of the state requiring me to stay and protect our interests against the Warsaw Pact invaders.'

It could be true, it could be false, it could be somewhere in between. The point was to draw Challoner in, to make him live those times before showing him his involvement now.

'Enemy of the state?' Challoner said. 'You were working in the Finance Ministry. How could an enemy of the state be instructing you to do your duty?'

'He was in the Finance Ministry too. Shall we move on? Keep the blood circulating.'

Broucek linked his arm through Challoner's and the banker didn't resist. Together they strolled towards the entrance. Broucek pulled them up.

'That building there is a sort of museum or permanent exhibition. It deals with the last war – I don't mean the Russian-led invasion, the last world war. It's our fate to sit in the middle of Europe and anyone who's going anywhere has to visit us. There's a display of photos, drawings, poems. It deals with Terezin concentration camp. Children a speciality. Do you want to go in?'

'You didn't fly West. You did what this enemy of the state told you. You stayed here. You grew in importance in the ministry. Even now you're on your own you know people of influence. How is past history about to trip you up?'

'Us,' Broucek said. 'Us.'

'Running dogs, paper tigers, the Chinese are poets,' Broucek said, 'poets with machine-guns. But "enemies of the state"? That's the phrase of a man with a cement soul. Enemies? Realists would say they created a parallel state that worked.'

'Have you been to Latin America?' Challoner asked. 'When you need to change money you go to a bank or you use the *paralelo*. The *paralelo* has a fine ring to it.'

Challoner's face had begun to show understanding.

Wariness was in his eyes. Broucek had chosen to conduct his business in the street. How was he different from the money-changers in Wenceslas Square or Havana?

'I like your George Orwell very much,' Broucek announced. '*Animal Farm* was banned so naturally people knew it must tell the truth. Four legs good, two legs bad. Four legs good, two legs better.'

To their left was the synagogue called, in Prague fashion, the Old-New Synagogue. Long before the communists, double-speak had been raised to a minor art form. Broucek swung away from it, leading Challoner towards the city centre.

'In this case, central planning good, private enterprise bad. Of course capitalism is the official religion now, but twenty-five years ago? Well, there was a group of people who knew what a disaster the economy was going to be so they set about creating a parallel economy. You may think that is overstating their achievements. It was certainly a parallel network of like-minded people, individualists, achievers, you know what I mean?'

He meant: All animals are equal but some are going to claw and bite their way on top of the pack. But Challoner simply gave a brief encouraging nod.

'It was just before the time of the Soviet invasion that I joined them.'

They paused while a crocodile of Japanese crossed in front of them. There was nothing Challoner could say to fill the silence. It was Broucek who had a deal to propose. Challoner already knew there was a deal coming and in a boardroom or across a desk he could be preparing his response. But now? He waited for Broucek and the Japanese. The group guide held a walking stick up in the air. It carried a red and yellow pennant of a rising sun. She was a local woman.

'This way, please.'

The Czech spoke English to the Japanese.

'To say we were a parallel state is only a mild exaggeration. The official state passed laws; we had our own rules and customs. The official state had a President, a Party chief, a Prime Minister; we had a leader. The state had its police; we had our own men. The state had its courts, though their judgements would be skewed by political considerations; our justice was not blinded by dogma. The state had its ideology, its theorists, its party line; we knew it was money made the world go round. The state had its informers and secret agents; but we had penetrated every area of the state so we knew what was going on. As you see I am being frank and open with you.'

What Challoner saw was a man describing something very like the Medellin drug cartel. Why should he make a confession like this?

'In those respects we were the parallel state. In one important way we diverged at right angles: the state lost money and we made money.'

'In legal ways?' Challoner affected a lazy tone.

'There were no legal ways for private individuals to go into business like that.'

'Well, I rather thought not.'

'Plumbers would come after hours on a private basis. Your car would be fixed on a private basis. The country would have come to a halt without such people. There

was blind eye acceptance of the little men. But when it
came to other, bigger affairs . . .'

'Of interest to you and – did your organization have
a name?'

'Not an organization,' Broucek said, 'not as struc-
tured. Oh I know, I said we were a parallel state but it
was not so formal. We simply acted in each other's
interests.'

Two phrases jostled in Challoner's mind: one of us
and *cosa nostra*. The Thatcher ethos embraces the mafia.

'I'll give you one example,' Broucek said, 'so you'll
see how we worked and understand how you are
involved.'

Challoner stopped dead. Involved? Does lunching
with Broucek involve him? It was his first visit to
Prague. His bank's business initiatives were still in his
briefcase. He stared into Broucek's eyes, trying to read
the future. He saw tiredness and tension, of course.
Was there something more? Was there a dread back in
the shadows? Did it involve him?

'Oh yes,' Broucek said.

'Do you know Presov?' Broucek asked. 'No?
Unimportant town in the east. You can smell Russia
from there. There is some industry – engineering, tex-
tiles. Salt mines too, though it's hardly Siberia. There
are little wooden churches round about. It has a history
of uprisings and workers' movements. Typical crappy
Slovak place. A long way from Prague, a long way from
interference, a long way from anyone checking up
what is going on.'

They were strolling again, ambling, two old pals

sharing a memory, a secret, a scandal. Challoner was listening, Broucek was talking, and twenty paces behind them a honeymoon couple were enjoying their trip to the capital. Broucek's easy tone was at war with the twists in his stomach. How to start? How to draw Challoner all the way in? No more pussyfooting. Launch into it.

'The actual beginning is a year before I became involved. There is a river to the north of Presov, the Sekcov it's called, and a plan was drawn up. Trade, Agriculture, Energy, Industry, all were involved, but the Ministry of Trade finally got a grip on it. Trees cover the hills to the north, pines, but also some beech woods. Beautiful in the autumn, so I'm told. According to the plan a sawmill was to be built. A dam would be constructed to provide hydro-electric power for the sawmill. As a bonus, a couple of neighbouring villages would be electrified. Of course building the dam will flood the valley and some peasant farms will be under water. Still, omelette, breaking eggs, that argument.

'A road was bulldozed through the hills, a more detailed survey done than just a blueprint drawn up on a ministry desk. What is going to be done with the timber? The pine can be used locally for furniture but the beech is valuable hardwood. Exports to Germany and Austria and England would bring foreign currency. That interested the Finance Ministry. And it was round about this time that the planning file was quietly closed and construction around the site stopped. Other work continued. Certain people in the Finance Ministry were making plans. When I caught wind of it, I became one of them.'

They walked a few paces in silence before Broucek stopped to stare at a shop window. He was showing unsuspected cultural depths – it was a display of sheet music to celebrate Mozart's bicentenary. Moving across the plate glass window was the reflection of a car. It passed slowly. Broucek could see a face he recognized at the passenger window.

'In those days,' Broucek picked up his story as he began moving again, 'to spend foreign currency you needed to fill in a dozen forms and go begging to the Finance Ministry. There was an application for just over four hundred and fifty thousand dollars. Nothing so alarming as five hundred thousand, no half a million – the million word flags attention. Purpose of foreign currency: purchase of Swedish automated sawing machinery. There is a rubber stamp and an illegible signature from someone in the Trade Ministry. There is approval from a certain party in the Finance Ministry. The money is transferred to London. You're frowning. Are you puzzled why the money goes to London and not to Stockholm?'

'I am puzzled,' Challoner said, 'but you're going to enlighten me.'

'The dollars didn't stay in London. They went to Zurich. Your Mr Wilson was Prime Minister then and used to talk of the gnomes of Zurich. So I imagine these little men burying the four hundred and something thousand dollars in a secret place. The account in the Zurich bank was in the name, not of a Czech ministry or purchasing agency, but of a Czech private citizen. Not legal for a Czech. A reference for this private citizen was given to this Swiss bank by a merchant bank in London. Your bank, as it happens. The money which went from Prague to Zurich via London was handled also by your bank. So there we have it.'

'Yes, well,' Challoner considered, 'all this was a long time ago, hardly of great—'

'One moment please.' Broucek produced a folded document from an inner pocket. Challoner hesitated – was he being served with a subpoena? He accepted and read the document with a frown while Broucek added a commentary. 'Your bank's headed notepaper at that time. Details of the currency transaction. You will notice there is no mention of purchasing Swedish sawing machinery – that has quite faded away. On the contrary, confirmation of the opening of the Zurich account. Also confirmation of the famous Swiss secrecy in banking matters. A paragraph on the "arranger's fee" deducted by your bank. Five per cent is high for doing little more than be a pipeline to Zurich but the people here were in no position to argue. Then signed by – notice the name?'

Challoner had noticed the name. For a moment he had gone still, seemed even to have stopped breathing.

'Done well in his career,' Broucek said breezily. 'Made a lord, contributed to Conservative Party funds – I'm not saying the two are connected. Now he's chairman of your bank.'

Challoner was tilting the letter for the best light.

'The signature is quite genuine. Oh, he's older, more distinguished, so his signature has developed a little. Now he's so important and so busy it's become more of a scribble. But he signed it.'

'Why have you told me this?' Challoner's lips pressed tight together. He had been expecting a deal. Now the ground seemed prepared for – blackmail was an ugly word – prepared for arm-twisting.

'Back in nineteen sixty-eight an inquisitive journalist started sniffing after this story. In the chaos after the Russian invasion he disappeared and his enquiry naturally stopped. Now, just in the past few days, people have been asking questions again.'

'Just a minute. You say the journalist disappeared. Did he reappear?'

'No.'

'So he died. Of natural causes?'

'Well, to stop breathing is to die of natural causes.'

'What you are saying, Broucek, is that he was murdered.'

'Thousands of people disappeared over the years. It's what happened. It is unfortunate that in this case someone is digging around. It affects a number of people, including myself. I could be dragged in. Then there would be more questions. Eventually your bank would become involved.'

'You're suggesting because we were the channel for a quite trifling sum of money to be invested in Switzerland there would be a scandal?'

'The money may seem small to you – two and a half million, three million in today's terms – but that is not how the average Czech will see it. Then of course it will lead to further enquiries, other possible transactions.'

'If I understand you right you could be sitting in the mire of a conspiracy to defraud the state.'

'And – your – bank.'

Broucek tapped Challoner on the shoulder to drive home each word. Challoner looked at the hand with distaste.

'Just imagine what would happen if this story came to light,' Broucek went on. 'You called it a conspiracy to defraud the state. Your bank was party to it. Do you honestly believe you would be allowed to do business here? And in the other capitals of the former Soviet bloc – do you think you would be welcome there? And think of your chairman's reputation. He was directly—'

'I can do nothing.' Challoner cut him short.

'Oh, but you can. You're seeing the Minister in an hour. You are uniquely placed to resolve all difficulties.'

Broucek wanted brandy, or better still Scotch – a bloody great triple – but the café only ran to wine. He drained the glass in one long swallow. If they'd produced a Johnnie Walker Black Label he'd have done the same. If it had been that Siberian White Lightning – one hundred per cent alcohol – he'd have done the same.

Broucek glanced at the wall clock. About now Challoner was entering the Minister's office.

Minister, thank you for making time to meet me. I appreciate how very busy you are, the important decisions blah blah.

Challoner would lay on the flattery, Broucek knew. We all had egos but politicians had bigger egos than anybody except pop stars.

Now, Broucek had said, there are no longer any files

relating to this matter in the Finance Ministry. But there is one in the Trade Ministry, quite a fat file, marked the Sekcov Project. It will be locked away along with a mass of others pending possible investigation by the new democratic régime. In most cases nothing will happen because they don't want to open up a lot of old wounds. In a couple of years it will all be forgotten. But right now – if there's a stink – the zealots will get busy.

Locked away? Challoner had at last spoken. Then I can do nothing.

Broucek drained his glass again and refilled it from the bottle. Another glance at the clock. It had stopped. No, it had moved three minutes. Three minutes of social chat. If the Minister was showing off his broken English, good. Use that as an excuse to get rid of the interpreter. Challoner had to choose his own words but in essence his job was clear.

It needs a minister's signature to get the file out, Broucek had said. What you must do is suggest to the Minister that the Sekcov Project deserves another look. Say that your bank was involved many years ago and felt the communist authorities lacked the imagination to see its potential. Ask for the file to be brought from the Ministry of Trade. If they cannot get it for you at once, have it delivered to your hotel. Then on the day you leave – not before – write a note which will arrive too late for them to stop you. In the note you say you are taking the file to London for further consideration.

And I throw the file away, Challoner had said. Just like that.

No. You have a letter written – some date in early

nineteen sixty-eight – saying that in view of the cancellation of the project you have arranged for the repayment of the money lodged in a Swiss bank pending the purchase of Swedish machinery. Insert this letter in the file and send it back.

Challoner had looked at him for a long time and then checked his watch. He said he had to leave for his appointment and walked away.

So at this moment Challenor was saying: Minister, I congratulate you on your wonderful English. Before we begin official business may I suggest a one-to-one talk for a few minutes . . .

Raising his glass, Broucek also raised his eyes. At the café window peering in were the honeymoon couple from the cemetery. They were not smiling for the camera. The woman beckoned with one finger.

'I hear what you are saying,' Pepa said, 'but I also hear other things.'

They had driven through Nove Mesto and then through a district of factories and warehouses and waste land. But who was looking at the view? Pepa and Broucek sat in the back seat, a thick-necked man was behind the wheel. It was a Skoda Favorit, anonymous, unmemorable.

'And what I hear is disturbing. I hear you are never in your office so my messages are ignored. I hear you have been running all over the country, making a spectacle of yourself with playboy soldiers. I hear you've been involving a ministry driver. I hear you are drinking all day – hear it, I can smell it. Picking up girls. And now, the most stupid, killing some old woman. No, you let me finish. I don't want to hear excuses. You never used to make excuses, never. You didn't need to. Do you understand what I'm saying? You were hard, direct and got results. But what have we now? There is still this threat hanging over us: that some country priest is going to expose you and the ripples will spread wider until all of us are touched. Those new democratic bastards would smile and rub their hands at the prospect of seeing me charged with corruption and you in the dock for murder.'

'It's being taken care of,' Broucek said. 'Right now.'

'Now? While you're sitting with me?'

'The British banker is—'

'The British banker!' Pepa chopped him short. 'What are you doing about the priest? People listen to a priest.'

This was where they had arranged to meet, Kampa Park. In normal times – or what had passed for normal times when God was in the Kremlin and the Communist Party ruled the Czech world – Kampa Park had been an island. But in these heady days when nothing ran normally the channel leading off the Vltava had been blocked and repair work was under way on the walls. Out in the main stream of the river was a weir where gulls perched and argued among themselves.

'You see that weir?' Challoner said. 'Let me tell you the reason they put it there.'

Broucek stared at him, surprised at this scrap of local knowledge.

'Did you say something?' Challoner asked.

'No. No, I didn't say anything. Tell me why they put the weir there.'

'It's to catch the bodies floating downstream. Bankers who've been pushed out of Finance Ministry windows.'

'What happened?'

'What happened? Nothing happened. But I could have been in the river swimming for my life.' There was anger still boiling in Challoner. Not since he'd been a young man had he felt this pressure inside him, the knots in his stomach, the galloping heartbeats. 'Let me tell you something. When we met yesterday I thought you were a successful operator – by Czech standards – who wanted to better himself. Good suit, haircut, shoes, know your way round a wine list. Now I understand what you are: you're a tough who's scrambled out of the gutter. I've met a number like you. In London, I mean. Brass nameplate outside the entrance, couple of secretaries in the outer office, one for work and one for play, the big desk, the firm handshake, the sincere smile, and the hard eyes and the bullshit. I've looked at your knuckles and I've seen the scars there. You've been physical in your time but that time has passed. You're a hard man gone flabby. There's nothing more pathetic than that. You're all voice and no muscle. You've got nothing to offer any more. Not to me, not to the crooks you work with. Just thought I'd tell you that so that we know where we stand. You've lost your balls, Broucek.'

Broucek clenched his right hand into a fist. Yes, there were scars. He should smash Challoner in the teeth and get more scar tissue. Challoner seemed to understand this and stood with his legs apart, his hands moving loosely in front of his chest. He no longer looked like a banker, he looked a boxer, and one who would welcome some exercise.

'You spoke to the Minister,' Broucek said. 'What did he say to you?'

'I said how much I had enjoyed my visit to Prague, how impressed I was with the progress they were making towards a market economy, how we wanted to help but felt we needed a little more time to view developments and then we would make concrete proposals.'

'I meant the Sekcov file.'

'Did you imagine for one minute I was going to do what you asked? You'd be blackmailing me the rest of my life.'

It was a grey world. The stone bridge was grey, the river was grey, the buildings on the far side were grey, the sky was grey, the smoke drifting up from Broucek's cigarette was grey. He was numbed. There was movement in front of him.

'Where are you going?'

Challoner stopped and turned on Broucek. 'Home. Catch the British Airways flight and I can be there tonight. Take the dogs for a walk. Drop in at the Rose and Crown for a pint. Eat steak-and-kidney pudding. Sit in front of the fire with Rosemary. Watch a repeat on television. You don't know what the hell I'm talking about, do you?'

'What are you going to do about that file?'

'No, Broucek, what are *you* going to do about the file? I'll tell you what I shall be doing. First thing tomorrow morning I'll see our chairman. I'll advise him to hire the best lawyer money can buy. If there is one blackmailing peep out of you, then he will nail you to the wall. There will be a bigger explosion than anything you've ever experienced. If the story comes out, my guess is you'll find yourself facing a murder charge. Think about it.'

Challoner started to walk again.

CHAPTER FIFTEEN

St Provop did not look like a church but a factory. It stood on an island, isolated by traffic. It was large, daunting, constructed of smoke-blackened bricks. What was manufactured here? Shoes, paint, souls? Corrugated-iron sheets formed a wall head-high around it. Glimpsed through the cracks were heaps of tiles and pipes for scaffolding. There was a forgotten weed-covered look to them, as if the roofers went off to some local hostinec to celebrate the Velvet Revolution back in 1989 and hadn't yet returned.

Fulnek tried the handle and found the door locked. A sign promised services at 11 and 6 but like everything else about the church it carried no conviction. If the door had been left unlocked, Fulnek reasoned, the pews would have disappeared for furniture or firewood. This was Zizkov, after all. Thieves and gypsies.

He'd wanted a few minutes of quiet, alone with the Madonna. Many people asked favours of her, seeking a mother's intercession with God. Hail Blessed Virgin Mary, Mother of Jesus, listen to my prayer, help me in my hour of need, help Jan to pass his exams, help Jan survive his operation, help Jan see the evil in that Jezebel, help Jan this or that, amen. A candle lighted, a promise of abundant future Aves. But Fulnek had been after a spell of solitude, excluding the outside world. A time to sit alone and restore himself. He would ask for inner strength to face his future, ask the BVM, ask God, ask it even of himself.

He crossed the road between trams with angry bells, heading back towards the city centre. The Poles had kept their snow. Weak sun gave the illusion of early spring. He pulled up at a hotel of sorts which shared an entrance with a club. This didn't cater for fancy foreign tastes, this was to satisfy honest Czech needs.

'Come in, friend, the show is just about to begin.'

A glass display cabinet showed photos taken on a bare stage of equally bare women. Their nakedness was emphasized by silvery stars bursting from their nipples and a piece of card over their pubic area. The card read: STRIPTEASE.

'You're interested, you're a man of taste. Wait till you see Maria. She's got great big ones. And when she moves . . .' The doorman kissed his thumb and forefinger. 'She's no snob either. She's not waiting for Fritz from Frankfurt to make her an offer. Know what I'm talking about?'

'Thank you,' Fulnek said.

He pushed into the hotel entrance. A lounge led off the empty reception lobby. Through the open doors a young woman smoked and watched him. Her lips and eyelashes were aubergine, her nails silver.

'*Ahoj*,' she called out. 'Are you looking for someone?'

'The telephone.'

She smoked and carried on looking at him. 'Up the passage.'

The telephone sat on a shelf in front of a wall covered

with graffiti promising a variety of experiences. *Gretchen and Verushka – two for the price of one*, he read. *Have you tried Round-the-World?* He was searching in his pockets and didn't hear the footfalls. When she spoke the woman's voice was close to his ear.

'It's something special you're after?'

'This.'

Fulnek held up a sheet torn from a notebook on which he'd scribbled the number. The woman moved in front of him, leaning an arm against the shelf. One breast was dangerously close to the telephone as he began to dial.

'Why bother?' she said. 'Everything you need is right here.' She put a hand on his wrist to slow his dialling. 'What's the matter? Don't you like me?'

'Please,' Fulnek said.

'What's your name?'

'Alois.'

'Alois. I'll call you Lojza.'

Lojza echoed inside his head, a scream.

'I'm Maria,' she said.

'Maria,' he said, and tried to erase the vision in his mind of a mother and child.

'Don't you like me?' she asked again.

'I'm sure you're very nice.'

'Nice?' she said. 'Nice?' She sighed.

'Please,' Fulnek said and finished dialling. He waited. He tried not to look at Maria, so close. His eyes roamed the graffiti. *Forget '68! Enjoy 69!*

'Do you like my perfume?'

He'd not been able to avoid it. 'Please.' Fulnek kept saying it. 'I have to speak to someone. It's private.'

'It used to be called Mille Nuits de Baghdad until that stupid war. Now it's Marrakesh Mon Amour.'

Fulnek could hear the ringing tone.

She said, 'Your hand is trembling. I can guess why.' She touched the hand that held the receiver, ran one finger slowly over it.

He could still hear the ringing tone.

She said, 'She's not in. Don't worry. Forget about her.'

Fulnek said, 'Leave me alone. Please go away.'

'Hello,' a voice said on the telephone.

'Hello,' Fulnek replied. 'You know who it is?'

There was a pause while each man identified to himself the voice at the other end. Music began from the club next door. Fulnek in the past days had seen a side of life that was totally strange to him. Now, at one remove, he was in the audience for striptease. Mick Jagger was singing *I Can't Get No Satisfaction*.

'I was wondering when you'd call,' the voice said. 'Where are you?'

'In Prague. I'm telephoning from a hotel.'

'I can hear music.'

'From next door. There's some sort of club.'

'I have to go,' Maria said. 'I'm on soon. I'll see you later if you're still here. Take that tremble away.' She pressed a kiss to her fingers and then touched Fulnek's cheek.

'That's a woman's voice,' the man on the telephone said. 'You're with a woman?'

'Just one moment.' Fulnek covered the mouthpiece and gave his full attention to the woman. Close to he could see where the blonde of her hair stopped and the dark roots showed. 'I'm trying to have a private conversation.'

'I'm going. I'm going. Come and watch. You'll like what you see and when I've finished . . .'

Her eyes travelled up towards the hotel bedrooms above but Fulnek was already giving his attention to the telephone again.

'Jarda, I apologize for the interruption.'

'An interruption, was she? You've been making new friends in Prague?'

'It's nothing like that,' Fulnek said. He closed his eyes. He could hear Mick Jagger's voice rising, rising. The photos had shown such a bare stage, such a bright pitiless light on the bodies.

'Believe me, Jarda,' he said. 'Believe me.'

Jarda was rapporteur of the synod that was sitting in judgement on him. Friendships formed at college or seminary were strong enough to stand up to the blows of life.

'You're still there?'

'I haven't gone away. How have you been passing your time?'

A dozen images jostled for Fulnek's attention. He saw the face of a strangled woman, a woman leaning from a window and flicking an envelope at him, a woman's puzzled reaction when she tried to kiss him, a woman holding a bathrobe together while she abused her husband, young women with painted eyes, a woman with her dress pulled up on the floor behind coats, a woman lifting a breast out of a bra to show him a scar. So many women.

'I've been examining the past,' Fulnek said.

'Good. And?'

'Searching for the truth.'

'Have you found it?'

'I'm almost there. I know his name but I still have to find him. Soon, I'm sure of it. Very soon.'

'Alois . . .' The voice was hesitant, puzzled. 'Are you positive?'

'No doubts,' Fulnek said. 'Jarda, I rang about the synod.'

'I know.'

'They said a week, maybe two weeks. But I thought after a week I'd ring you.'

'The decision is being made public tomorrow afternoon. They expect you here.'

'I was hoping for a word in my ear now.'

'I'm afraid . . .'

'You're afraid you can't tell an old friend?'

'I'm afraid the news is bad for you, Alois. The worst.'

If Broucek told anyone about Frantisek Moravek he would start off: This is a true story.

Moravek had owned a successful textile factory. The small business he had inherited from his father Jiri had doubled in size in the first ten years he had run it after his father's death; and doubled again in the next five years when he began exporting. Czechoslovakia in the first third of the twentieth century had been one of the most prosperous countries in Europe and Moravek had grown rich. In 1925 he developed the urge to put some distance between himself and the source of his wealth and he decided to move from Cheb to Prague. He employed servants to run his house, he would employ servants to run his factory.

Moravek arrived in Prague and consulted various authorities. No, he didn't want a damp and crumbling mansion whatever its illustrious history. He would build. The head of the meteorological service, after lengthy calculations, announced that the low hills in the district called Troja overlooking the city had the perfect climate. The prevailing winds came from the west and noxious fumes from any industrial development would be blown away. Moravek was pleased. He'd made his money from industry but he didn't need to smell it day and night. He built a huge villa and moved in. What nobody had foreseen was that in 1948 the prevailing winds would change and blow, cold and harsh, from the east. Before the end of the year the elderly Moravek, his wife, three dogs and a number of servants were evicted. The grand villa was declared the property of the state, specifically of the Finance Ministry.

It was divided into three apartments. In 1973 Broucek moved into one of them. There was something about him – his brusque manner, the sort of women he brought home, the floods he caused by leaving the bath tap running – that made the other families move out. Perhaps it had been the suggestions he had put to the wives. In any event by 1978 the whole villa was Broucek's.

Yes, it was a true story, Broucek would say, and it gave him a certain satisfaction.

The afternoon was well advanced when he arrived home following his meetings with Challoner and Radl. In the road outside there was some work being done on the drains, or at least canvas screens had been erected and the heads of two men watched him over the top. They'd been there when he left in the morning. They'd arrived some time yesterday for their screens had been up when he got home at 2 a.m. Should he offer them a drink? Radl wouldn't like that.

It was just Pepa putting pressure on him.

In the house Broucek went to the sideboard where the bottles stood and poured himself the Johnnie Walker Black Label he'd been promising himself. He went to the kitchen for ice cubes and finally he went to his study. The light was blinking on his answering machine. It was Petr, not the one with grenades, the one he'd rung in the night. He played the message through twice and went to refill his glass. He came back and played the message a third time, and then he laughed. He slumped down in his chair and put his head back and laughed until he choked. Petr was the one he'd asked to find out about Fulnek, where he was priest of, any dirt he could dig up.

'Well, well, Father Fulnek.'

He should tell the watchers outside.

Broucek swirled the whisky round his tumbler, listening to the ice cubes. They clinked, they chuckled, they said: you're not alone, we're here, we're your friends.

'Father Fulnek, fancy that.'

He pulled the telephone directory across the desk, looked up the number and dialled. Was he in? Was she in? Would she speak to him? Prerova had a hot temper. Always had. He had gone once to a meeting where she had made a rousing speech. Free Bodnar!

Bodnar Must Live! He had stood at the back but could feel the heat of her there. Strangely the night he had sent for her was not burned into his memory. He had taken over the house beyond Smichov and she'd been brought there and when he'd seen her, he'd decided what needed to be done. Threats would not be enough. She had to be taught she was responsible for her actions, she had to be taught others could be hurt by her behaviour, she had to be humiliated, she had to understand his power.

Why wasn't she answering the telephone? Was she out, was she in the bathroom, was she afraid to answer in case it was him?

After the humiliation there had been the business with the barber's blade. Drops of blood had popped out the length of the slash. Her breast was crying red tears. He'd rubbed in the ash. The feel of her breast hadn't given him any pleasure. The violation was the important thing, to invade her, to show there was no hiding from him even inside her body.

Just so she could not hide now.

Nine times, ten times the telephone rang. She's there, he decided. She doesn't want to answer. But it's hard to resist a telephone's clamour. It insists: I have news for you. Good news, a disaster, but it's just for you.

The ringing tone stopped. She'd picked up the receiver. She was listening. She was suspicious.

'*Ahoj.*'

Prerova's voice gave nothing away. It was neutral. It said: I am not here if it turns out I don't want to speak to you.

Broucek waited. Now what's she doing? She's waiting for a sound. He put a cigarette between his lips and clicked his lighter several times. She'd hear that. She'd be wondering.

'It's you.'

'And who am I?' Broucek asked.

'I'm not talking to you.'

'And I don't want to talk to you. But I do have things to say to Father Alois Fulnek.'

'Alois – he's not here.'

'Isn't he? Listen, I know where he's been. I know who he's seen. I know what he's done. I know what he's running from. Something hangs over his life while he goes after me. Tell him I want to see him.'

'I told you: he's not here.'

'When he comes, tell him I'll be in touch. Tell him to wait.'

'How do you know he's coming here?'

'He has nowhere else to go. Tell him.'

There was a click as Prerova cut the connection.

Would she tell him? Prerova was wild, unpredictable.

Broucek looked round his study. The shelves were crammed with books. When others had been learning Russian, he'd been learning English. He seemed to have time then, even with his work, even with Pepa, even with his women. Usually they'd look through the door and gape at the books. Have you read them all? Yes. They're in English? Yes. Say something in English.

It was only the really dumb ones who'd ask him to speak English. He could say anything. He could say: The square root of minus five was logically impossible.

He could say: The capital of the province of New Brunswick is Fredericton. It made no difference. The really dumb ones would sidle up to him and murmur: I know what you're saying. They thought everything was sex.

And sex did get into everything.

Suppose she didn't tell Fulnek. Suppose she warned him to get out.

God damn women. He got out of his chair and left.

There were wire-guarded lamps in the stairwell but one of the bulbs had gone. It was dusk outside, the streetlamps on, and a patch of light was thrown against one wall. Prerova's door was in almost total darkness. Fulnek was bent over, peering for the keyhole, when he saw the shadow thrown against the wall. He turned and the man stopped.

'You're Fulnek? Alois Fulnek?'

'Yes.'

'Finally we meet.'

Broucek moved forward another step and Fulnek saw the gun in his hand. Fulnek had seen police with pistols in their holsters but never one in a man's hands. He expected something bigger. Broucek took another step and he was out of the light and into the dark.

'I should kill you now. Get it over with.'

Fulnek's throat was dry. He tried to swallow. 'But you wouldn't get it over with.'

'I could kill you before you even had time to shout for help.'

'Do you think a dead body doesn't speak?' Fulnek said. 'Do you think Bodnar's corpse isn't shouting after all these years? It would be one more murder charge when the police finally arrest you.'

From below came the sound of voices. Two men began to climb up the stairs. Broucek slipped the gun into an outside pocket of his jacket.

'I want to talk,' Broucek said. 'We can go into the apartment. She left about a quarter of an hour ago.'

Fulnek had a key in his hand. He could feel it, a little slippery from the grip of his fingers. He dropped it back in his pocket.

'We'll talk outside.'

The two men had appeared on their landing.

Fulnek said, 'Good evening,' and, 'Excuse me,' and was past them and going down. Broucek followed.

Out in the street Broucek said, 'We can drive somewhere.'

'No.'

'Somewhere quiet where we can talk.'

But Fulnek was already walking. He didn't want to be in any room or car with this man. He didn't want to be confined with him, didn't want him too close, didn't want to be shut away with him out of sight. He thought of Prerova's slashed breast. That had been a long time ago. He thought of Hasslerova, head twisted, one eye bulging. That was this morning.

At the end of the street Fulnek turned left past the darkened Supraphon offices and crossed the main road that led from the station. There was a public garden no bigger than a tennis court, with a pair of benches, beds of earthed-up rose bushes, litter bins the Zizkov residents lobbed their empty cigarette packets at. Traffic passed, crowded buses and trams, women on foot with string bags of food. It was safer than being shut inside with a murderer, though not by much. Fulnek caught himself with the thought and had to marvel. His life was upside down and inside out.

They sat together on a bench, closer together than Fulnek would have liked, but it meant they could talk without raising their voices. A man had stepped out of some doorway and followed them and was now easing himself onto the other bench. Even here, Broucek thought. Bloody Pepa. Well, he'd get a first-hand report.

'I've always got this,' Broucek said, tapping the pocket he'd slipped the gun into. 'Don't forget.'

Fulnek said nothing.

'I'm not going to kill you. Not if things work out. I'm going to offer you a deal.'

Fulnek waited but Broucek seemed to expect some response. Fulnek said, 'A deal?'

'Yes. You see, I know about you. I've found out.'

Fulnek was silent again. He'd been searching for the murderer of Vaclav Bodnar but without any clear idea of what would happen then. He'd been doing it for reasons of justice, he could tell himself, a one-man truth commission. But it was more to fill the time while his future was decided, to blot out the thoughts that came into his head. The trouble was the truth was not enough. A scrap of a love letter was not enough to take to the police.

'Even last night,' Broucek said, 'I would have killed you because that would have kept you quiet. Now I know different.'

And Fulnek knew different now. Justice would be

done in a rough and ready way. First he would hear the man out.

Broucek was lighting a cigarette. He was fiddling with the lighter, flicking it as he had done over the telephone to Prerova. 'There was a time when you would simply have vanished, been packed away in a hole in the ground. That was the old Czechoslovakia. Won't work any more.'

Fulnek said, 'The new Czechoslovakia is going to be different?'

'The new Czechoslovakia is about doing deals. We each do something to help the other.'

Fulnek knew what was expected of him: forget Bodnar. He asked, 'What do you propose to do for me?'

Broucek said, 'As I understand things, you're about to be kicked out of your job? Is it right to call it a job?'

God existed. Fulnek had no doubt of that. He needed God more than ever. He needed the strength that his faith in God gave him. But the church he saw as something else. The church was bishops, organization, bureaucracy, history, dogma, jobs. How much did he need the church? He made some sort of gesture with one hand.

'All right,' Broucek said. 'You're going to lose your job because of a woman – or to be precise because of what a woman says, what she alleges. She is pregnant and says you are the father. Father Fulnek. That's what I found out today. The bigger she gets, the more noise she makes. She'd found out where your bishop lives and gone along to see him and pointed at her belly – Look! She'd read about something called genetic fingerprinting and demanded a blood test for you and the baby when it is born. And certain people have said, Yes, she did call on that priest a lot, and at night too. And when questioned, you refused to co-operate, wouldn't even call her a liar.'

'Enough,' Fulnek said.

It was a matter for God, not for a church synod and certainly not for a murderer, to judge. Fulnek stared at the traffic but saw a mouth open in a scream: *Lojza, I hate you.*

'She says when the baby is born she will put Alois Fulnek down on the birth certificate in the place where it says: Father's name. Now,' said Broucek, who didn't accept he'd said enough, 'if I closed my eyes and concentrated very hard I might just be able to imagine how that would affect you. Might be, might not be, because I don't think like a priest. But I think like a man and I think that would devastate you. Your work, your home, your reputation, your whole life out of the window. Yes?'

Fulnek kept staring ahead. Silence was a priest's strength.

Broucek said, 'What you have to do is buy her. Everybody has their price. All right, it won't be a pair of Italian boots. It may need to be a house. Or a ticket to America and a green card. These things can be arranged. I can do it, that'll be my side of the deal. She also has to deliver. She has to withdraw all allegations, apologize, say she was temporarily unbalanced by her situation. On the birth certificate will go: Father unknown.'

Fulnek turned to look at him. 'There's the difference

between us. You think money can solve any problem. But with her I think the problem is in her soul.'

'You can buy a soul,' Broucek said.

Not this one, Fulnek knew. You couldn't buy this one with anything he'd be willing to pay.

Anna Kadeckova, aged twenty-eight, was a widow. Fulnek had met her dressed all in black, her face and her large dark eyes shadowed by a black veil, at her husband's funeral. It had been just over a year ago and he'd conducted the service.

'*Libera me, Domine, de morte aeterna in die illa tremenda . . .*'

It was a month later that she came to his house. She'd asked why he'd used the Latin rite instead of the Czech. Because to speak Latin was more mysterious and therefore in some way more of a comfort because death itself was a mystery. But how could he explain that? He'd said: 'Because it's beautiful.' She looked at him and her eyes had grown huge as if he'd said: 'Because you're beautiful.' Then she began crying. Her own handkerchief was frilly and too small to wipe away the tears. He'd given her his. She was crying, she said, because her husband's death was her fault. They'd quarrelled and he'd gone out angry and driven too fast and couldn't take that corner by the supermarket. Fulnek had comforted her, tried to.

A week later she came back. She'd gone off with his handkerchief and now she returned it, washed and ironed. It smelled very slightly of the perfume she wore. She'd been sorting out some of her husband's things: letters, photos, a carved wooden bear from a skiing holiday in the Tatras. It had upset her. Fulnek didn't want her crying again and took one of her hands in both his, held it tight, tried to pass some calmness and strength to her.

She came the next week because she needed someone to talk to, and the next week, and then after only two days. Could a man who murdered in cold blood understand her? She was getting frustrated, he would say, she was missing it. Could he understand Fulnek? Could he understand the loneliness, the sense of life passing by, the knowledge that in a world of rich possibilities he was a pauper? Middle-aged menopause, he would mutter. No, he could not understand. He could not understand how, against all reason, all training, all Catholic ruling, he let it happen. Quite simply Fulnek needed love and thought that was what Anna offered.

The evening when it happened she'd asked, 'Alois, why are you not married?' I am, he said. She looked at a loss. I'm married to the church, he explained. 'You are married spiritually to the church,' she'd said, 'but a man should be married emotionally and physically to a woman.' She'd touched his cheek, rested a hand on his chest, but no lower. She went and closed the curtains of his sitting-room and he let her instead of telling her to leave. The evening was cool. She put a match to the fire and when the logs were blazing she took her clothes off. She folded them neatly on to a chair. It was done without frantic hurry. She'd thought it all out. 'Alois, come and lie with me in front of the fire.'

Anna Kadeckova, widow, became the mistress of Alois Fulnek, priest.

'I'm your Anicka, aren't I?'

Yes.

'I'm the one you need, the one you've been missing in your life.'

Yes. At least, he thought so.

'I can move in here. Then we'll always be together.'

But that wasn't possible.

'Priests have housekeepers,' she said. 'To the world, that's what I'll be. To ourselves, something more.'

Priests did not have twenty-eight-year-old widows to be housekeepers, especially not ones with glowing dark eyes and bodies that seemed sculpted by suffering.

She thought about this. And with the same deliberateness with which she had taken off her clothes and folded them in a neat heap, Anna set about becoming pregnant. The Pope thundered against contraception and Fulnek never asked about it but he'd assumed she took precautions. That's what women said in the confessional – not that they used contraception but that they took precautions. Well, Anna hadn't.

'The baby will be ours,' she said. Her eyes were bigger and rounder than he'd ever seen. There was triumph in them. 'Now we must get married.'

But I can't marry you. A priest can't marry.

'Then stop being a priest. Don't you love me, Lojza? Was it just my body you wanted, a bit of pleasure?'

Had she forgotten how she closed the curtains and lighted the fire and undressed in front of him?

She kept coming to see him and he let her come into the house. It was better than having her stand on the steps, banging on the door. And he let her in because he knew he was to blame. He could ask God what to do but God replied he had chosen the path of his own free will so he must walk down it. Anna's eyes grew larger and darker, and when he peeped into them he saw the beginning of her madness there. It was then that she conceived the idea of his expulsion from the church and had gone to see the bishop. If Alois had to leave the priesthood, he would be free to marry her. She truly believed he would want to.

'No,' Fulnek said.

'What do you mean?' Broucek asked.

'I mean *No*. That's clear, isn't it?'

'You mean no deal?'

Broucek took a moment to try to understand. He had offered to spend whatever it took to have the woman withdraw her allegation, to let the priest's life run as before. They hadn't discussed Fulnek's side of the bargain, though it was surely understood: to drop his meddling into the death of Bodnar and the corruption he had been investigating.

There was the gun in his pocket. That solution was possible though not right now. It was the rush hour and at the tramstop twenty metres away a dozen home-going workers waited, too many witnesses.

'Why?'

'It's not what I want,' Fulnek said. 'What will happen because of the woman will happen. Let it. What I can do is redress my moral balance sheet by exposing you.' That was pompous. Fulnek knew it. He remembered Prerova saying she didn't want a sermon and he supposed it was a hazard of being a priest for so many years. What he wanted was that the man should know, should understand. 'You are a rapist, a sadist, a torturer and a murderer. I don't know how many people you've killed but I do know one: Bodnar. You should be put in prison for the rest of your life for that alone but the evidence has gone.'

Broucek said, 'You're holding back. There's more. I can tell it. What have you got?'

'There is a letter Bodnar was writing on the day he disappeared.' Fulnek dug a sheet of paper out of his pocket and unfolded it. 'This is all that seems left. He never finished it.'

Broucek took the paper. The street lighting was too poor so he flicked his lighter and read by its flame: *The long search is over, my darling, I swear it.* His eyes skipped down the paragraph. *His name, his name, you cry. I'll be blazing it soon enough: JOSEF RADL.*

Broucek read it again, all the way through. There was no mention of him. There was not a thing to link him, Broucek, to the murder of Bodnar. There was just the accusation without proof of corruption and the name Josef Radl.

And this was why he had been searching for the priest?

Broucek began to laugh, just as he'd laughed this afternoon when he'd heard what Father Fulnek had done. He laughed until people in the queue for the tram turned to look. It was so beautiful he had to swallow the laughter that welled up inside him. Not a damn thing connected him to Bodnar's death. The priest didn't even know his name. The name he knew was Pepa's. The file in the ministry had papers signed by Pepa. If the priest took the letter to the authorities, if the file became public, if Pepa was arrested – why, there would be a hole waiting to be filled and he could move right in. It was sweet. A bubble of laughter forced its way out.

'It doesn't prove anything, does it?' Fulnek said. 'I agree. But I have something else that does.' Fulnek took a scrap of paper from his pocket. 'I picked it up this morning. It was left in my bedroom. Hasslerova was on the floor and this was on the chest of drawers.'

Broucek flicked his lighter again. He saw the note of the train times to Kutna Hora and the line that read: FOR MR ALOIS FULNEK.

'It had been left for the police to find: the corpse and this note. It was a way of giving the police my name. Not very subtle, as if I would leave my visiting card after killing someone. You added that top line. It's nicely printed except for the last letter in my name. Suddenly that's done in normal writing, quite distinctive, as if you were in a hurry to get out. And of course there'll be fingerprints. I was just leaving so I had on my coat and my gloves when I picked up the note. It'll be your fingerprints the police find because I don't think you wear gloves to strangle someone.'

Broucek let Fulnek finish before he said, 'I didn't write that.'

Fulnek frowned. 'You murdered Hasslerova.'

'I didn't write that.'

'You murdered that woman.'

'But I didn't write that. I wouldn't be so stupid.'

Fulnek had to think about this. He said, 'Someone you knew went in there. Someone obeying your orders. I don't know why. Clearing up after you. Or you forgot something.'

'They're not my fingerprints. It's not my handwriting.'

'Suppose I go to the police,' Fulnek said. 'Suppose I give them the note. I'll be in a bit of trouble . . . But those fingerprints . . .' Fulnek was still having to think things through. 'The kind of person you could call up to go to a murder scene, he would probably be a criminal. His fingerprints would be on record. Then they'd get a sample of his writing for an expert to compare. Look at that "k" with its loops.'

That bloody Karel. Broucek had told him to remove the guest book where visitors sign in, not to forge evidence.

'When the police arrest him,' Fulnek said, 'and accuse him of murder, how long will it be before he tells them he never did it, you did?'

That clumsy shit-kicker.

'The police will be interested in why he was covering up for you, what you were so desperate to hide . . .'

Broucek could picture the scene. The police would get Karel to sign his name to something and then they'd match the "k" in Karel and the "k" in Fulnek. It would take about fifteen minutes to get the whole story out of him.

Broucek gave a short 'Ha!' without any of the exuberance of his earlier laughter. He snapped his lighter and touched the corner of the paper. When the flames were licking round his fingers, he dropped the paper on the ground and watched it burn to ashes.

'I was afraid you'd do that,' Fulnek said. He got up and started to walk away.

Broucek stared after him. There was something wrong. Fulnek should have been shouting, trying to beat out the flames. 'Wait a minute. What do you mean?'

'Do you think I'd let you handle the evidence? I had a photocopy made.'

'Wait. I want to talk.'

Fulnek had joined the group on the pavement. A tram was coming up the hill and slowing. Broucek had his hand in his pocket but even if he took his gun out he'd have no clear shot as people jostled together. The tram was packed but the doors opened and people struggled to get on. There was a shout, the bell clanged, the doors closed and half a dozen people were left standing on the pavement. Broucek could no longer see Fulnek.

Fulnek, jammed between overcoated bodies, didn't know where a number 21 tram went to but that scarcely mattered. Out of a window he had a glimpse of Broucek running alongside, mouthing something, then falling back, and finally being lost to sight.

Broucek watched the tram disappear. Dear God, that oaf Karel would be bowled over the first time the police shouted at him. He had to chase the tram. His Mercedes was parked two blocks away, but if he could find a taxi . . . He looked around but Zizkov didn't run to taxis. The man who'd sat on the next bench stood just behind him.

'That tram goes all the way to the cemetery,' the man said.

So what? Broucek stared at the man. Fulnek could get off at any stop along its route.

'Goodbye,' the man said.

CHAPTER SIXTEEN

Broucek drove the length of the number 21 tram route. He slowed to a crawl at each stop as if Fulnek might have got off and be waiting for him. People queuing for trams stared at the Mercedes. A girl in a very short skirt smiled at him. The skirt stopped high up on her legs, just below her buttocks, about a hand's reach below her buttocks. A miniskirt in weather like this. The things a girl would do to get a man.

He thought of the woman who'd got pregnant so she could trap Fulnek. Why did she want Fulnek? What was special about him, apart from being a priest? And he wouldn't be that much longer. He'd said 'No' to Broucek. Just that. No.

Broucek still found it hard to take in.

No. No deal.

He left the car in the service area beside a concrete apartment block, a modern ruin already crumbling, and went to a café for a drink. He would have to speak to Pepa.

'Where's your telephone?'

'The public telephone is—'

'Yours. Where is it?'

The barman looked at him, reached under the counter and brought out the instrument. It had been dropped at some time, the mouthpiece cracked and now held together with sticking plaster. God, everything was falling apart.

'There's some spilt beer down there needs mopping up,' Broucek said.

'What?'

'Leave me alone. It's a private call.'

When he got through to Pepa, Broucek said, 'I'm looking for the priest.'

'You found him and you lost him.'

'I'm looking for him again.'

'I'm told you talked together and he went off and you let him go. You're finished.'

'No, I'll find him again. It'll just take a little more time and then he'll see sense.'

'I said you were finished. You were never like this. You never talked about making a priest see sense. You'd have got rid of him. End of the problem. And the woman, got rid of her. Even the English banker if it was necessary. Everybody walks away from you and you let them.'

Czechoslovakia was different now. Broucek was going to say this but the phone had gone dead.

He drove back and parked outside Prerova's apartment. Looking up he saw her windows were still dark. He walked the two blocks to the small garden where he'd talked with Fulnek.

It was the tone of Pepa's voice he didn't like. He didn't like the way he'd said, 'You're finished.' Pepa didn't understand about the new Czechoslovakia. He had men and he could give orders and it made Broucek uneasy. But suppose the police were to call on Pepa, start questioning him about the Sekcov project, lock him away pending further investigation . . .

Broucek looked for the love letter that Bodnar had been writing. That plus an anonymous note saying to look at a certain file in the Ministry of Trade should be enough. He hadn't seen Fulnek put the letter back in his pocket. In fact he was certain it had been left lying on the bench. Now it was gone.

He left the Mercedes in the taxi rank and ignoring the shouts of the drivers went into the station. He found the telephones but had to look up the number.

'Are you receiving me well?'

There was a pause so long he almost hung up.

'I hear you're in trouble.'

'Petr, we all have trouble from time to time. I need a name from you.'

'Pepa is not happy.'

'Then don't tell him I called.'

'It's serious.'

'Petr, I need the name and, this time of day, I guess the home telephone number of someone helpful in the Ministry of Justice. It's got to be someone with good police connections and access to the fingerprint archives. I need someone's prints removing.'

There was another pause. 'I'll need to ask Pepa.'

'Ask Pepa? Why, for God's sake?'

'Because perhaps Pepa doesn't want anybody to help you any more.'

Broucek put the phone down. Forget it.

The station had been rebuilt with a central concourse

bigger than any cathedral. Lights hung down from a
dark void and it looked as if the whole of the ceiling had
been lifted off or blown away.

Karel's fingerprints were on file not because of any
criminal past but because the authorities, in their paranoia, had fingerprinted the entire Finance Ministry. If
the priest handed in that note, if the police checked the
fingerprint archive, if Karel was asked why he'd been in
that room and had he done the murder . . . But did it
matter? If Karel gave the police his name, Broucek
would deny it. It would be his word against Karel's, and
Karel's prints were the ones in the room.

He felt drained. He'd been running about for days.
The Hotel Esplanade was just down the road and they
stocked Johnnie Walker Black Label.

Three hours later he got behind the wheel of his
Mercedes and headed down into Wenceslas Square. On
the top of the buildings you could still see the metal
framework where revolutionary posters had been displayed. There'd been a big revolving red star, but that had
come tumbling down. Wenceslas Square was really a
short boulevard with the bottom end barred to traffic. He
turned west and never questioned the impulse that made
him drive that way. He crossed the river and turned off
Ujeho into the alley where cobbles thumped his tyres.
The alley narrowed and he stopped the car and looked
ahead to the building where Olga lived, perhaps with a
blind lover or perhaps with a man who howled at the
moon or perhaps on her own. He forgot which was her
window, if he ever knew. Somewhere up there.

Broucek left the comfort of his car and stood under

the lamp. He bent backwards, raised his head towards the lamp and howled like a wolf. He took a deep breath and howled again, longer. Nobody was curious about a wolf howling in central Prague, nobody peered out except from the window at the top. A head appeared and Broucek howled again.

'Stay there,' Olga said. 'I'm coming down.'

It had begun to snow, not big lazy flakes but hard little pellets. Broucek stood in the entrance to the building, looking out, listening. When Olga came up to him he said, 'I never heard snow make a noise before.'

Olga listened. The sound was like grains of sand sifting. 'It's Polish snow,' she said, 'always grumbling about something.'

She wore black: black leather jacket, black jeans, black plastic boots, black headscarf.

'You're different tonight, all in black.'

'In case I have to jump out and walk,' she said. 'I'll show up against the snow.'

She moved over to the car and ran a hand along the bonnet, her head on one side.

'Have you ever driven a Mercedes?' he asked.

'No.'

'Do you want to drive us?'

'The way you are, I think I'd better.'

She reversed out of the alley and started slowly down the main road.

'Which is the button for the radio, Tonda?'

'How do you know my name?'

'You told me yesterday.'

Was it yesterday? He felt exhausted.

'The radio, Tonda.'

'There.'

'What kind of music do you like, Tonda?'

She wore no make-up round her eyes tonight. They were almond-shaped, almost oriental. Someone took a sword, he thought, and made two quick slashes. Even when she was driving and facing forward he had the feeling she was watching him out of the corner of a sword-slash.

'Tonda . . . music.'

'Anything. Whatever you like.'

'You mightn't like it, Tonda. You like Heavy Metal, music like that? No, you don't understand. A really big sound. There's Heavy Metal, then there's Brutal Metal, but best of all there's Bulldozer Metal. That is Heavy Metal with balls.'

Shit, things were going on that he no longer understood. Prague wasn't Prague any more. People played at being Civil War soldiers. Girls painted their faces like savages. You could buy Russian uniforms, Russian guns, Russian toilet seats. Corpses began talking of the past. Mozart turned into Heavy Metal with balls. He shook his head.

'Can't take it. Why don't you have a little nap, Tonda?'

'Where are you driving?'

'Where do you want to go?'

Broucek stared at her profile, the pert nose, the wide mouth, the eyes with corners like sword-slashes. He'd had the idea while he'd been drinking whisky at the Esplanade, it just came as a flash. Now, in the car with Olga, the idea was no longer a whimsy, it was firmer, made flesh.

'Budapest, maybe. I've got friends there.'

'Are you joking?'

'I'm getting out,' Broucek said. 'Are you coming with me?'

'Am I what?'

'I have to leave Prague. I feel cold here, cold. Looking at you at the wheel, dressed all in black, gives me an idea. You're my chauffeur. We could even get you a cap.'

'I'm not wearing any bloody cap. I don't know, maybe I'd wear one of those Soviet officers' caps.'

'It would have to be black with a little rim.'

'You're crazy.'

Not crazy. He'd had the thought and it made sense. He'd leave the country and be out of Pepa's reach. He'd take Olga with him and then contact Prerova: don't cause any trouble, don't let the priest cause any trouble, because now your daughter is together with me. Olga could telephone Prerova: Mama, I'm happy, don't spoil it. Crazy? It was perfect.

'Jesus, scary,' Olga whispered. 'Light me a cigarette.' She drew hard on it and the glowing tip lit up her mouth and nose. 'Tonda, Tonda, Tonda.'

She's thinking about it, Broucek thought. Good.

'Hey,' Olga said, 'I don't think I want to go to Budapest.'

'Well, Vienna. Maybe Milan.'

'Getting better. When you reach California let me know.'

'Got to go home first and pick up some stuff.'

'Does the Mercedes know the way or are you going to tell me?'

*

They drove up U Vltavy and turned left into a cobbled road with white globes of lighting. There were chalets on both sides, weekend *chatas* with cherry and plum trees and vegetable gardens. The houses thinned, the lighting and the cobbles gave out, the road narrowed to a track between a bank and a bramble hedge.

'Tonda, what happens when we meet another car?'

'He has to back up.'

'You live in the country?'

'This is a shortcut.'

The track joined a tarred road and passed through great fruit orchards. Abruptly the orchards stopped and a suburb of bungalows began. There were small houses with winter-bare gardens. Olga drove slowly, peering out.

'What do people want to live here for?'

'There's no pollution.'

She laughed. 'That's the first joke you've made.'

'I'm serious.'

'I was afraid you were. It's all dark. They're all asleep. Shall I find some Bulldozer Metal and shake them up?'

'It gets better.'

They dipped over the brow of a hill and got a view down to Prague. At once the houses grew second storeys, even third storeys for the maids. The gardens boasted large trees, rusting children's swings and swimming pools under winter wraps.

'There,' Broucek said. 'Turn in by those screens where they're supposed to be doing something to the drains.'

Were they still there? The headlights swept across

the screens and then it was dark again. Broucek looked
back and was no wiser.

Olga looked round the living-room, the dining-room,
the kitchen and saw there were still more doors and
gave up.

'You live here alone? No Mrs Tonda locked up? No
French maids with feather dusters?'

'I don't like to feel cramped. What do you want to
drink?'

'I don't know.'

'Anything,' Broucek said.

'Dragon's Breath.'

Broucek was breaking the seal on a new bottle of
Johnnie Walker Black Label. He looked at her. 'What's
that?'

'The man says anything . . . I'll have what you're
having. What's through there?'

'My study.'

'Your study? What do you study?'

She opened the door. The light on the telephone
was flashing.

'Someone's left you a message.'

Broucek passed her in the doorway and stood by the
desk. He stared at the telephone while the little light
winked at him. He could think of no one he wanted to
listen to, no message he wanted to hear. He had to get
out of Prague. He had no future here. He'd leave Prague
to the tourists and the gulls and the new politicians
and Pepa. And if anyone came to ask Pepa questions
about the Sekcov project and all the other foreign currency contracts and bank accounts in Zurich and the

Caymans and Gibraltar and about the death of Bodnar and then went on to the deaths of Hosnedl and Rubin and Zoul and Stur and Svabinsky and Zizka and the four Romanians and Krcin and Jakubickova and her two daughters and Jurkovic and Holub and Steinhart and a few more – well, Pepa would make some arrangement. He'd telephone one of the new ministers. 'Are you receiving me well?' He knew secrets about some of the new democratic ministers too.

'Aren't you going to listen to your message?'

'I think not,' Broucek said. 'No.'

'When are you leaving to go to Budapest or Vienna or Milan?'

'Tomorrow.'

'Well, then.'

'Where are you going?'

Olga looked back over her shoulder, glancing at him from the sword-slash corner of one eye.

'Upstairs,' she said. 'Bring the whisky if you like.'

'So,' she said, 'here we are. This was always going to happen, wasn't it?' She'd kicked her boots off against the wall and thrown her leather jacket on to a chair. Now she perched on the edge of the bed in black jeans and shirt, with the scarf tied loosely around her neck. 'A man like you with a Mercedes. Just a little while ago only rich communist bastards had Mercedes. Now any rich bastard can drive round in one.'

'You enjoyed it,' Broucek said.

'Okay.'

'Come with me tomorrow and you can drive all the way.'

'Budapest.'

'We can go south. Down through France to Spain.'

'Getting warm.'

'Morocco, if you like.'

'I like.' She walked to the window. 'Have you got curious neighbours? Can they see in, hear things?'

'There's nothing out that side.'

'Well,' she said, 'there's Prague. You've a good view from the window when you're tired of playing games.' She peered down. 'Oops, there's nothing below.'

'The house is built at the top of a cliff.'

Olga turned away from the window. 'Tonda,' she said, 'frankly I think you're a bit creepy. You know nothing about me and yet you want to go driving to the moon with me. Don't you even want to see what I look like?'

Broucek sat on the bed with the whisky bottle in one hand and a glass in the other while she stood in the middle of the room. He took a sip of whisky and held it in his mouth, savouring its taste and the prickle the alcohol made on his tongue. Leaving Prague had a very positive side. She'd be his chauffeur, his protection against Prerova and the priest, and more.

Olga unbuttoned her shirt and dropped it on the floor. She unzipped her jeans and wriggled to free her body from them, stepped out of one leg and then the other. Her bra and knickers were black too. She cocked a hip at him.

'The show's all right so far?'

She could see the beginning of a shine to Broucek's forehead. It was the excitement in him or else all the whisky he had drunk. She put her hands behind her back, unhooked her bra and held it up in the air a moment like a trophy before letting it fall. She slipped both hands inside her knickers, paused to give Broucek a grin, then pushed them down, bending over as she stepped out of them. She tossed them at Broucek.

'There,' she said. She put one hand on her hip, the other behind her head, and turned round in a full circle. 'Not bad, huh. What do you think?'

Broucek swallowed. Was she like her mother? He seemed to remember full breasts, wide hips and slim firm legs. Was that Prerova or another woman or all women in one? He said, 'Come here.'

She walked to the bed. He put down the bottle and glass and tried to take hold of her.

'Tsk, tsk,' Olga said. 'We should be on equal terms. Take your clothes off. I'll help you.'

It took a little while. Broucek let her do it all, watching her unbutton, untie, unzip, unclothe him. She said, 'You look quite perky. The whisky hasn't affected that.'

Broucek reached for a breast but she took a step back. She smiled. 'We have a special relationship, don't you feel?'

'If you don't come here . . .' Broucek started to get off the bed.

'Don't rush it,' Olga said. 'You're like the boys at school, always eager, desperate. It's better to build up to it.'

He said, 'You've had a lot of men?'

'But you're special. I think, for you, there should be something special, something different.'

Blondie, a rosebud. He said, 'Tell me.'

'You're a powerful man,' Olga said. 'You dominate,

give orders. You have it all your own way with a woman, do this, do that. It's too easy for you. But suppose we turn it about – that would be new. Now you would be in my power. Do this. Do that. Let me have my way with you. What will I do? What demands will I make? Will you be able to meet my needs? Does that excite you, Tonda? Yes, I think it does.'

'What do you want to do?'

She'd ransacked his closet, tossing things out.

She'd said, 'We're not having any rubbish, nothing that came from Kotva or Maj. Christian Dior, that's good. Got to be silk, I feel, silken knots. Pierre Cardin – oh, Tonda, I am surprised. Hermès, a woman's scarf, who was she? It'll do.'

Now he was stretched naked on the bed, the ties and the Hermès scarf bound round his wrists and ankles and tied to the brass rails at the foot and the head of the bed.

'That'll do,' Olga said. 'In fact I'd say it was perfect. Don't you find your position intriguing? Piquant? You can still move your body, can you? Yes.'

'Come here,' Broucek said. 'Lie on top of me.'

'Tonda,' she said, 'you've forgotten. I'm the one who gives the orders now. You are my slave. Or something.'

She perched on the edge of the bed. Broucek raised his head as far as he could, his mouth almost reaching a nipple. She bent a little towards him before pulling back.

'Bitch.'

'Tonda, you have to get it into your head. It's me who is in charge. Do you want a drink?'

'How can I hold a glass?'

She picked up the bottle. 'Open your mouth.' She poured whisky in his mouth. He swallowed, gagged on the whisky, spluttering. She poured and poured, over his face, over his chest, over his stomach. The last drops she shook into his navel.

'Imagine – if you were a lizard with a long tongue, you could reach down and drink out of your belly button hole.'

'You're crazy. Why did you do that? The bed will stink for weeks.'

'But you won't be here to smell it.'

He would be in Budapest or Spain or Morocco. Something in her tone started him thinking. She had outlandish ideas. The blind man who was her lover, the other lover who howled because she covered a street-lamp, the lizard. 'This is stupid. Untie me.'

'Hmmm.' She made a face, pretending to consider. 'Tonda, I like you like that. In fact, I wouldn't have you any other way.'

'Where are you going?'

'Downstairs this time.'

'Why? Why are you leaving?'

'I'll be back. You'll see.'

'I'm not going to be tied up any more. I'm not some bloody chicken trussed for market.'

Olga came back from the doorway but it wasn't to untie him. She slapped his cheek. It wasn't hard but it shocked Broucek. When he looked in her face it had changed. The mocking expression had gone and her eyes were direct and hard.

'Do you want to know why you are tied up? Do you? This morning I had a cup of coffee, a glass of fire water and a heart-to-heart with my mother. Finally, finally. The first time I met you I thought I'd walked in on a lovers' quarrel. The atmosphere had built up and it could have ended in something physical. Punching and kicking or tearing each other apart in bed, either way. No, she said, the physical part was a long time ago, nineteen sixty-eight, when you raped her. Rape? I couldn't take it in. Rape? Really rape? She told me about it, told me enough anyhow, explained how you gave her that scar that runs down under her tit. And she told me another thing. Pay attention, Tonda, this is important. She told me it's possible you are my father. She simply does not know. It could be Venca, it could be you. What do you say to that, Tonda? Hello, your little fellow has gone to sleep. He's shrivelled right up and is trying to hide in there. Think about that while I'm gone.'

Broucek was straining at the knots when she came back, twisting and tugging. They were holding though the knot round his left wrist had slipped a little. It would last long enough. Broucek went rigid.

'Jesus, what's that?'

'Like it?' Olga asked. 'Maybe you've forgotten what she looked like.'

A gash went down her chest and curved under her right breast.

'Strawberry jam,' she said. 'Do you want to lick it off?'

Two dabs of jam made eyes above a nipple which could have been a button nose. Her breast was changed into a face, grinning at him.

Broucek's eyes slipped down from her breast to the hand which held a kitchen knife.

'You think I'm going to kill you,' she said, 'and there's not a thing you can do about it. You're wondering how you could have been so stupid to have got yourself tied up. I thought of other ways. I wanted revenge for my mother and for Venca and this seemed perfect.' She tested the blade with her thumb. 'This isn't sharp enough so I'll use one of your razorblades.'

When she came back from the bathroom the knot on his left wrist was loosened some more. Perhaps silk had been a mistake, too slippery.

'Damn Christian Dior.' She wound the ends of the tie round his wrist and did another knot. 'What do you think, Tonda? Am I going to stab you in the chest or cut your throat? Watch.' She held the razorblade between thumb and forefinger and made one flowing stroke down his chest and curving under his right nipple. Blood spurted and Broucek arched his back and threw himself to one side as far as he could. 'You're a fool. You made it worse.' In several places the blood made trickles down his skin. Then with the razorblade she made a cut on her own forearm and cut it deeper a second time to make the blood flow. 'We don't know if you are my papa, do we? But I decided we ought to share our blood.' She rubbed her arm against his chest, smearing her blood down the length of the razor-slash she'd made. She rubbed and rubbed while Broucek struggled, not understanding what she meant or what the hell was going on. 'Now you are my blood father. There, I think that'll do. That's over, Tonda. Now it's just a question of time.'

*

She'd washed the jam and the blood off her body and got dressed. She stood looking down at Broucek.

'You don't speak much, Tonda. Don't you say anything to your ladies? Don't you whisper sweet words or dirty words? I don't imagine you'd be much fun in bed. You'd only be thinking of yourself. Well, I'm leaving you now.'

'Tied to the bed?'

'You'll get loose. Or your cleaning woman will find you. I'll leave a note. When you read it you may decide you can't face waiting for the inevitable. The future is up to you. You'll have a choice, like you gave my mother a choice once.'

She took a pen from his jacket and used the back of a bill from a restaurant. She wrote a few words, thought of signing her name and decided against it. She used the kitchen knife to spear the note to the bedside table.

'That's it, Tonda. I was special, wasn't I, different from your usual ladies. You'll remember this night for the rest of your life. So . . . goodbye. I'm going to borrow your nice Mercedes to get home. You won't be needing it.'

Broucek got one leg free without much fuss. He tugged and tugged and unexpectedly his foot popped through the Hermès scarf. He was using that foot to try to push down the tie that bound the other foot to the rail. When he had both legs free he'd be able to swing his body off the bed and maybe wrench a wrist out of the tourniquet Olga had made. That's when he heard the footsteps down below.

She'd come back. She'd forgotten something. She wanted to do some more cutting, more blood mixing. What had that been for? The thoughts vanished when he heard two voices, male. They climbed the stairs and came into his bedroom. They both carried pistols, just in case. The last time Broucek had seen them they'd been behind the screens erected in the road. They were Pepa's sewage workers in the same way Pepa had gardeners.

'He's been having a party,' one of them said.

'You should have invited us, Mr Broucek,' the other said.

'What do you want?' Broucek asked. He was naked, smeared with blood, reeking of whisky, tied by both wrists and one ankle. No dignity or authority was possible.

'What do we want? Nothing. We're not taking anything. We're here from Pepa – don't think it's anything personal to us. You see, what Pepa says is you've been running round like a headless chicken and it's got to stop.'

'Mirek, did he really say "headless chicken"?' his companion asked.

'God's truth. So he sent us to stop it. He gave us some discretion but he said when we do the job to make it look like you did it yourself.'

'How does a chicken cut off its own head?'

'Jarda, this is no time for jokes.'

'I want to speak to Pepa,' Broucek said. 'I can clear this mess up.'

'Mess is right,' Jarda said. 'Why did she do this?'

'Then in a day or two,' Mirek went on, 'there'll be a

whisper – funny the way whispers start and spread – that you jumped because all the things you did a long time ago were bubbling up.'

'Just a minute,' Jarda said. He pulled out the knife and held the note up for Mirek to read. 'Nice girlfriend you had, Mr Broucek. Perhaps we needn't bother.'

'She did that on purpose? That's a really dirty trick to play.'

'There ought to be a law against it.'

'But I don't think Pepa wants to wait round for Mr Broucek to die. It could be years and Pepa's not that young himself.'

'Old man in a hurry,' Jarda said.

He went to the window and opened it. Mirek used the kitchen knife to cut through the ties that bound Broucek. When Broucek began struggling, he delivered a sharp chop to the back of his neck at the base of his skull. Weak in his limbs and groggy in his head, the last thing Broucek saw was Olga's note on the table: WELCOME TO THE WORLD OF AIDS. NOW WHAT ARE YOU GOING TO DO?

Chapter Seventeen

It was the shouts outside that woke Olga. Dagmar didn't stir. She could give him the elbow and say, 'Dasa, see what it's about.' But why disturb him? Sleeping was Dagmar's talent: it was easy and he enjoyed it. He worked late at the Makaskar, lighting the candles, choosing the music tapes and washing dishes and he needed to sleep late.

She heard a man shouting, 'It's a disgrace. This would never have happened before.'

There was shouting from time to time in the building and sometimes it spilled outside. Olga had a theory that old buildings made people shout; men and women had lived too close too long and the old bricks and stones had absorbed every grunt and swear word and recrimination and betrayal until the walls could take no more and everything erupted in cries and yells and flung glasses. Then the walls felt better except where the glasses had smashed.

Well, that was her theory.

'It's not mine.'

'I'll call the police unless it's moved.'

'Tell me why I should move something that's not mine.' She recognised Zupky's voice. He lived on the floor below her. 'Tell me how I can move it since I don't have a key.'

Oh-oh. Olga got up and draped the bedspread round her shoulders against the cold. Opening the window and looking down she saw that Tonda's Mercedes had a companion. Another Mercedes was nose to nose with it. They seemed good friends, almost kissing. But the owner was unhappy. He'd driven out of the fancy apartment block and met Tonda's Mercedes jammed in the alley.

'Hello,' Olga called out.

The two men looked up.

'Is this yours? I'm going to call the police and have it taken away.'

'Please, don't do that. I'll come down and move it. Give me two minutes to get dressed.' Olga pulled the bedspread and nightdress down to give a peep of bare shoulder. There, that should hold him for a couple of minutes. The last thing she wanted was the police coming and getting nosy about Tonda's Mercedes. Or Mr Broucek, as she knew from the insurance document in the glove box. Why have you got Broucek's car? Perhaps we should go over and check everything is all right because he doesn't answer the telephone. She'd have to leave the car somewhere else, not outside her own flat.

'Thank you for waiting,' she said when she got outside. 'Sweet of you.'

He wasn't sweet, he had a sour face. One of Them, the old guard. She could see his brain turning over: Why was she living in that crumbling building when she had a Mercedes? How old was she? Twenty-two?

How could she afford it? It was so predictable. It was the way They thought.

He began, 'Is the car yours?'

Olga said, 'I borrowed it from this rich bastard I know.'

She got in the Mercedes and reversed out of the alley. She'd have to get rid of it but it would be fun to show it to her mother, maybe take her for a drive in it while she told her what had happened last night. She crossed the river and headed towards Žizkov. Thieves and gypsies. She should never have left.

She turned on the radio. It was too early in the day to take Bulldozer Metal but she'd find something. There was pushbutton tuning and every bloody station had news. In the morning people liked to hear about bombs and famines and plane crashes and stock market crashes. Oil was up. She'd hardly be able to afford to fill the Mercedes. The Slovaks were threatening to break away and do their own thing. Some threat. Perhaps Zupky would have to go back to Bratislava. She hoped so because Zupky cooked a lot of stinking cabbage. She heard that the Afghans were killing each other, the Ethiopians were killing each other, the Liberians, the Angolans, the Cambodians, the Salvadoreans, the Peruvians – dead bodies were piling up everywhere. It hardly seemed important to report the one dead body that had been found, apparently fallen twenty-five metres from a window in Troja. She couldn't believe her ears, but there it was. Name of Broucek. There were suspicious circumstances. Police were investigating and for the moment withholding further details.

'Tonda, shit,' she whispered. 'Jesus.'

She pulled over to the kerb and braked abruptly, to the anguish of the drivers behind. She sat staring through the windscreen, gripping the wheel tightly to control the shakes in her arms.

It was too soon. She hadn't prepared herself, got her reaction ready, known how to deal with it. She'd written the note, told him he'd got AIDS, but that was the kind of shock that took time to take hold. Disbelief, panic, terror. She didn't know but she imagined it would take days to prey on him, maybe weeks. Even then she'd had no certain idea how he would react.

Twenty-five metres. Jesus.

She couldn't face her mother now but she'd telephone. His name was Broucek, mama. I wanted to put a scare into him and I did. Jesus, I did.

A policeman was walking towards her. She was sitting in Broucek's car, her fingerprints were in his house, her blood on his body. She had been insane, thinking of nothing except what her mother had finally told her. She moved the Mercedes out into the traffic again and in the mirror saw the policeman turn to stare.

Sexy woman driving a sexy car, she told herself. That's all.

Fulnek unlocked the door inset into the gate and walked inside. To him it had been a seminary, to others a place of interrogation, to Bodnar a place of execution. The buildings looked at peace now. What would become of it? Did the church have plans to claim it back? Would it be turned into a hotel, a retirement home?

He found a broom in the kitchen and went to the chapel to sweep it out. He started at the back and went methodically forward, sweeping up broken wood, cigarette ends, matchboxes, pigeon droppings, leaves, chewing-gum wrappers, dried human shit and smeared paper from the confessional stalls, pages torn from magazines, plum stones and beer bottle tops. He wanted to do something physical. He wanted to clean up some of the mess in the world.

This afternoon he would take the bus from Kutna Hora to Brno and listen to the official ending of his vocation. Would Anna be there, tearful, smiling, hysterical, silent, accusing? He would have to face that.

Tomorrow he would go to the police, explain about Hasslerova, try to convince them, show them the note of the train times. He didn't know about fingerprints. It was a possibility. He'd show them Bodnar's last letter. It was proof of nothing but it did give a name.

There were two days he had to endure. He remembered Bodnarova telling the future from her Tarot pack. She'd turned over the Eight of Swords. Problems and difficulties. He saw plenty of those ahead. But she'd said – if you believed that nonsense – that better times were already coming. Fulnek didn't see that. Perhaps it was like sitting in an autumn storm and seeing the barometer rise and saying tomorrow would be fine.

Pushing the pile of rubbish out through the chapel door he paused. A car was coming up the hill. It stopped outside the wall and he heard the slam of a door. Oh Lord, he prayed, not Them again.

It was Olga who passed through the gate. She

stopped, peering round the buildings, and saw Fulnek standing by the chapel.

'*Ahoj.*'

He watched her walk towards him. She was a good-looking young woman and he could see Prerova in her and glimpsed something of what had driven Bodnar to love her.

'Did you know I'd be here?' Fulnek asked.

'My mother told me. She said she'd never given the old priest back his key and this morning you asked for it.'

Fulnek spread his arms and she came into them. He gave her a hug, a priestly hug, a hug for her and her mother.

'Call it a pilgrimage,' Fulnek said. 'I started here as a priest and I shall end here. This afternoon – did she tell you?'

'Yes.'

'This afternoon is just for bureaucrats.'

Olga went inside the chapel and inspected the empty space. 'Well, as they say, it's got possibilities.'

'That's what life is, possibilities. We choose. We have to live with our choice.' Stop, he told himself, no sermons.

She wandered off to inspect graffiti on the walls, licking a finger to see if it would rub off. She turned round. He was staring at the roof of the chapel and then all round. What was going to happen to him, the end of this period of his life? He'd been sleeping in her mother's apartment, in the room which had once been her own. And now?

She took a breath and said, 'I was hoping I would still find you here. You see, I want to confess.'

His attention came back to her.

'I mean, you are still a priest.'

'I didn't know you were a churchgoer. Your mother isn't.'

'I don't go to church.'

'I am – still, as you say – a priest. But if you are not a practising Catholic . . .' He stopped. He was turning into a bureaucrat himself. 'Of course. When one is troubled, one needs to talk. It may be called confession, but leaving aside the religious aspect it is sharing a burden. You cannot make an act of perfect contrition but what does that matter? God hears what you are trying to say.'

They crossed the chapel to the confessional stalls. Fulnek sat and Olga had to kneel with the grille between them.

'It smells terrible,' Olga said.

'It used to be worse. You have asked to make a confession in the presence of a priest and of God and I hope you understand it must be full and honest and in the expectation the sin will not be repeated. For many people that pledge is nothing more than a ritual and they go away in the knowledge that they will repeat the sin. The circumstance of your coming here is unusual, so unusual that I feel I should stress that confessing is more than being sorry, it is to commit yourself to a better way.'

'I feel so bloody shaken, do you see?'

'Is it a sin of the flesh you wish to confess?'

Was it? Olga thought of the razorblade slicing the skin of Broucek, thought of smearing her blood with his. That was of the flesh, but it wasn't that. She thought of his body lying twenty-five metres below the bedroom window. But even that physical outcome wasn't on her mind.

She said, 'No.'

Fulnek said, 'In that case I assume it is a sin of the spirit you wish to confess.'

A sin of the spirit? She didn't know. All she knew was she had done it. But she said, 'Yes.'

She closed her eyes and saw Broucek tied to the bed and the blood on his chest.

'Tell me,' Fulnek said.

Speared into the table beside the bed was the note she had written.

'You see, I lied to him . . .'

She laid her cheek against the grille and told him. She had driven a man to suicide and the reality of that horrified her. 'Jesus,' she whispered through the grille, 'twenty-five metres. How long does it take to hit the ground? What goes through your mind?' And again the awed 'Jesus', not a prayer. She had wanted revenge for her mother's rape, wanted to cause him anguish and suffering. This had overwhelmed her.

Fulnek said, 'So he's finally dead?'

'Haven't you been listening? He jumped out of the window. Surely any rational man would go to hospital and have the tests to see if he'd really caught AIDS.'

'Tell me about it.'

She was quiet and it seemed for a while she wouldn't tell him.

'You must,' Fulnek said, 'even if it is very bad.'

'For him it was going to be a new sexual kick,' Olga

began. She paused, got up her courage and then told it as it happened. She was twenty-two years old, a woman in body, but a child who could play a practical joke that had spun out of control.

'What you did was cruel, it was wrong. It had terrible consequences that cannot be undone. It is something you will have to live with.' Fulnek understood she needed the disapproval first, the comfort second. 'We all carry the burden of our wrongdoing. Yes . . .' His thoughts flashed to Anna and this afternoon's bureaucratic judgement. 'Yes, we all do. However, God knows the provocation you felt. God understands you wished to punish Radl for the extreme evil—'

'Hold on a minute. Radl? Who's this Radl?' Olga got off her knees and squatted instead on the floor. 'His name was Broucek but I called him Tonda.'

The letter in Fulnek's pocket gave the name Josef Radl. 'Are you positive?'

'Of course I'm bloody positive. You don't think I've done the wrong . . . Look, Broucek is the name of the man who raped my mother, murdered Venca and now has fallen out of a Prague window. That's not some mistaken identity. My mother saw him, knew him. She was in no doubt at all. Raped her on the floor, cut her up, ruined her career, twisted her life. He was a bastard and I wanted to pay him back for the shitty way he behaved.'

'It's just I had the wrong name,' Fulnek said. 'I don't doubt you had the right person.'

'Well, that's a relief.'

Somehow, talking about it, rehearsing Broucek's evil, the confusion over names, brought about a change in

Olga. Her feelings of remorse for the lie grew less, her enthusiasm for life returned.

She said, 'I've got to get back to Prague and see my mother. Oh God, I've got to ditch the car too just when I'm getting used to it. Maybe sell it. Petr knows some Germans . . .' She kissed Fulnek on both cheeks. 'Ciao. I think I shall see you again, perhaps.'

Perhaps.

Fulnek left the chapel and climbed upstairs to look one last time at the room where he had prayed and studied. He perched on the narrow bed where he had tussled with the devil until sleep released him. He looked at the dusty outline where the cross had been nailed to the wall. He looked at the closet where he had hidden with Prerova pressed close against him.

Yes, perhaps.

It was the barking of dogs that took him into the corridor to open a window and peer down. A pair of red setters raced in circles, chasing each other and their own tails. They showed the surplus energy of dogs or children who have been locked up. Catching sight of Fulnek at the window they stopped running and barked at him. Their owner stood by the entrance gate. Directed by the dogs he walked forward until he stood under the window.

'They said in the village that you hadn't left. They said a very pretty girl came in a large car but even she hadn't been able to persuade you to go with her.' The man smiled up at him. 'You're Father Fulnek, I'm told. At my age I find shouting tires me. If you were to come outside we could talk in normal tones.'

'And you are . . .?'

'Don't you know? My name is Radl, though people call me Pepa.'

This was the day for visitors to the former seminary. For the second time in an hour Fulnek found his thoughts in disarray. Radl here? How did he know to come? He answered himself: In the same way Broucek knew that Prerova and I had been here – a village informer. The next question was impossible to answer: Why has Radl come?

Radl started the moment Fulnek appeared. It was as if his voice was a force that could knock Fulnek off-balance, shooting out statements, firing direct questions. Then, in silence, waiting for Fulnek's response.

'The dogs have been shut up in the car, and before that shut up at home. I should exercise them more because that means I get more exercise. Where does youth get its energy from? What happens that we lose it? Though I will say you have been showing commendable energy. Hello, how are you doing? Well met.'

To his surprise Fulnek found himself shaking hands with Radl.

'You came to see me,' Fulnek said.

Radl waited to see what question Fulnek would ask. 'Why?'

'You've already answered that: to see you.'

'But why?'

'If our police force showed half the zeal you have, no crime would go undetected. So I was curious to see what kind of person you were. In fact I do know some things about you. I know, for instance, that you have problems with your superiors, that someone has been making unsubstantiated accusations against you. What do you propose to do about this woman?'

'Nothing.'

'Wise. The rights and wrongs of the matter have nothing to do with it. She sounds a hellcat and in her rage she will kick and scratch and bite and you would suffer terrible wounds. Shall we see where they've got to?'

The dogs had disappeared into the chapel. Turning to follow after them, Fulnek caught sight of two men near the gate. They simply stood and waited. Two of Them, Fulnek understood, two of the old watchers. There was sudden barking from the chapel and sounds like pistol shots. Hurrying to the chapel door they saw the dogs alternately running and pawing at the walls while pigeons wheeled above, clapping their wings. At the sight of Radl and Fulnek the pigeons flew out of one of the broken windows.

'Despite hundreds of generations of domestic life with men,' Radl said, 'dogs have never lost their hunting instinct. Nor have men, come to that. Would that explain your pursuit of Broucek, would you say?'

The name was slipped in without any fanfare but Fulnek had the impression that antennae were twitching in the air, seeking the slightest quiver. Once more he faced the question: why had he gone in search of Bodnar's killer? Was it for an ideal of justice? Because of a more personal feeling towards Prerova? To stop his mind brooding in this gap while his fate was decided? Unable to decide, he deflected the question.

'Actually it was you I thought I was after.'

This drew a reaction. Radl wheeled and directed an unflinching stare at him. 'Explain.'

'The reporter Bodnar had been inspecting some great financial scandal. This happened a long time ago but the truth is only now coming out. Because of his prying he was killed. Just before he was abducted he wrote a letter, half a letter, giving your name.'

'Ah, you mean this.'

Radl produced the photocopy which Fulnek had made.

'You left it on a bench and it was brought to me. Do you still have the original? Do you ponder over it at night?'

Radl had turned aside as if his attention was caught by the graffiti but he kept very still waiting for the reply.

'I destroyed it this morning when I heard the news.'

God would forgive the lie. God would understand.

Radl took a moment, mulling over this news, and went on, 'Bodnar was not as good an investigator as he thought. It turns out Broucek was at the heart of the corruption, whatever it was. Has your detective work uncovered that?'

'No.'

'Shame. I was curious to know what it was. Lucrative, certainly. You haven't been to Broucek's house?'

'No.'

'He lived in some style. Just himself, apart from fleeting partners, in a house big enough for a dozen. Expensive car, expensive taste in clothes and restaurants.'

'You knew him well.'

'At one time we had a professional relationship. But

I would not have expected him to do what he did, so obviously I didn't know him well at all. You, whom I have only just met, I feel I know better. I would say you were a romantic, which is an uncomfortable position for a priest. I would also say you are determined, obstinate even, a fighter. These are admirable qualities in anyone, Father Fulnek, unless taken to excess.'

Radl walked away a little, inspecting the confessional stalls and a mural, a recent one, a pornographic fantasy. He was giving Fulnek some moments on his own to reflect. I am being warned, Fulnek told himself, just a hint, nothing overt.

'What sort of person would do a drawing like that?' Radl asked.

'Someone like Broucek.'

'Broucek had more accurate knowledge of female anatomy. Nor would he have gone in for this random destruction. Destroy for a purpose is how I would judge him. Certainly he was flawed with a broad red streak of violence. In the end he turned it on himself.'

Radl didn't appear to expect any response. Fulnek was silent, waiting.

'This is something of a fleeting visit,' Radl said, 'just a detour because I wanted to meet you. Unfortunately I have some business in Prague to attend to. I wonder if we shall meet again. It would be interesting to have a talk. Your experience of life has been so very different from mine, yet our conclusions might not be so different. Take that woman who is causing you so much trouble. You are not concerned with rights and wrongs but what is most advantageous: in this case doing nothing.'

Radl gave Fulnek one of his unwavering stares and then abruptly clapped his hands and called to the dogs. They frisked about them as they left the chapel. Radl gave a brief glance at the white X on the wall before making for the gate. The watchers still stood there. 'Nobody goes in, nobody gets out.' Fulnek remembered hearing that order on his last visit.

'So now the search is over,' Radl said. 'Now you can rest. I understand – it is one of the other things I have heard about you – you have a friendship with a woman who lives in Zizkov.'

Anger, warm and generous, welled up in Fulnek. What spying had been going on. With an effort he said nothing.

'Soon, very soon, your life will be less . . . restricted. May I wish you happy days and the peace to enjoy them.'

Once again, to his surprise, Fulnek found his hand grasped. Then Radl was gone. Fulnek watched him climb into the back of his car. The two men, the watchers, twins in dark suits, gave Fulnek a final look and got into the front seats. Don't think, Fulnek said to himself, wait. Wait until the car starts, then wait until it moves off down the hill, then wait until it vanishes round the corner. So . . .

A new excitement grew out of the anger Fulnek felt. Radl had come for no purpose other than to warn him: do nothing more. The matter was closed by Broucek's death. He, Fulnek, should now find delight in his newly granted freedom. Yet the fact of his coming meant the opposite. Bodnar had been right and had paid for it by being killed by Broucek. But the heart of corruption was Radl.

Fulnek would use this new period of freedom to uncover the truth. How, he didn't know. He had the licence number of Radl's car, and Weiser could help there. Fulnek would know where Radl lived. He would find out the connection between Broucek and Radl. He would find out what Radl had been doing in 1968 when Bodnar had written that letter. In effect he would be completing the work that Bodnar had started.

He and Prerova would do this together. It would be a monument to Bodnar. It would be a bond between them.

Satisfied, Fulnek closed the door set into the seminary gate and locked it.

Warner Books now offers an exciting range of quality titles by both established and new authors. All of the books in this series are available from:

Little, Brown and Company (UK),
P.O. Box 11,
Falmouth,
Cornwall TR10 9EN.

Alternatively you may fax your order to the above address. Fax No. 01326 317444.

Payments can be made as follows: cheque, postal order (payable to Little, Brown and Company) or by credit cards, Visa/Access. Do not send cash or currency. UK customers and B.F.P.O.: please send a cheque or postal order (no currency) and allow £1.00 for postage and packing for the first book, plus 50p for the second book, plus 30p for each additional book up to a maximum charge of £3.00 (7 books plus).

Overseas customers including Ireland please allow £2.00 for postage and packing for the first book, plus £1.00 for the second book, plus 50p for each additional book.

NAME (Block Letters) ....

....

ADDRESS ....

....

....

☐ I enclose my remittance for ....

☐ I wish to pay by Access/Visa Card

Number ⬚⬚⬚⬚⬚⬚⬚⬚⬚⬚⬚⬚⬚⬚⬚⬚

Card Expiry Date ⬚⬚⬚⬚